D0374840

The Treason Trials of Aaron Burr

LANDMARK LAW CASES

&

AMERICAN SOCIETY

Peter Charles Hoffer
N. E. H. Hull
Series Editors

For a complete list of titles in the series go to www.kansaspress.ku.edu

PETER CHARLES HOFFER

The Treason Trials
of Aaron Burr

UNIVERSITY PRESS OF KANSAS

Published by the University Press of Kansas (Lawrence, Kansas 66045), which was
organized by the Kansas Board of Regents and is operated and funded by Emporia
State University, Fort Hays State University, Kansas State University, Pittsburg State
University, the University of Kansas, and Wichita State University

Library of Congress Cataloging-in-Publication Data

Hoffer, Peter Charles, 1944–
The treason trials of Aaron Burr / Peter Charles Hoffer.
p. cm. — (Landmark law cases & American society)
Includes bibliographical references and index.
ISBN 978-0-7006-1591-9

Printed in the United States of America

Book Club Edition

CONTENTS

There is something almost seductively attractive about Aaron Burr. Slight and short, with a high brow and piercing eyes, no one who met him ever forgot this founding father. A trusted and admired friend to some, a feared and reviled adversary to others, no founding father provoked such strongly divided opinions in his time—or in ours.

Nor did any of the revolutionaries experience such dramatic swings in their fortunes as he. Accused variously of a harebrained plot to "revolutionize" the West and detach it from the rest of the nation, of an invasion of Spanish Mexico that would leave him its king, and of a variety of more mundane canal, land development, and banking schemes, he seemed to combine in his life all the virtues of honor and vices of ambition common to his contemporaries.

Historians and biographers still debate whether he was a misunderstood patriot or a scheming traitor. Had he only been less secretive about his intentions! Nevertheless, his trials for treason and high misdemeanor are worth a fresh look. The trials attracted more attention than any others in the first four decades of the new nation. They caused the first media frenzy in the nineteenth century, bringing newspaper correspondents to Richmond from all over the country. They also brought together Burr, Chief Justice John Marshall, and agents of President Thomas Jefferson, who watched the course of the trials from afar. Hovering over them, like the ghost of Banquo at Macbeth's coronation feast, was the rival Burr killed in a duel, Alexander Hamilton.

The two great political parties of the day, Jefferson's Republicans and the Federalists, had equal if divergent stakes in the outcome of the trials. The Federalists had supported Burr when he and the Republican Party leader Jefferson received an equal number of presidential electors' votes in 1800 but had now turned against him. Jefferson's dislike for Burr had grown, and the Republican press insinuated that Burr could never be trusted. The world was watching too, for Britain, France, and Spain all had imperial interests in North America, and Burr had connections to delegates from all three.

But something more was at stake in the trials than the fate of Burr and his alleged fellow conspirators. The politicization of the law was a dangerous precedent for a nation supposedly founded on a rule of impartial law. From their inception, the accusations against him were as motivated by personal and partisan spite as by anything that Burr did or could have done, and the trial became a test that those in power might use treason charges as a political weapon. Here John Marshall and Thomas Jefferson played roles as or even more important than that of Burr himself. Jefferson branded Burr guilty before the trial had begun, and Marshall's abilities were never more in evidence than in his management of the trial and his rulings on the law.

Finally, Marshall's opinions in these cases created important precedent on substantive and procedural grounds. Today the notion of the law of evidence—what was admissible in court and what was not, which party in court bore the burden of proof at any given time in the trial—is a major part of law school curriculums and the subject of many treatises as well as a set of Federal Rules. But in 1807, the law of evidence was not well established. Hearsay and rumor, suspiciously produced documentary evidence that one party could not produce or the other party could not see in advance, could all be entered at trial. Marshall's rulings on the admissibility of oral and written evidence would become the bedrock of an American law of criminal evidence.

The author's contribution to the extensive literature on the so-called Burr conspiracy includes taking the arguments of counsel and the rulings of the court seriously. He has reproduced them with a running commentary, linking them to prior and future cases. Insofar as the counsel were among the leading legal thinkers of the day and one of the titans of American constitutional jurisprudence sat on the bench, the give and take in the court demands close reading. The author has one more trick up his sleeve before he is done: an explanation for Burr's otherwise bizarre conduct that no one has yet proposed, but in light of all the circumstances, one that cannot be ignored.

Introduction

One might, given the notoriety of the treason trials of Aaron Burr in their time, assume that they were "political trials." Although all criminal trials are the result of government prosecutions, three criteria are necessary for a criminal trial to be a political trial. The first is that the trial be politically motivated; the second criterion is that the outcome of the trial be affected by political considerations; and the third is that the trial have a significant impact on politics.

Some political trials have become infamous for their unfairness to the accused. Treason trials may take this form. The treason trial of Socrates in ancient Athens was arranged to quiet him when he pressed for war against other Greek city-states. The treason trial of Sir Walter Raleigh in the first years of James I's reign in England was James's way of preventing Raleigh from becoming the head of an opposition faction. Were Burr's trials similarly political?

The state is supposed to be neutral in criminal trials, with no particular bias or animosity against the defendant. But what if the very existence of the state is at stake? If Burr plotted to sever the union, Jefferson's administration had no choice but to find him, arrest him, and bring him and his allies to trial for treason. The Constitution of the United States only defined one crime — treason — because that crime was so dangerous to the nation. In fact, the Constitution's framers devoted an entire section (section 3 of Article III) to the crime. At the same time, the definition was limited and specific: "Treason against the United States, shall consist only in levying war against them, or in adhering to their enemies, giving them aid and comfort. No person shall be convicted of treason unless on the testimony of two witnesses to the same overt act, or on confession in open court." But what did "levying war" mean, and what was an "overt act"? Both Congress and the federal courts would bear the burden of applying the language of the Constitution in Burr's case.

Not every trial for treason has a political animus behind it. Sometimes the defendant really did commit treason. Did Burr? Or was he the victim of a political hatchet job? Thomas Jefferson, the president of the United States at the time, told Congress and the judges that he thought Burr was guilty even before the federal grand jury handed down an indictment. Jefferson sent a confidential agent to gather evidence against Burr and offered complete pardons to anyone who would testify against him. Had Jefferson, who thought Burr a dangerous political figure, rushed to judgment? If so, Jefferson's personal bias would have fulfilled the first criterion for a political trial.

Supreme Court Chief Justice John Marshall, on circuit with federal district court judge Cyrus Griffin, presided over the treason trials and the accompanying trials for violating the Neutrality Act of 1794. Marshall did not like Jefferson and thought that he had misused his presidential powers. Jefferson was one of the founders of the Republican Party. Marshall was a stalwart of the Federalist Party. The two parties hated and feared one another. Did Marshall interpret the law at the trials in order to strike at Jefferson? If so, Marshall's actions would have fulfilled the second criterion for a political trial.

The political consequences of the trial were equally marked. The West, described by one leading historian of these events as a "cauldron" of ambitious and divisive schemes, quieted. The Jeffersonian Party firmed its control of federal politics on the eve of the new nation's most perilous diplomatic crisis. The careers of a number of leading politicians ended. These events were sufficient to fulfill the third criterion

But in the end, the Burr trials were not political, and that is the most important legal story from the early nation that one can learn. Burr never made his purposes clear, and in the dangerous times of the 1800s, his secrecy worried many of his contemporaries. Jefferson had good reason to be concerned, for the West was rife with conspiracies. Marshall may have had strongly antipathetic views of Jefferson, but his handling of the case and the professionalism of counsel (including Burr's part in his own defense) converged to set an enduring precedent against political trials.

What was on trial then, and why? Even in the context of the fast and loose practice of commerce and law in the early nation, Burr's maneuvers were hardly commonplace. To be sure, law was not simply books and courthouse rhetoric. The lawyers of the early republic were entrepreneurs who saw law as a way to power, wealth, and security. They used law to their own ends as well as that of their clients.

The four principals in the story were all lawyers, and all vaulted from successful law practice to public life. As counselors, Alexander Hamilton was a fiery advocate, Jefferson a studious pleader, Marshall a highly successful litigator, and Burr a quicksilver courtroom performer. Burr chose a legal career precisely because he loved the give and take, the battle itself, where he could represent one side or the other with all of his skill.

The law was contest, and Burr found it life giving. Lawyer-entrepreneurs like Burr were a regular feature in the legal landscape. Lawyers not only set up deals, they also participated in their fruition. The modern Model Code of Ethics prohibits the mingling of funds and self-dealing. In post-Revolutionary New York, these were the rule. Aaron Burr merely took this show on the road. Had he gone too far down that road, to a place where ambition and greed verged on treason?

Certainly Burr contributed to his own travails by planting false trails that led, in some contemporaries' minds, to a treasonous project. Historians still debate his motives and aims. Whether Burr actually raised rebellion or merely talked about it, or whether he was merely perceived by some to have conspired to some illicit purpose, Jefferson could hardly ignore Burr's Western adventure. One might say that peace occasionally broke out along the Mississippi. Five hundred years before Burr was born, the Mississippi had become a cockpit of rival Indian factions. The arrival of the Spanish and French sent the Choctaw, Chickasaw, Natchez, and other native groups into perpetual competition for European arms. The huge and largely unpopulated trans-Appalachian West gained in the Paris Peace Treaty of 1783 was doubled by the purchase of Louisiana in 1803. By the time the United States purchased the Louisiana Territory, New

Orleans and the surrounding lowlands had been a burned-over region of imperial contest and local unrest for a hundred years. Far from the Atlantic coast and largely unconnected to it (only three rough overland paths broke through the Appalachians to the lands of Ohio, Kentucky, Tennessee, and western Georgia), settlers, trappers, and merchandisers depended on north-south river courses to bring their goods to market. Surely someone who could put together a small army of desperadoes and cool-eyed adventurers from the frontiersmen and the ex-army men who lived on the Western rivers posed a danger to the new nation. Was it Burr?

The Spanish certainly feared him. The ominous shadow of Spain, an unwilling ally in the War for Independence, also fell across these river passages. Spain's North American empire abutted the Louisiana Territory. The Spanish government knew about the Lewis and Clark expedition and must have been concerned for the security of California when Jefferson claimed that the Louisiana Territory ran all the way to the Pacific. American "filibusterers" nibbled at Spanish Florida, Texas, and New Mexico. Men dreamed of great wealth through land speculation; the possibilities of Florida, Texas, and even Mexico beckoned. They did for Burr.

Added to Jefferson's worries were the Napoleonic wars raging in Europe, with both Britain and France soliciting trade, then unconscionably stopping U.S. ships on the high seas or confiscating their goods in port. Jefferson preferred peace to war, and he staved off further involvement in Europe's wars though diplomacy. However, a full-scale war against the Indians in the Northwest edged closer, and English outposts in Canada were safe refuges for Indian raiders. Westerners were angry that Jefferson did not secure their settlements against Indian incursions. Were they so disaffected that someone like Burr could induce them to declare their independence?

Some defenders of Burr have suggested that Jefferson's part in the case was untoward, an expression of his personal partisan animus against Burr. To be sure, both Burr and Jefferson had been scarred by the bitter political combat of the late 1790s. Then the dominant Federalist Party had used its majorities in both houses of Congress to harass the opposition Republicans, including the two men. Burr was Jefferson's vice presidential running mate in both 1796 and 1800. In the former election, Jefferson, gaining the second largest number of electoral votes, became vice president. He and President John Adams came to detest one another, and the two parties grew even farther apart. When in 1800 Jefferson and Burr received the same number of electoral votes and Burr did not publically step aside, Jefferson barely concealed his dismay. Burr refused to surrender any of his electoral votes, and only after a prolonged debate in the lower house did Jefferson best his former running mate nine states to six. The two men, never close, became even less cordial. So it was that Jefferson came to believe Burr to be a cool and cunning adversary, never trustworthy. This may explain the vigor with which Jefferson pursued the prosecution of Burr, but it does not make that prosecution unwarranted. Putting oneself in Jefferson's shoes, one can understand why Burr's conduct in the waning days of 1806 might have seemed so dangerous.

And what if—as is disputed to this day—Burr's grandiose aspirations went beyond entrepreneurship, beyond filibuster, to turn a war with Spain into an opportunity for personal gain that may have edged into treason? Burr's case is still proof that all the rules of due process, as well as the limitations of law and the importance of judicial interpretation of law, did not fail, even when a president and a congressional majority played fast and loose with law. Law and the republican leaders' shared commitment to legal process held the nation together. Without the Constitution, the confederation of little republics would have shaken itself to pieces. Without the novel ideal of fundamental law, government could persecute those whose opinions it disliked and whose purposes it distrusted. Without lawyers, courts, or judges, the ambitions of men would have known no limits. Without law—or, that is, the fidelity to law—the nation would not and could not survive. The statesmen of the United States rightly boasted that we were a nation of laws, not men.

This said, one cannot overemphasize the continuing importance of Burr's trials. Too often and too easily those whose opinions we oppose or suspect become "traitors" in our minds. The harmful misuse of the term becomes far more serious when the executive and the Congress—the elected branches—fear for national security, engage the nation in war, or seek out internal enemies. Then the cautions of the Burr trial are set aside intentionally. The demand for quick and certain justice overwhelms the far more subtle (if far more fundamental) claims of procedural fairness and right. The blindfold is tightened on the statue of Justice, and the scales she holds are loaded down on one side with panic and partisanship. The rights of defendants have little weight when laid in Justice's other pan. Yet surely this makes the Burr trials even more important to us, as an object lesson in the dangers of hasty judgment, colored by political and personal animosity.

Whatever the merits of this book, it has benefitted immeasurably from the kind and wise comments of William Nelson, Daniel Hulsebosch, Tim Milford, Lloyd Bonfield, and Lauren Benton, all members of the NYU School of Law Legal History Colloquium; Keith Dougherty and the members of the University of Georgia American Political Development Working Group; Charles Hobson, Nancy Isenberg, and David Konig, the readers for the University Press of Kansas; and Williamjames Hoffer and N. E. H. Hull, my collaborators in this and other projects. My debt to Mike Briggs and the wonderful folks at the University Press of Kansas I am happy to acknowledge once more.

CHAPTER I

A Meeting in the Eagle Tavern

Richmond, Virginia, at the falls of the James River on March 30, 1807, pulsed with excitement. Around the Eagle Tavern at the foot of the hill above the river, at the top of which sat the Virginia statehouse, spectators and residents gathered in anticipation. The town was filling with visitors who had come to see a man denounced by the president of the United States as a traitor, Aaron Burr, and to hear the state's foremost courtroom orators. Every bed that could be rented in town was spoken for, and every tavern filled at evening with thirsty patrons. Richmond was happy for the clientele, though not so pleased with the hundreds of visitors' tents that appeared on the banks of the James. No one realized at the time that the spectacle would last well into the fall.

In the Eagle Tavern's back room, two men faced one another across a table. One was Burr, rumpled by travel and care but still alert and graceful, almost birdlike in his movements. He had taken the time to change his clothes and powder his hair — reappearing as a gentleman. A contemporary described his appearance some months before: "of meagre form, but of an elegant symmetry . . . fair and transparent" with an "erect and dignified deportment . . . his presence is commanding . . . mild, firm, luminous and impressive." His deep-set, hypnotic eyes "glow[ed] with all the ardor of venal fire, and scintillate[d] with the most tremulous and tearful sensibility." He was taciturn in company, yet when he spoke, "his voice was clear, manly, and mellifluous." In all, he was the epitome of a gentleman, to the eye and ear frank and honorable, but to Judge George Adams, who had observed Burr on that earlier occasion, the overall impression was a man "reserved, mysterious, and inscrutable."

Burr had not come to Richmond willingly but under arrest, accused of the highest crime against the nation: treason. Could he still gain his freedom on bail? That was the question that John Marshall had come to Richmond to hear and decide. Tall, broad shouldered, with loosely hung limbs, dressed neatly but not elegantly, the Chief Justice of the United States Supreme Court would preside over the circuit court, a trial court, in his hometown. With federal district court judge Cyrus Griffin, Marshall would spend nearly half a year on the case. Marshall had already distinguished himself as a litigator, legislator, and diplomat, and since 1801 had been the highest judge in the land, but the case would try his patience and skills to the utmost.

Marshall knew of Burr, but of the man himself, Marshall knew little other than Burr's public reputation for scrupulous impartiality and dignity sullied by a flirtation with the presidency in 1801 and a notorious duel with Alexander Hamilton in 1804. Marshall had even hoped, for a fleeting moment, that had Burr won the highest office, the New Yorker might favor him with continued patronage. In 1801, Marshall might have anonymously penned an encomium for Burr in the *Washington Federalist:* "He never shrank from the post of danger. He is equally fitted for service in the field and in the public counsels: He has been tried in both: in the one we have seen him an able and distinguished Senator — in the other a brave and gallant officer."

At that time Burr's rival for the presidency had been Thomas Jefferson, and Marshall hated his fellow Virginian. To Marshall, Jefferson's well-known "foreign prejudices seem to me totally to unfit him for the chief magistracy of a nation which cannot indulge those prejudices without sustaining deep and permanent injury." That was unfair, for Jefferson's sincere belief in human equality and dignity shone through his private writings and his public conduct. In a world of aristocracy and prejudice, he had truly meant "that all men are created equal, that they are endowed by their Creator with certain unalienable Rights, that among these are Life, Liberty and the pursuit of Happiness. — That to secure these rights, Governments are instituted among Men, deriving their just powers from the consent of the governed." A man of many passions, Jefferson found it hard to forgive Burr, and according to Dumas Malone, Jefferson's foremost biographer, the president "was convinced that the security and unity of the country were imperilled" by Burr's actions. In the fall of 1806, Jefferson had sent an emissary to follow Burr's footsteps and gain evidence of his guilt. In January 1807, Jefferson addressed Congress, accusing

Burr of the most hideous offenses, and throughout the trial, Jefferson would direct the prosecution.

Others in the small room were determined to punish Burr, or to save him from the gallows. Virginia federal prosecutor George Hay wanted to proceed with haste and firmness. For Hay, Burr's former position as vice president made his alleged crimes all the more dangerous. Hay sat across from Burr's own counsel team, led by former Virginia governor Edmund Randolph. Randolph had written the constitutional provisions defining — and limiting — treason, and perhaps equally important, he had faced a daunting inquiry into his fiscal probity as attorney general of the United States. They were adversaries this day, though they had great personal respect for one another. Unlike some of the lawyers in the case, political differences had not made them into personal enemies.

There was one other man in the room, but he could not have been seen with the naked eye. Alexander Hamilton, dead nearly three years, was present wherever Burr went. Everyone in both political parties and all of the reading public knew that Burr and Hamilton had met on a sandbar at the foot of the bluffs of Weehawken, New Jersey, on July 11, 1804, at the end of which meeting, Hamilton lay dying on the sand. Hamilton was the founder of the Federalist Party and no friend of Jefferson's, but in 1804 Hamilton had exceeded the bounds of what former officers and gentlemen might say about one another's politics and character, all but forcing Burr to demand satisfaction. Hamilton then refused to accommodate Burr, though Burr would have withdrawn the challenge had his adversary offered any form of apology. Nevertheless, the Federalists blamed Hamilton's death on Burr.

Those in the room and those keeping vigil without knew what was at stake. The federal Constitution defined treason — the only crime the Constitution defined — and an act of Congress in 1790 had made treason a hanging offense. Marshall had already heard and disposed of similar charges against Burr's colleagues, Samuel Swartwout and Erick Bollman (or Erich Bollmann, depending on who spelled his name in the documents). Burr himself had already faced and narrowly escaped two formal judicial inquiries into his supposed plot to sever the Western states from their Eastern siblings and create a new nation. With good reason, the eyes of the nation were focused on the Eagle Tavern and the men within.

Burr's life begs for explanations, for from his first steps on the public stage until this moment, he was a riddle wrapped in secrecy and charm. For his premier biographer, Nancy Isenberg, Burr was "a Christian man of action" and the avatar of "a new democratic ethos." Unlike some among the founders, Burr was a republican "natural aristocrat," whose energy and optimism gained him lifelong friends, and whose opposition to slavery and belief in the equality of women were far ahead of his time.

Roger Kennedy was only a little less fulsome in his praise of Burr as "a romantic," for whom "conviction" and "conscience" shone through a "calm" and deliberate demeanor. Burr would not give offense by action or speech, though others might see his reformist views as "dangerous to the plantation system." Nathan Schachter saw in Burr "essentially a practical man, not an idealist," whose achievements included the foundation of "modern machine politics." But Burr was "singularly faithful to his code" of conduct and "to his friends." As Jonathan Daniels concluded, Burr was simply a "witty, headlong, and courageous man" capable of true "dignity" in the face of injustice and danger whose reputation suffered the "connivance of such masters in the shaping of history" as Hamilton and Jefferson.

But Burr has as many accusers among his chroniclers as admirers. Edward Larson concluded that "few politicians fully trusted Burr and many actively disliked him," because in an age when private virtue was much extolled (if often only a facade), Burr "enjoyed a self-gratifying life punctuated with extra-marital affairs." When faced with crucial decisions, he wavered or "equivocated." For Gordon S. Wood, Burr's "behavior challenged the basic premises of the [founders'] thinking and violated the fundamental values of their experiment in republicanism." He was a "free-thinking, free-spending aristocrat who lived always on the edge of bankruptcy . . . a notorious womanizer . . . who used public office in every way he could to make money." Burr had no public vision and acted always in "haste and secrecy" to gain his ends. For Buckner Melton, Burr was "a puzzle," and "getting a handle on him" was "impossible," although one thing was certain — Burr was a "traitor."

If the child was father to the man, Burr's childhood — filled with promise and travail — forecast the course of his adult life. Burr, born in 1756, was surrounded by piety, books, ill health, and genteel poverty. His father, also named Aaron Burr, was one of the leading New Jersey Puritan ministers. His mother, Esther, was the daughter of the Reverend Jonathan Edwards of Stockbridge, Massachusetts, a foremost figure in the Great Awakening of evangelical piety and preaching. But both mother and father died before Burr was two years old. For a brief time he and his sister were cared for by a family friend, then both became part of the family of uncle Timothy Edwards. Children's personalities may be formed by the fear of separation, and surely Burr's desire to excel, to prove his place in his new family, owed something to the loss of his parents. But loss can also breed a secretiveness and a restiveness. Burr's adult life featured both.

Money remained a problem. Burr was a voracious reader and precocious student, but there was never enough money for books, and hardly any of the trappings of aristocratic ease in his new family. Gifts and an inheritance helped, but did not allay insecurity as he went to school in New Jersey, apprenticed in Connecticut, started his legal career in New York, continued his political career there and in Washington, D.C., and thereafter traveled by boat, carriage, and horseback all over the country.

Burr made friends easily and held them close, a hedge against the terrors of separation and loss. The sons and daughters of his friends became his assistants and followers. He befriended immigrants from England, Ireland, France, and the German states, drawing them into a warm and confiding circle. To his surviving daughter, Theodosia, on whom he doted and with whom he later shared his innermost feelings, he transferred this attachment. Her son, little Aaron, was the apple of his eye, but both would be lost before their time. If there is such a thing as fate in men's lives, Burr was fated to lose what he loved most.

Burr was a rebel, too, against his Puritan upbringing. He found the company of women reassuring. They replaced beloved mother and aunt. He rebelled against British authority and heroically served in the Revolutionary armies. He rebelled against the rigidities of all orthodoxies, religious and secular, supplanting the passionate ideologies of the day with a calculating realism that made him, long before his time, a modern.

Burr roared through the College of New Jersey, entering at age thirteen and graduating at sixteen, in 1772, with 10,000 pounds' colonial money his father had left in trust for him to study for the ministry. He then left for Connecticut to further his studies, but religion did not attract him for long, and he switched to law. He read law under Tapping Reeve, one of the foremost law teachers of the day, but at nineteen, he was swept up in the Revolutionary fever.

Burr was not a supporter of the movement for independence from its inception. According to Herbert Parmet and Marie Hecht, the young Burr was not attracted to ideals of liberty and equality, and he had no affection for the "rabble" who seemed to enjoy pulling down the symbols of British authority. But with his friend Matthias Ogden, Burr journeyed to the Continental army engaged in the siege of Boston. A stop to seek a commission in the new army and a rebuff from its commander, George Washington, left Burr with a lifelong distrust of Virginia aristocrats. Endorsed for officer's commissions by New Jersey leaders but not provided with salaries for the commissions, the two men found Washington unwilling to make them officers. He could only commission those men whose states had promised to pay salaries. A stiff man and a stickler for the rules, Washington had to turn down both the volunteers. Burr would tangle with Washington on later occasions.

Burr idled away the time in Cambridge, Massachusetts, with no official duties, perhaps ill (as many were with camp fevers), perhaps sulking. The opportunity for honor and advancement came with the invasion of Canada. Without any formal standing in the army, Burr joined the regiment marching through Maine to assault Quebec. The commander of this body of men was a Connecticut merchant, Benedict Arnold, who had talked his way into the role. Perhaps Burr thought he could do as well. Dressed in a forester's outfit, proving that his frail frame was up to all hardships, Burr pressed on when others faltered or returned home.

His reward was his own store of courageous acts, a far better fate than befell the expedition. It failed disastrously. The Americans could not lure the English and French from Quebec, and winter, disease, and lack of siege weapons eventually told. The commander of the combined force, Richard Montgomery, was killed in a last-ditch effort to breach the walls. Ogden was wounded, as was Arnold. Others were taken prisoner. Burr was lucky to come out alive.

His service with the army in the disastrous battles of Long Island and New York City brought the energetic young man (now commissioned) greater opportunities for personal heroics, but ended with Washington's enmity and slow advancement in rank. As a regimental commander in New Jersey and Westchester, New York, Burr excelled, however, and found time to spend with his future wife, Theodosia Bartow Prevost, while her husband was abroad. He married her in 1782 after she became a widow. His role in the Revolutionary armed forces ended when in 1777 ill health forced him to resign his colonelcy.

Poorer than when he entered the service, Burr at first found his prospects uncertain. In 1781, the state legislature had barred loyalists or crown sympathizers from practicing law for five years, allowing young men like Burr to seize an opportunity to rise quickly in the profession and gain political office. He ran his health ragged preparing for the bar exam in Albany, New York, but he passed with flying colors and was admitted to the bar in 1782. The successful practice of law required sponsors, for sponsors brought rich clients, and both demanded that Burr pay court to powerful families like the Morrises and the Schuylers. Burr also made friends with leading lawyers like William Livingston and Melancton Smith.

Asking the powerful for favors meant obligating oneself to perform favors, and Burr was as good as his word. There was no clear line between law practice and politics on the one hand, and law practice and peculation on the other. The legislature, the courts, and family ties formed a triangle that enabled a man to move up, move in, and make it. Burr's abilities as counsel were immediately clear. In court, as he had been in uniform, he proved a master of the quick riposte, the unexpected ambush, the relentless pursuit of an adversary on the run. He was elegant but not condescending to juries, not an orator (and never became one) or a notable writer, but in person-to-person conversation highly persuasive. As Burr's biographer and younger friend Matthew Davis wrote of Burr's courtroom skills, "As a speaker, Colonel Burr was calm and persuasive. He was most remarkable for the power which he possessed of condensation. His appeals, whether to a court or a jury, were sententious and lucid. His speeches, generally, were argumentative, short, and pithy. No flights of fancy, no metaphors, no parade of impassioned sentences, are to be found in them."

One believed what Burr said in court because Burr plainly believed it. Burr faced many more experienced counsel in the courtroom, and usually bested them. His fees grew apace. This enabled Burr to take on students, for the usual course from apprentice to lawyer was "reading law" with an established member of the bar. Davis recalled that Burr's choice of "assistants" was realistic. "When learning was required, he selected the most erudite. If political influence could be suspected of having effect, he chose his lawyers to meet or *improve* the supposed prejudice or predilection. Eloquence was bought when it was wanted; and the cheaper substitute of brow-beating, and vehemence used when they were equivalent or superior. In nothing did he show greater skill than in his measurement and application of his agents; and it was amusing to hear his cool discussion of the obstacles of prejudice, or ignorance, or interest, or political feeling to be encountered in various tribunals, and of the appropriate remedies and antidotes to be employed, and by what persons they should be applied." Much the same could be said of Burr's appreciation of political assistants to help him with his Western plans in later years.

Rewards for the rising legal star were political as well as financial. In 1784, he became an assemblyman. There he moved with swift and bold steps to oppose slavery. For favors real and anticipated, Governor George Clinton appointed Burr state attorney general in 1789, and Burr used his office to reward and promote his corps of followers — the "tenth legion," his daughter Theodosia called them. Some were family, others were old friends. But rising in politics meant making enemies too. In 1791, Clinton's opponents, gathering around young and able Alexander Hamilton and his emerging Federalist Party, supported Hamilton's father-in-law, Philip Schuyler, for a newly created U.S. Senate seat. Burr beat Schuyler and earned Hamilton's undying animosity.

Marriage to Theodosia Prevost had brought more family, more bills, and more connections. He bought Richmond Hill, then a country home at what is now the intersection of Charlton and Varick Streets at the edge of Greenwich Village, to entertain and impress, but Burr was often absent. Nevertheless, the mansion became a refuge for migratory and temporarily abandoned young people, servants, tutors, distant relatives, clients, penurious friends, and three slaves. Confined to the house and grounds by frequent illnesses, his wife was often ill at ease. She pleaded with Burr to spend more time at home. Little Theodosia barely survived the illness that took her younger sister. His son died next, and his wife, her ailing constitution weakened by grief and loss, followed in 1794. Burr was away again, in Philadelphia, chasing something — power, wealth, honor, fame — that was always one step ahead, and chased in his turn by misfortune and sadness.

The balm was politics. For others of his generation, politics was a galling necessity or a duty of honor. For Burr, the nitty-gritty of political action was a refuge from his demons. But a gentleman must not show his fascination (much less his obsession) with power. The delicacy of reputation, the modest gentleman pose, suited Burr. As Joanne Freeman has suggested in her study of honor in the founders' generation, a public man could not appear weak, nor could he be too aggressive. There was a code, broken or transgressed more often than obeyed, but still a code. Burr's personal opinions of his opponents might be scalding, as he revealed in his deathbed *Memoirs*, but public expressions must be carefully composed. Indeed, the almost dainty aristocratic tone of his public comments on others scarcely matched what he said about them in private.

For others of his generation, politics was the outward expression of political ideologies. Not for Burr. As Matthew Davis judged, "Colonel Burr's mind cannot be said to have been a comprehensive one. It was acute, analytical, perspicacious, discriminating, unimaginative, quick to conceive things in detail, but not calculated to entertain masses of ideas. He would never have gained celebrity as an author; but as a critic, upon whatever subject, his qualifications have rarely been surpassed." In politics, Burr was a modern, a hands-on party manager. No detail was too small, no press release too obscure, for his attention. Too disillusioned by the conduct of the ordinary man in the Continental army to believe in democracy, too familiar with poverty to believe in its virtues, Burr still loved the game of politics. He would have been perfectly at home in the next generation, when party loyalty far outweighed ideology.

Burr's attitudes toward life did not derive from a single inspiration. Though he understood honor, he was not bound by anything more than its outward forms. Though he was a gambler in love and a speculator in lands, he did not allow himself to be consumed by avarice. He could be distant and cold, but the young men who followed him were not drawn to him because he was a model, like Washington, of disinterested virtue. Instead, Burr formed attachments because he gave back full measure of friendship and loyalty to those whose sought it from him.

Burr had not supported the federal Constitution, but as a realist, he accepted it when it was ratified. In the U.S. Senate, Burr sided with the emerging Republican Party against Hamilton's Federalists. In this affiliation, Burr was careful not to be seen, or to be, too partisan. But he was Thomas Jefferson's running mate for the nation's highest office in 1796. Jefferson received the second highest number of electoral votes and became vice president under John Adams. Burr went away empty-handed.

Often sick and always in need of money, he spent much of his energy in these years trying to obtain back pay owed him for his wartime service. He hungered for higher office, perhaps as governor of New York, for then state office was more prized than federal posts. That he had no chance to gain the office and did not see it was another of Burr's weaknesses — a realist in his own mind, he was never realistic about his chances or his business practices. For example, he involved himself in a banking scheme of grand proportions. The Bank of Manhattan was supposed to become the safekeeper of the city's revenues. It foundered. He took part in a land speculation scheme, the Holland Land Company, that brought more debts (and some suspicion of corrupt misconduct). Speculation of all kinds was the sin and the siren of the lawyer class. As shrewd as he was in his politics, Burr was wildly overenthusiastic in his market dealings. He even speculated in Canadian land and tried to negotiate with foreign government agents for loans and gifts to pay his debts. Finally, Burr speculated on the value of state and federal debts, a volatile and unpredictable money market.

But first, more politics, and a glimpse of the highest office the country could offer. Burr was at times a strong supporter of the Republican Party; at other times, he listened and perhaps leaned to the moderate wing of the Federalists. Recall that he was not ideologically inclined. Perhaps one should conclude that his political attachments followed his personal attachments.

He endeared himself to the Republican Party when he argued the case for his fellow senator Albert Gallatin's citizenship. In 1794, Gallatin was elected to the Senate from Pennsylvania, but the Federalists did not want to seat him. They challenged his naturalization. Burr insisted that citizenship rested on the newcomer's desire to be a citizen. What was more, Gallatin had resided in America from 1780 and fought on the Revolutionary side. Who could have a better claim to the rights and privileges of citizenship? Gallatin lost. The Federalists held the majority of the seats, and every Federalist voted against him.

Burr and Gallatin became fast friends, and from Gallatin, Burr learned a great deal about Western land speculation and finance. In defending Gallatin, Burr joined with young Edward Livingston of New York, a radical Republican and scion of the state's Livingston clan. The Livingstons were one of the ruling families of New York, with political and economic tentacles reaching out to Western lands. Livingston himself was another member of the College of New Jersey circle, graduating in 1781. In 1803 he would relocate to New Orleans, drawing Burr's attention to the prospects of the lower Mississippi.

Burr attracted unwanted attention from the Federalists. It may have been his high profile in the key state of New York, or it may have been his low profile in the Senate. He campaigned actively in New York for the governorship, and his style of going to the people nettled the Federalists. The attack on Burr was vicious and unprincipled, decrying his ambitions as a demagogue and at the same time denouncing him as a crypto aristocrat — surely some of the mud would stick. His opponents belittled him for his small stature and his imperturbable demeanor. Against such an improbable variety of insults and smears, Burr might have taken furious action — though the catcalls were published anonymously, he knew who his detractors were. But his response to the insults was cool imperturbability.

Burr's place in the Republican Party, however, was never as secure as the Federalist smear campaign would indicate. He favored the democratic initiatives of the Republicans but did pay homage to Republican love of the French Revolution. He visited Jefferson, in 1793 retired from his post as secretary of state, and later recalled the great civility of his host. Surely they shared estimates of the prospects of an opposition party in the upcoming elections, but Burr was unlikely to have expressed any ideological commitments.

His Senate term done, Burr returned to New York and his mountain of personal debt. Speculations in land and banking had failed.

Burr had invested in stocks that friends had touted and then defaulted. He sold his home and its furnishings, and thereafter was perpetually chased by creditors. Yet he remained generous to his friends and friendly to strangers. To pay for past debts, he borrowed. Hence Burr was driven to engage in a number of questionable financial deals. His assistant in these was John Swartwout. They dabbled in municipal bonds and banking and land purchase schemes, and they used political connections in Albany and the city to outflank rivals, including Alexander Hamilton. Was Burr corrupt? No more so than his contemporaries, men like Hamilton, Robert Morris, and James Wilson. They did not have the security of landed wealth and slaves, like Washington, Jefferson, and the other planters. They had to hustle, and they did.

Ironically, for a time in 1798 and 1799, some of the state's Federalists began to trust Burr—at least Hamilton did. As America prepared for war against France—the ministry in charge of its diplomacy having offended American diplomatic emissaries by demanding a bribe— Burr joined with Hamilton to prepare New York's defenses. But the Federalists in Congress went too far. They passed a series of laws curtailing freedom of speech and used these to silence Republican editors and editorial writers who opposed the war scare. Burr, serving in the New York assembly, denounced the acts, though characteristically his language was far more temperate than Jefferson's secretly authored "Kentucky Resolution." Jefferson called for state interposition between its citizens and the federal government, demonstrating a profound ignorance of (or antipathy to) the very idea of federal sovereignty. When president, he would retreat from such extreme views of state's rights and would outdo the Federalists in imposing central power on the states and their citizens. For now, Burr's return to the Republican fold convinced Jefferson that Burr was still a good running mate.

Burr was as energetic in the 1800 presidential campaign as ever, but summer brought another challenge. Burr was good with children, and his surviving daughter, Theodosia, was the apple of his eye. He believed that young women should be as well educated as young men, and he prepared a rigorous course of reading for her. Though like her father she was often ill, she became his companion and hostess, and a charmer in her own right. That summer, she met and fell in love with

Joseph Alston, a wealthy rice planter from South Carolina and the son of one of the Republican leaders of the state. Young Alston would carry off Theodosia in 1801, and in the coming years, he would underwrite the Burr family finances. Though Theodosia was rarely at Burr's side thereafter, Burr took great delight in his daughter's match. His letters to her show a side of Burr that is warm, generous, and confiding. As he wrote to her on the eve of his duel with Hamilton, "I am indebted to you, my dearest Theodosia, for a very great portion of the happiness which I have enjoyed in this life."

The election of 1800 resulted in one of the more bizarre episodes in presidential history. Jefferson and Burr received the same number of electoral votes, and both more than Adams and Charles Cotesworth Pinckney, the two Federalists. Under the constitutional provisions for the election of the president, all candidates were eligible for the highest office, even those who ran for the vice presidency. The vice president was simply the man who got the second largest number of votes. (The Twelfth Amendment to the Constitution, framed and ratified after the election, told electors to cast separate ballots for president and vice president.) With the two top vote getters receiving the same number of votes, the House of Representatives had to choose the winner. Each state's delegation voted, and each state had one vote. The winner would have a majority of the states—nine. In effect, it became a second electoral campaign.

Privately, Burr wrote to Republican friends like Samuel Smith of Maryland that he would "utterly disclaim all competition" with Jefferson. He later added that it was "ridiculous" that he should be elected president. These were nondenial denials of his intent. He never said never. As Jefferson and others in the party like Delaware's Caesar Rodney began to worry that Burr had unprincipled ambitions of his own, Federalists Robert Goodloe Harper of South Carolina and Delaware's James Bayard began a correspondence with Burr, hoping to find him more amenable to Federalist policies than Jefferson was likely to be. Personal friends like Swartwout urged Burr to go to Washington and persuade key members of swing delegations to vote for him. But he did not—odd that a man who always campaigned hands on, personally directing and appearing in person to sway voters, on this one occasion refused to campaign for himself.

Hamilton played his part in these later episodes, persuading Federalist congressmen that Jefferson was the better choice in 1801. Jefferson might be a radical, but Burr was a scoundrel, another sinister conspirator like the Roman villain Cataline. When Burr ran for the New York governorship in 1804, Hamilton told a public meeting that Burr's ambition had no bounds, and he hinted that Burr wanted to sever the union to make himself a president of one of its parts. In private, Hamilton told anyone who would listen that Burr was a dangerous man, and word was soon abroad that Hamilton was sharing his opinions widely. Hamilton admired Burr, but hated him. Perhaps, as some have suggested, Hamilton had none of the gentleman in him — he surely was not born to it.

Born on the Island of St. Kitts in 1755 to a local white woman whose first husband, a womanizing Danish bird of passage, may or may not have terminated the marriage legally, and reared by James Hamilton, the second son of a lesser Scottish gentry family adept at finding ways to fail at business in the islands, young Alexander should have been doubly cursed. But he had dutiful tutors, some of them Jews who had found life in the mixed-race islands a haven. And he had a wonderful imagination, a precocious energy, and the ability to detach himself from ill fortune, including the permanent departure of his stepfather and the early death of his mother, that would carry him through a life of adventure.

That adventure began with books. Like Burr, Hamilton was an omnivorous reader of everything, willing to pore over volumes for hours at a time. Not able to retain even his mother's meager estate, Hamilton had to rely on the generosity of neighbors to pay for her funeral. The pastor would not allow her burial on church grounds, perhaps the cause of Hamilton's almost lifelong refusal to support organized churches (though in his last years he became deeply religious). Apprenticeship in business followed for a time, then off to sea and finally, arrival in New Jersey to attend the College of New Jersey. Hamilton was self-taught, immensely intelligent and energetic, schooled in the casual cruelties of life, and, most unfortunately, a young man who had learned how to hate.

Presbyterian connections ensured that he attend a preparatory school in New Jersey. Unlike Burr, Hamilton had no family ties to the College of New Jersey, but he did have an ability to impress older men of affairs. He had found sponsors in the West Indies, and now he found them in New Jersey. Burr and Hamilton crossed paths in 1773, but their meeting was not recorded. Hamilton may have been too busy courting William Livingston, a lawyer practicing law and raising political mayhem in New Jersey. Hamilton attached himself to the squire's circle, Whig lawyers opposed to parliamentary taxes on the colonies. But Hamilton was not accepted at the college, and matriculated at Kings College (later Columbia) in New York City instead. Whether Hamilton nursed a grudge against the College of New Jersey and its graduates, including Burr, is speculation, but he never became close to the members of the college's tightly knit coterie.

Kings College was not a hotbed of protest against parliamentary and crown impositions on the colonies. Hamilton's two years there brought friends and contacts, however, with what would become the Revolutionary party. He practiced oratory, read and attended lectures, and enjoyed himself in the company of the protestors. His first published work, two pamphlets vindicating American rights, catapulted him to the attention of the colony's Whig leaders and led him to singular notoriety as a twenty-year-old, still virtually penniless immigrant. In the spring of 1776, he was named a captain of a volunteer artillery unit that he helped raise, and though he had no formal military training, his men and his superiors soon recognized his energy, goodwill, and ability. In short, he shared many of the same virtues, and vices, as Burr. He had an easily wounded pride, a need to excel, and great energy. What he did not have was Burr's cool calculation and secretiveness. Hamilton said what he thought.

A bit of a dandy, a gentle disciplinarian, a courageous and loyal officer, Hamilton distinguished himself at the battles around New York City in the summer and fall of 1776. He caught Washington's eye and joined the general staff in 1777. There he became something of the son that Washington never had. He was Washington's pen, and to some extent the older man's eyes and ears. Like Burr, he lectured generals and governors — youth was no object. It never had been.

In battle, he was fearless to the point of reckless disregard. At his studies, in the moments of leisure he could steal, he was indefatigable. He still wrote, under assumed names (as was the custom in an age when words might lead to duels or imprisonment for libeling the government), passionately argued political tracts. Often his targets were other Revolutionary figures.

He married well — into society, power, and wealth. Elizabeth Schuyler would bear him eight children and outlive him by nearly a half century. She was everything that Burr's wife was not — pretty, a wonderful mother, healthy, and above all loyal. She defended him when he admitted an adulterous affair, demanded that he receive credit for his political achievements, and did not blame him when their adored oldest son fought and died in a duel — a duel that Hamilton might have prevented. She kept house at The Grange, built for her by Hamilton, but his debts, like Burr's, placed a great and unrelenting burden on her domestic finances. Like the Burrs, the Hamiltons were always just a step away from bankruptcy.

With peace, Hamilton finished his preparation for the bar and became a leading figure in New York's courts. He and Burr, both learned, fluent, and brilliant, were sometimes rivals and sometimes paired. He defended the loyalists when they returned from their exile, and British creditors seeking payment for prewar debts. He greatly admired Britain and its economic success, even though he had fought Britain. With both integrity and ability on his side, his reputation grew faster than his bank account.

Like Burr, Hamilton parlayed contacts and proven abilities into a government job — collecting taxes. Elected to Congress under the Articles of Confederation, he was aware from the start of the weakness of the Confederation government. It lacked an executive, a judiciary, an independent source of income, and clout with foreign nations and the states. No man did more to bring about the Constitutional Convention and the ratification of the federal Constitution than he.

Hamilton showed more interest in the ideology of governance than in its practice. Here he totally differed from Burr, for whom the give and take of party combat was an elixir. Hamilton believed in active government, girding its credit at home and abroad with wise investments, support for industry and commerce, and recognition of the key role that the monied classes must play in a solvent and progressive economy. His *Federalist* essays promoting ratification of the federal Constitution in New York still stand as unrivaled defenses of American federalism and constitutionalism, equaled only by James Madison's essays on the same subject.

Hamilton wrote the *Federalist* essays that defended the federal judiciary, an innovation (for the Confederation had no judicial branch).

He commented that the Supreme Court and any inferior trial courts the Congress might erect would not endanger the liberty of the people because the courts were "the weakest branch."

At and after the New York ratification convention, he was characteristically eloquent, but the habit of command and the tendency to denounce those who did not obey, practiced as Washington's aide-de-camp, served Hamilton ill. Always respected and sometimes admired, he made lifetime enemies for no gain. John Adams was one of these. James Monroe felt Hamilton's wrath, and Burr interceded to prevent a duel between the two men. Hamilton was involved in eleven such contretemps, seeking or being sought in duels. Burr's dignity was as often assaulted as Hamilton's, and with less reason, but he refrained from issuing or accepting challengers — until one persistent critic's continued slurs could no longer be borne.

When Washington became the first president and his first choices for secretary of the treasury turned him down, he asked Hamilton to fill the office. Hamilton worried that the new federal government's indebtedness would destroy it. He argued for a national bank, bounties for manufacturing, protective tariffs, and the funding and assumption of state war debts, to be paid by federal bond issues. To ensure that his programs passed Congress, Hamilton assembled a congressional following that would become the first national, standing political party. In older Anglo-American ideology, such standing parties were at best regarded as corrupt, and at worst as conspiratorial cabals. But Hamilton argued that his Federalists were neither — they were the government.

Controversy and conflict dogged the new party nevertheless, and soon its ideological and political opposite appeared. Representative James Madison, Hamilton's former ally, along with Secretary of State Jefferson, formed a Republican Party. The Hamiltonian Federalists favored Britain, the banker-creditor interest, a strong national government, and loose construction of the Constitution. In loose construction of the Constitution, the various agencies and officers of the new federal government could expand their powers through interpretation of the letter of constitutional law. For example, Hamilton found room in the "necessary and proper" clause of Article I, section 8, for Congress to charter a national bank.

The Republicans favored revolutionary France, a limited federal government, the debtor-farmer interest, and strict construction of the Constitution, a position that weighed the balance in federalism in favor of state power. In strict construction, the branches of the federal government were limited to the powers explicitly given them in the Constitution. These "enumerated powers" could not be expanded by the branches themselves. Thus, for example, because nothing in Article I gave to Congress the authority to charter a national bank, such an action violated the Constitution.

If as President Washington's Secretary of the Treasury Hamilton made his greatest contribution to American governance and finance, as President John Adams's foe, Hamilton nearly brought the nation to war and ruin, and doomed the Federalist Party. Hamilton intrigued with members of Adams's cabinet to undermine the feisty New Englander, and Adams despised Hamilton for it. Hamilton was to be the second in command of the army Congress created to fight the French in 1799, but Adams pulled the plug on the war machine by making peace of a sorts with the French. Hamilton responded by convincing Charles Cotesworth Pinckney to run against Adams in 1800, splitting the Federalist Party, costing Adams reelection. To top it off, Hamilton openly published a pamphlet denouncing Adams and his policies. When the election was over, like Burr, Hamilton had burned his political bridges, and he returned to his law practice full time.

Hamilton was a land speculator. Everyone who could cobble together the credit invested in Western lands. They were the El Dorado of the new republic. But while Hamilton saw the West as a field for investment, Jefferson saw the West as the salvation of the republic. Transplant the republican values of the yeoman farmer to the West, replicate that process over and over, and no monarchical cabal could ever usurp power. Long before historian Frederick Jackson Turner called the frontier the laboratory of American democracy, Jefferson had arrived at that conclusion.

Jefferson intensely disliked Hamilton, but everyone knew where Hamilton stood. Jefferson profoundly mistrusted Burr, for no one knew where Burr stood. When Burr failed to renounce his chance at the presidency, in 1801, Jefferson publicly professed confidence that Burr had not meant to replace him at the head of the party ticket, but privately, the new president seethed.

Jefferson was born on his father's Piedmont, Virginia, tobacco plantation. Not quite a member of the Tidewater aristocracy, but certainly part of the gentry, Jefferson was bred to a gentleman's ways. Unlike most of his cohort, however, Jefferson took the life of the mind seriously. Educated by tutors and then at William and Mary, the tall, rawboned redhead was a voracious reader and kept thorough notebooks with quotations from books he admired. Throughout his life, Jefferson would collect books, finally giving his library to Congress when its own library was burned by invading British troops in 1814. In these notebooks and in his library collection one can see the radical inclinations of the man: a belief that reason could and should win out against superstition, a faith in the power of the ordinary man, and a commitment to republicanism's central tenet of government by the people.

Jefferson studied law with George Wythe, whose liberal principles (including antislavery) Jefferson admired. It was this Jefferson who defended a bondsman who was falsely reenslaved, and who wrote in his *Notes on the State of Virginia* (1786) that slavery was an evil. Yet Jefferson was truly, as his brilliant biographer Joseph Ellis has written, "the American sphinx." This man, so deep and convoluted in his thinking, and perhaps so determined to conceal those twists and turns, remains a puzzle. The same Jefferson who publicly denounced slavery and the slave trade only freed a handful of his more than two hundred slaves, and those were his consort Sally Hemings and his children by her.

The paradoxes of his life and thinking did not stop with slavery. He was a brilliant writer but a poor public speaker. He was almost studied in his lack of pretension, but easily offended and slow to forgive. He was a modern in many ways, envisioning a genuine democracy; erecting a wall of separation between church and state; calling for a continuing revolution against tyranny of all kinds over the human mind; and advocating in the essential relation between an educated citizenry and republican virtue in the promotion of public schools. But he embraced the older plantation ethos of big house, fine wines, and parental authority over children and servants. He could be evasive as well: he denounced parties and expensive intrusive government, and then became one of the most committed party leaders in our history, using party to fashion a federal government far more costly and intrusive than Hamilton's.

Like Burr and Hamilton, Jefferson found politics congenial. As a penman for the American Revolution, his contributions were unparalleled. His *Summary of the Reasons for Taking Up Arms* (1775) and his draft of the Declaration of Independence (1776) were to political theory what Hamilton's *Federalist* essays were to constitutional theory. Jefferson was not a particularly able governor of Virginia during the Revolution, but he proved a very able diplomat in France during the 1780s.

As secretary of state and a founder of the Republican Party, Jefferson supported the French Revolution and the cause of French republicanism. When Great Britain joined an alliance of aristocratic European nations to invade France, Jefferson favored the French. Within a year of taking his place in Washington's administration, Jefferson found himself estranged from Washington, furious at Adams, convinced that Hamilton was a corruptionist, and sorry for himself. Merrill Peterson, Jefferson's biographer, described the "fruitless recriminations" that marked his service under Washington.

But one achievement marked that tenure, and Jefferson was duly proud of it. He worked unceasingly to quiet the border between the new nation and the Spanish North American possessions, and there was peace. If he did not conclude the treaty defining the boundaries (that came in 1794), he correctly and consistently recognized that American commercial interests required peace. A decade later, as president, he kept the peace in the Southwest.

Winning the second largest number of electoral votes in 1796 elevated Jefferson, who had campaigned for the highest office, to vice president. He presided over the Senate with aplomb and skill, writing a manual for proceedings that is used to this day. But the vitriol of politics during Adams's term would have daunted any man, and Jefferson had little power to dampen the rhetoric or mediate the conflicts. Jefferson believed in the ultimate value of human reason, which meant that men must be free to think and speak, but he regarded his enemies, both personal and political, not with tolerance but as evil men. Once consigned to this status, almost no one could win back Jefferson's favor.

For Jefferson's views of the Federalists were learned in a hard school. A faux war scare against France allowed the Federalists to humiliate and harass the Republicans. The Federalist majority in both houses passed, and Adams signed acts designed to crush the Republicans. Jefferson concluded that the Federalists wanted a return to a monarchical system. Free thought, free speech, open opposition to government would vanish.

The Sedition Act of 1798, the centerpiece of this legislative program, had two sections. The first section dealt with conspiracies, the second with publication of seditious libels. "If any persons shall unlawfully combine or conspire together, with intent to oppose any measure or measures of the government of the United States, which are or shall be directed by proper authority, or to impede the operation of any law of the United States, or to intimidate or prevent any person holding a place or office in or under the government of the United States, from undertaking, performing or executing his trust or duty; and if any person or persons, with intent as aforesaid, shall counsel, advise or attempt to procure any insurrection, riot, unlawful assembly, or combination, whether such conspiracy, threatening, counsel, advice, or attempt shall have the proposed effect or not, he or they shall be deemed guilty of a high misdemeanor." The act was broad enough to encompass the meetings of the Republican clubs.

The second provision of the act was even more chilling. It was a crime for "any person [to] write, print, utter, or publish, or . . . cause or procure to be written, printed, uttered or published, or . . . knowingly and willingly assist or aid in writing, printing, uttering or publishing any false, scandalous and malicious writing or writings against the government of the United States . . . with intent to defame the said government . . . or to bring [it] . . . into contempt or disrepute; or to excite against them, or either or any of them, the hatred of the good people of the United States, or to excite any unlawful combinations therein, for opposing or resisting any law of the United States." The act duplicated almost to the word (substituting the word *president* for *king*) the English seditious libel act, saving only that truth was a defense (if opinions could be proven true), and the punishment was not death, but fines and imprisonment.

The statute was an end run around the First Amendment's provision that "Congress shall make no law . . . abridging the freedom of speech, or of the press; or the right of the people peaceably to assemble, and to petition the government for a redress of grievances." The Sedition Act violated every one of these guarantees, though Federalists smugly insisted that it only applied to unlawful speech, publication, gatherings, and petitions. That was, of course, a perfectly circular, and hence fallacious, argument. But with control of all three branches of the federal government, who could stop the Federalists from doing what they pleased with the Constitution? Twenty-five Republican publishers, writers, and editors were indicted under the law, fourteen were tried, and ten were found guilty.

With all three branches filled with Federalists, the Republicans had to find allies in the state governments. Jefferson drafted a protest in the summer of 1798 and gave it to a friend, John Breckinridge, to present as his own to the Kentucky state legislature. The assemblymen there were already agreed that the Federalists had gone too far, copying the most barbarous features of English common law. Jefferson's document went further than any other leading Republican's — indeed, further than Jefferson the president would have permitted. He called the Constitution a compact among sovereign states and would have allowed any of those states' governments the authority to interpose themselves between the federal courts and the citizens of the state. It was a poor reading of what the framers had written. The federal government was a sovereign government and its will could be impressed on its citizens, whether or not a state government objected. Jefferson used the word *nullification*, and the Kentucky legislators adopted it in 1799. As a sitting vice president, Jefferson had to keep his authorship of the resolves a secret, but he made no secret of his opposition to the Federalist laws, which he made a target of his second run for the presidency. Not only did the Republicans win that office, they gained a majority in both houses of Congress.

As president, Jefferson preferred writing to oratory, and private consultations to plenary meetings of his cabinet. He would not tolerate ill manners among his senior appointees or at his small dinner parties. His republicanism sometimes had a forced quality, in part because he was still an awkward conversationalist and a poor public speaker, in part because he only trusted his pen and a few good friends like Madison, Albert Gallatin, and Henry Dearborn, his secretaries of state, the treasury, and war.

Jefferson's first act as president was the repeal of the Judiciary Act of 1801. That last-minute Federalist enactment would have ended the justices' hated practice of circuit riding by appointing inferior circuit court judges for each of the five judicial circuits: "There shall be in each of the aforesaid circuits, except the sixth circuit, three judges of the United States, to be called circuit judges, one of whom shall be commissioned as chief judge; and that there shall be a circuit court of the United States, in and for each of the aforesaid circuits." The newly appointed circuit court judges would replace the Supreme Court justices in the existing circuit courts. These were the trial courts that heard cases of federal crimes, among other types of cases. But Adams and his secretary of state, John Marshall, with the advice and consent of the outgoing Federalist Senate, had filled every one of the new posts with loyal Federalists.

That was the straw that broke the act's back. For even if Jefferson conceded the intrinsic value of having a Supreme Court act in a purely appellate capacity, and even if he set aside his fears of an overweening federal judiciary, the crassness of the defeated Federalists finding sinecures for themselves in the courtrooms was too much to swallow. When the new Congress met in December 1801 (the constitutional amendment ending the lame-duck Congress, the Twentieth Amendment, was not passed until 1933), Jefferson asked for the repeal of the Judiciary Act, and in March 1802, the deed was finally done. "It is dead," Jefferson reportedly crowed.

It was ironic then, and perhaps still is, that Jefferson was sworn into his office by newly confirmed Supreme Court Chief Justice John Marshall. The two men resembled one another in many surface ways, but they were not at all alike below that surface. Cousins, both gentry, both sure of themselves, both vulnerable, they might have been allies. They grew up in similar settings, chose law as a career, and then dedicated themselves to public service. Both believed in the culture of public virtue. But there the similarities ended, for by 1801, they viewed one another with suspicion. By the end of the Burr trials, they would cordially hate one another.

Marshall was born on his father's frontier farm on September 24, 1755. He was a generation younger than Jefferson. His father owned land but did not regard it as defining one's status. Instead, he was the agent for the powerful Fairfax family, a surveyor, vestryman, and lay justice of the peace. Marshall's father owned twenty slaves at his death, and young John inherited two.

There the dissimilarities from Jefferson began. Marshall never had more than one or two slaves, and they worked in his house or accompanied him in his travels. Jefferson owned, at any one time, nearly two hundred. John Marshall worked the farm with his father, while Jefferson never had to till the soil with his own hands (though he retained an active interest in botany throughout his life). Jefferson covered gentry pride with simple cloth; John Marshall wore simple pride. Jefferson had won no military laurels; Marshall would see service with Washington's flying camp, survive Valley Forge, take orders from Alexander Hamilton, and after the war, move to Richmond to practice law. He had studied with George Wythe at William and Mary, just as had Jefferson, but his course of study was framed by his wartime service and was not especially intensive (little more than a month). He never shared Jefferson's love of books or learning.

Marshall was licensed to practice in his home country of Fauquier — not a difficult task given his family's influence — but in Richmond he could practice in the state supreme court. The fees were better, and so were the clients. He quickly found a place among the leaders of the bar, and his practice grew. The move to Richmond also brought him closer to his life partner, Polly Ambler. She was the love of his life, though never very healthy and in later years homebound. In Richmond he could be near her, and he took every opportunity to be in her company. Her medical problems did not prevent the couple from having ten children, four of whom died before adulthood.

Otherwise, Marshall's headquarters was Statehouse Hill. The courts were in the statehouse, and the atmosphere among the lawyers and judges was one of polite informality. Marshall fit in perfectly. He did not grub for fees. He did not have to, for as a war hero, a man whose trustworthiness was soon well known, and an able advocate, he soon had a thriving practice. His father's connections brought important clients, including the heirs to the Fairfax lands on the Northern Neck. Other clients included George Washington, James Monroe, and Thomas Jefferson.

Never stodgy, never standoffish, Marshall was soon an important figure in state politics. He found legislative activity alternatively boring and corrupt, however. "Our prejudices," he complained, "oppose themselves to our interests." For Marshall, those prejudices included the mistreatment of minorities, domestic abuse, and overly punitive sentences for petty crimes. No liberal, he was a conservative in the best sense of the term.

He supported the federal Constitution, for it seemed to him to ensure the safety of the nation, and therefore the security of the gains of revolution. At the Virginia ratification convention, he persuaded Edmund Randolph, governor of Virginia, to lay aside his doubts and agree to ratification. Randolph had helped draft the document, then refused to sign it, and then, with Marshall and Madison, guided the ratifying convention to adopt the new frame of government.

As his defense of the new Constitution demonstrated, Marshall was at home with nuance and subtle distinctions. He was a far better and far more successful lawyer than Jefferson. Although that skill was not based on book learning, Marshall knew his classic texts. His greatest skill, however, was his ability to see the root question in the mass of detail, and to find the resolution of complex questions in easy-to-follow principles.

Unlike Jefferson, who feared federal power (until he became the head of the federal government), Marshall reckoned that only a strong central government could hold the union together. Thus in 1797 he reluctantly agreed to John Adams's request to serve in a diplomatic mission to France. When the French Directory insulted the mission in the XYZ Affair, Marshall kept his head. He returned to honors but did not join in the clamor for war with France. He had mixed opinions on the Sedition Law, and when he ran for Congress in 1798, he publically disclosed that "I am not an advocate for the . . . Sedition Law[s]. Had I been in Congress when they passed, I should . . . certainly have opposed them." What was more, if elected, he would oppose continuing the law beyond its March 1, 1801, end.

Marshall was sincere in his doubts, and privately reiterated them to Washington. His stand infuriated the hard-liners in the Federalist Party, including Hamilton, but endeared him to Adams. Marshall won the election and found himself sitting in Congress. There he proved to be an independent-minded representative, voting with the Federalists on most issues but defending Adams against the Hamiltonians when they sought to censure the president. He voted to repeal the Sedition Law, joining with the Republicans. Though called "indolent" by some and castigated as indecisive, he was also much liked and his honesty valued. For this, as much as for his loyalty, Adams named Marshall secretary of state, and the Senate confirmed the nomination. A scant six months later, Adams named Marshall to replace Oliver

Ellsworth as Chief Justice of the U.S. Supreme Court. On February 4, 1801, when Adams's reelection bid was already lost, Marshall was sworn in.

The Republicans were understandably upset. Jefferson in particular had developed strong antipathies to Marshall that events would only worsen. All of this came to the test in *Marbury v. Madison* (1803). William Marbury's appointment as justice of the peace for the District of Columbia had been another of the Federalists' midnight moves to fill the judicial offices with Federalists. Marshall, outgoing secretary of state, failed to send it on, and the incoming secretary of state, Madison, with the assent of President Jefferson, did not remedy Marshall's oversight. When he did not get the commission, Marbury filed suit with the clerk of the Supreme Court under the provisions of the Judiciary Act of 1789. Section 13 of the act gave to the Supreme Court under its original jurisdiction the power to issue a writ (a judicial command) "of mandamus" to Madison to deliver the commission.

The Constitution spelled out the original jurisdiction of the High Court—that is, the suits that could be filed directly with it. These included "all cases affecting ambassadors, other public ministers and consuls, and those in which a state shall be party." Nothing was said about Congress adding writs of mandamus to this list, but Charles Lee, counsel for Marbury, filed it with the clerk of the High Court.

The issue before the Court, as Marshall framed it, was whether the Court had jurisdiction over the case. Although the political overtones of the case, in light of the repeal of the Judiciary Act of 1801, were obvious, Marshall ignored them. In a very long opinion for that day (twenty-six pages), Marshall wrote for a unanimous Court. He ruled that the justices could not issue the writ because it was not one of the kinds of original jurisdiction given the Court in Article III of the Constitution. The Constitution controlled or limited what Congress could do, and in particular, it prohibited Congress from expanding the original jurisdiction of the Court. Congress had violated the Constitution by giving this authority to the Court. In the end, he struck down that part of the Judiciary Act of 1789 as unconstitutional.

The power of "judicial review" that Marshall assumed the Court possessed to find acts of Congress unconstitutional, and thus null and void, was immensely important. First, it protected the independence of the Court from Congress. Second, Marshall implied that the Court was the final arbiter of the meaning of the Constitution. This vital pronouncement of "judicial supremacy" would be elaborated and extended in the coming years to include state legislation and state court judgments. Finally, Marshall reminded everyone that the Constitution was the supreme law, and that every act of Congress had to be measured against it.

Although Marshall would have been the first to deny it, he had substantially enlarged the jurisdiction of his court and thereby changed the meaning of Article III of the Constitution. Its framers had not given to the High Court the authority to strike down acts of Congress. They could have given the Court the authority to review federal law, but they did not. *Marbury* did.

Marshall was aware that *Marbury* opened wide his conflict with Jefferson and protected the opinion in two ways. First, he wrote as if the plain logic of his decision simply could not be gainsaid. Second, he made the ruling self-executing. That is, because the Court refused to help Marbury, its ruling did not require Madison or Jefferson to do anything. They might reject Marshall's arguments, but they could not directly oppose them by refusing to obey a Court order — there was none to disobey.

By 1804, the paths of the four men present or represented in the Eagle Tavern had crossed and recrossed. They had joined or opposed one another in legal practice. They had vied for office or allied to help one another gain office. Marshall and Jefferson were careful not to publically give offense. Burr kept his own counsel. But Hamilton could not stay his temper or temper his language. Over and over in his career he had insulted Burr, and in the New York gubernatorial campaign of 1804, he went too far.

There are many accounts of the events leading up to the duel that Hamilton and Burr fought that insufferably hot morning of July 11, 1804. The sand spit in Weehawken on which they stood is still there, bisected now by light rail tracks. What caused the two men to row across the Hudson from their New York homes, and what happened in those brief minutes, may never be concluded.

The most recent biography of Hamilton, Ron Chernow's *Alexander Hamilton* (2004), tells the story this way: Early in January 1804, Burr, knowing that he had no chance of running on the Republican ticket, asked Jefferson for some post of honor and remuneration. Jefferson was cold to the idea. Burr decided to try his luck with the New York governorship, which he had previously sought in vain. DeWitt Clinton would have outmaneuvered Burr without Hamilton's help, but Hamilton could not forbear. He openly and privately warned about Burr's perfidy at a time when Burr's cup of bitterness had run over. He believed (wrongly) that Hamilton was writing anonymous attacks on him. So long as he had hope of winning in New York, however, he kept his peace with Hamilton. He lost, more because of Jefferson's influence on Republican voters than Hamilton's on Federalists, but Burr blamed the loss on Hamilton.

In the meantime, after the election, Hamilton's private conversations, long circulated, found their way into an Albany newspaper. Reading a copy anonymously sent him, Burr "flew into a rage." There was, in addition to the usual political accusations, Hamilton's insinuation that Burr was guilty of a more "despicable" act. On June 18, Burr demanded the Hamilton retract and apologize. He had begun "an affair of honor," whose roots lay in French aristocratic custom and had come to America with the French forces during the Revolution. Burr and Hamilton had been involved in many such affairs, Burr customarily trying to cool tempers, while Hamilton stoked them. But Hamilton had lost his beloved eldest son to a duel, ironically with a Burr follower, in 1800, and had lost his taste for this exotic repast.

Still, honor was honor, and Hamilton had to reply. Most often, the threat of the duel caused the protagonists to find some way out of the quarrel short of actual combat. Hamilton had invariably been the initiator of such challenges, and perhaps he was at a loss about how to respond to one. Perhaps he thought that Burr had nothing to gain by shooting to kill. In any case, Hamilton's stubborn refusal to concede anything showed that he did not expect Burr to close the final act.

Seconds for the two men, as was expected, attempted to negotiate a settlement short of the duel. Hamilton danced around technicalities — how could he apologize if he did not know what he was precisely accused of saying? His letters to Burr added more insults. Even his friends, privy to the exchanges, were worried. Burr had thrown aside all courtesies and demanded combat. Hamilton, who had privately denounced dueling, now felt he had to engage in one. He told a friend that he would go through the rituals but "waste" his shot.

In a letter left for opening after the duel, he revealed that he could not kill anyone and would not. Was he depressed? Was he already failing from some ailment? Did he simply "gamble that Burr would not shoot to kill"? He became fatalistic and passive, then wistful and tranquil. What would happen would happen. When they found themselves across the table from one another at a public occasion for veterans, Burr "averted his eyes" from his opponent, while Hamilton became uncharacteristically boisterous.

Nancy Isenberg's *Fallen Founder* (2007) paints a different picture: Burr was not openly antagonistic when he first asked Hamilton to explain what his "despicable opinion" could be. Burr had discussed the matter with friends before sending the letter to Hamilton, and he explained that he had on earlier occasions, in Burr's words, "forgiven Hamilton" out of a "sincere desire for peace." He hoped that Hamilton would make some gesture that would allow the two men to put the matter behind them. But Hamilton's reply was "evasive and disingenuous." How could he explain what he had said over a course of a decade and a half of rivalry? His closing was "provocative" and "brusque."

Burr replied "with surgical precision," another example of how sharp his legal mind could be. Hamilton should have spoken in the proper ritual fashion, as one gentleman to another, not dismissed Burr's note condescendingly. When Hamilton replied to Burr's second letter, he did it as offhandedly as he had to the first — he had nothing to add to what he had already said. He made arrangements for a duel before Burr had taken any steps other than writing letters. Isenberg sees the back and forth as a kind of legal contest, dueling over meaning. "For Burr, honor began with sincerity. For Hamilton, it was protecting one's public reputation."

If Isenberg is right, and there is much reason to accept her judgment, Burr's view of honor came not from his military experience, but from his religious beliefs and background. Honor was inward, a manifestation of a man's spiritual character. For the Puritan, true manhood was intertwined with a sense of guilt for one's inevitable missteps, the need to redeem the day and avert sin. Hamilton never had much time for religious observances. For him, honor was a matter of not shaming oneself, and not letting others shame one. This was far closer to the Southern gentleman's conception of honor. In a shame culture, one's merit was what others thought of one.

Or perhaps, as Joanne Freeman has written, the duel was part of the "larger grammar of political combat." Insults became challenges, and challenges must be met. It was an "intricate game of dare and counterdare, ritualized display of bravery, military prowess, and — above all — willingness to sacrifice one's life for one's honor." Both Burr and Hamilton subscribed to this vocabulary of early national politics. Both wrote anonymously. Both saw malice and evil in their opponents, rather than simple disagreements or alternative ideological postures. Their duel was "timed" when both men had left politics and had nothing but their honor to display to the public.

But in this game, no one was supposed to die. The precise events at the duel — who fired first, whether Hamilton wasted his fire or pulled the trigger instinctively as Burr's ball hit him in the hip and lodged in his spine — were then and are still matters of controversy. But no one can doubt the impact of the duel on the two men. Hamilton lingered in agony and died the next day. His last will and testament, when published, made him a martyr and Burr the villain. Burr fled because New York and New Jersey authorities sought to indict him for his conduct. Although he could, and did, sneak back, he could not carry on legal practice until a decade had passed. He removed himself to Washington to preside over the final session of the Senate, but his economic prospects looked as bleak as his political future.

CHAPTER 2

The Western Adventures
of Aaron Burr

The story of Burr's Western adventure in 1805–1806 is almost impossible to tell with precision. There were so many individuals telling so many contradictory stories, and so many parts of the story that we will never know, that any approximation of Burr's motives is pure guesswork. Even following him around is dizzying. But follow him one must.

Hamilton's death made him a martyr to the Federalists. Burr's reputation among the Republicans was already ruined by his vacillation after the 1800 election results were counted. His handling of the Senate in the trial of Justice Samuel Chase on a Jefferson-sponsored impeachment, his farewell speech to the Senate, and his announcement of the electoral victory of Jefferson and the new vice president, George Clinton, all gained him plaudits, but respect did not translate into popularity or trust. He told the assembled senators that they occupied "a sanctuary, a citadel of law, of order, of liberty," a safe haven against "the storms of political frenzy and the silent arts of corruption." But he had been accused of these very acts himself, and he was still regarded as Hamilton's assassin. His leave-taking moved some of his colleagues to tears, but Jefferson shed none.

Burr could not stay in Washington much longer. He told Charles Biddle at the outset of the new year that he feared to "go where I might be seized and confined in jail with felons." The fury of his enemies had not abated by March 22, 1805, when he wrote to Biddle "In New-York, I am to be disenfranchised, and in New-Jersey hanged. Having substantial objections to both, I shall not, for the present, hazard either, but shall seek another country."

Burr faced more immediate problems. He was broke. Unable to resume law practice in New York—indeed, unable to recover the legal papers from his office in the city—he could not collect fees or pay his own mounting debts. The West, with its vast lands beckoning for development, called to the speculator in him. Lawyers in Ohio, Kentucky, Tennessee, and down the Mississippi could make a fine living as entrepreneurs, as Burr's friend Edward Livingston was proving in New Orleans.

The Western prospect meant renewed contact with the senior officer in the United States army and soon to be governor-general of the Louisiana Territory, the ubiquitous James Wilkinson. Burr knew Wilkinson from the Canadian campaign, and later as a bluff storytelling veteran, a man of pride and somewhat suspect financial ethics. Wilkinson made the first move to establish a more personal relationship. In May 1804, when Burr's self-esteem was at low ebb, Wilkinson wrote and proposed that he "take a bed" in Burr's residence as Wilkinson was passing through D.C. Burr was flattered. Wilkinson was a superb flatterer. In the winter of 1804–1805, the two were closeted in Washington and shared evenings mapping out what might have been an invasion of Spanish Mexico.

Wilkinson, who rowed to his objectives with muffled oars, wrote vaguely about the plan to his old friend John Adair of Kentucky, lately elected U.S. senator. Adair assured Wilkinson that Kentuckians were spoiling for a fight with Spain. By March 1805, Burr and the general were on intimate terms, Burr telling Wilkinson of his "movements" and "plans." A year later, he was defending Wilkinson to Jefferson and Secretary of War Henry Dearborn, a Massachusetts Republican who served in the cabinet office for Jefferson's entire tenure.

Wilkinson appeared to Burr to be trustworthy, but appearances were deceiving. Though gossip circulating in New Orleans linked the two men (Wilkinson was supposedly Burr's right-hand man), Wilkinson was never anyone's man but his own. As Burr was telling Wilkinson about the likelihood of war with Spain, Wilkinson was intriguing with the Spanish — indeed, had been receiving regular payments from Spain for reporting on American aims and movements. This made him Spain's secret agent — number 13 according to their records — with a yearly stipend of $2,000, significant money in those days.

Though poorly populated and relatively underdeveloped, the West was a hive of conspiracies, and Wilkinson figured in most of them. Wilkinson emigrated from Maryland to Kentucky in 1784, when it was still a part of Virginia. He schemed with local land speculators and the Spanish governor of New Orleans, where Wilkinson had commercial interests, to sever the Kentucky region from the union. The so-called Spanish Conspiracy went nowhere, but the Spanish government was impressed enough with Wilkinson's bravado and his promise of further services to award him the secret stipend. After Wilkinson accepted an officer's commission in the new United States army, he persuaded the Spanish to pay him an additional $16,000 to help them protect the eastern flank of their empire from rapacious land speculators (like Wilkinson).

There was nothing new in Wilkinson's outside employment. In the early 1790s, Hamilton reported secret cabinet deliberations to the British ambassador, George Hammond. They even gave him a code name, Number 7. While in the administration as secretary of state, Jefferson was discussing confidential government matters with the French minister, Edmond-Charles Gênet. Hamilton and Jefferson did not make a practice of sharing government secrets with foreign emissaries for cash payments, however.

Wilkinson had a more serious rival in the conspiracy business in the person of William Blount. Blount was a North Carolina–born politician and U.S. senator from Tennessee who was trying to make a killing in Western lands. The value of the lands depended on safe navigation of the Mississippi and the "right of deposit" of goods in Spanish New Orleans. In the 1790s, Blount sought aid from the British government to invade Spanish Florida and Louisiana, a course of action that convinced the House of Representatives to impeach him for violating the Neutrality Act of 1794. The Senate tried him and disqualified him from future federal office.

Blount could not hold a candle to Wilkinson, however. With the Spanish ceding the Louisiana Territory to the French in 1800 (a forced transfer that Napoleon furthered by holding the Spanish king hostage), and the United States buying the Louisiana Territory from the French in 1803, Wilkinson saw another opportunity for honorable public office and dishonorable private pillaging. As a senior officer in the army, he joined William Claiborne, newly named governor of lower Louisiana, to accept the cession of New Orleans and the rest of the territory from the French prefect. The Spanish authorities were literally standing in the wings, watching, while the cession ceremonies went on, giving Wilkinson a chance to demand the arrears of his stipend. If they wanted him to help prevent an American thrust into what remained of their empire, they had better remit the balance. When they paid a portion, he responded by informing them to fortify the borders of Texas against filibusterers (like Wilkinson). So pleased were they with this tidbit that they agreed to restore his annual salary.

It was a Wilkinson skilled in dissimulation who suggested to Burr that they correspond in code. Burr had trouble deciphering Wilkinson's letters and begged him, "why put such a tax on the pleasure of your correspondence?" Burr was so careful in his spoken and his written language that he needed no cipher to conceal his purposes. When Wilkinson later wrote a defense of his own motives, his *Memoirs* (1816), he recast the story of his correspondence with Burr, making Burr look like the initiator of the code.

While Wilkinson intrigued with the Spanish, Burr met with Anthony Merry, the English minister to the United States. Merry, inaptly named, thought himself stuck in a third world country, slighted by its Anglophobic president, with little influence in his home country. He was receptive, not to say gullible, when Burr approached him. To Merry, Burr confided not "the exact nature and extent of his plan," but its general outlines, "to endeavor to be the instrument" for the "Independence" of the western parts of the United States. Burr wished from the English government funds and the promise of naval support for the venture. The funds were to come first — about £100,000, "sufficient for the immediate purposes of the enterprise." Merry was persuaded that Burr had "in a much greater degree than any other individual in this country, all the talents, energy, intrepidity and firmness which are requisite for such an enterprise" and forwarded it to his government.

Burr never did get a penny from the British, though he renewed his requests periodically. When Burr went West, his lieutenant Charles Williamson continued the importunities directly to the British. Williamson had come to the United States to represent British investors in the Holland Company, an awkwardly named and even more awkwardly managed New York land speculation scheme. Williamson was charmed by Burr and at his behest traveled to England to represent Burr's interests. Williamson's proposition to the English was a filibustering mission against the Spanish Empire, quite different from what Merry heard Burr say. Even after his American patron was discredited by the treason trials, Williamson continued to plead for a British subsidy for Burr.

Burr's declining political fortunes did not drive off the small group of men dedicated to his welfare like Williamson. Among them was Samuel Swartwout of New York, son of John, one of Burr's allies in the New York banking business and a former U.S. marshal in New York. Another was Peter Ogden, the son of young Burr's great friend and fellow veteran. Former senator Jonathan Dayton of New Jersey joined the circle. He had known Burr from their New Jersey days, and his fingers itched to get into the same pies as Burr's. Historian David Hackett Fischer judged that "the odor of corruption lingers over Dayton's career."

These "Burrites" were an odd lot, and to them he added others in the next year. They included Senator John Smith of Ohio, John Adair, Senator John Brown of Kentucky, Harman Blennerhassett, an émigré Irish lawyer, and perhaps the oddest, German adventurer Erick Bollman.

By the late spring of 1805, Burr was no longer tied down by official duties. Theodosia was in South Carolina, but she would come to him if he asked, and Joseph Alston and their son Aaron would come too. For Burr, the next year and a half were a whirlwind of motion, meetings, purchases, plans, and perhaps even plots. These included the chartering of a bank and a canal company, and buying a huge tract of land on the Washita (today spelled Ouachita) River in the Louisiana Territory. (The river passes by the modern town of El Dorado in Arkansas, surely an example of ironic convergence.)

Burr engaged in long conversations with men of affairs and men on the make about the shadowy great adventure that would make them all rich. Did Burr contemplate the invasion of the Spanish colonies of Tejas, Mexico, and New Mexico? Jefferson's purchase of the Louisiana Territory from France brought war with Spain closer, for the two nations did not agree on the southwestern border of the purchase. The Spanish were uneasy. Tipped off by Wilkinson, New Mexico's governor attempted to intercept Meriwether Lewis, William Clark, and their Corps of Discovery on their exploratory journey up the Missouri. Although the federal government had no control over the adventurers, speculators, and other "grey eyed men of destiny" casting hungry glances across the Mississippi, the Spanish spent and spied to find out America's official plans for the far West.

Perhaps Burr intended to take advantage of the unsettled state of the Southwest to filibuster or raid the enemy colonies. If so, he would need a war with Spain to make the enterprise legal. Congress in 1794 had passed and Washington had signed into law a prohibition on private wars, the Neutrality Act. Engaging the enemy in a time of war was a time-honored way to make a profit. At sea during the Revolution, American privateers had taken enemy ships as prizes and sold off the ships and their cargoes. But privateers become pirates when war is over.

A final possibility, which Burr's enemies claimed he had in mind all the time, was splitting the western portion of the new nation from its eastern neighbors. Western sentiment was never entirely in accord with the seaboard states' interests. Land sale policy and Indian policy divided the two sections. In 1804, as a concession to Westerners, the federal government sold pieces of the national domain a quarter section at a time (160 acres), at $2 an acre. Speculators and squatters wanted the size of the parcels and their cost reduced. To nominal Republicans like Brown of Kentucky and Smith of Ohio, a plan to create a separate nation in the West might have had more than passing appeal.

Whatever his motives at the time, Burr began his first trip through the West at Pittsburgh on April 29, 1805, traveling down the Ohio and then the Mississippi. On a small island in the Ohio River just west of modern-day Parkersburg, West Virginia, Burr berthed his vessel. It was locally known as Blennerhassett Island after the Irish émigré who had bought it and built on it an elegant estate home. Harman Blennerhassett was a highly educated man, resident in America for almost a decade. Portraits of him depict a long, narrow face with handsome features and romantic eyes. The mansion had fourteen rooms on a landscaped plot of 169 acres.

The mansion, isolated on purpose, concealed a secret. Harman had married his niece, his sister's daughter. Burr did not know — no one in the States did — and he found Margaret fluent in many languages, athletic, and comely. Though only twenty-eight years old, she was the mother of four sons. Burr's love for Theodosia was undiminished by her persistent ill health, and his adoration of his grandson Aaron was made stronger by the boy's sickly constitution — but how Burr must have envied Margaret and her sons. The Blennerhassetts gave the appearance of health and wealth, though in fact Harman had run through just about all of his inheritance.

Burr moved on to Cincinnati, where he joined Smith and Brown, the latter a College of New Jersey alumnus and lawyer, along with Dayton, recently relocated to Ohio. Dayton and Burr had long known and admired one another. The four men agreed to press for a canal that would ease travel down the Ohio. For this they would need the support of the Ohio legislature. They planned to create a bank to fund the project as well. Then the conversation turned to the likelihood of a war with Spain and the potential value of the Spanish possessions for men daring enough to mount a military incursion. All of the men were Revolutionary War veterans, and the hardships of their service, transformed by memory and desire into glorious years, beckoned. So did the prospect of Spanish gold.

Then on to Lexington, Kentucky, where Burr found a friend in Adair, like Wilkinson a Revolutionary War veteran and a man spoiling for a fight with Spain. Burr's next stop was Frankfort, Kentucky, the capital and the home of Senator Brown. From there Burr traveled on to Nashville and a warm welcome from Andrew Jackson. Burr's duel with Hamilton would not have disturbed Jackson, for he too had fought duels, and in one at least, shot dead his opponent. Burr stayed for four days at the end of May and the beginning of June, feted by the lawyer-planter and future president. If the country went to war against the Spanish, Jackson hoped for a command.

Burr would continue to court Jackson, writing him on March 24, 1806: "You have doubtless before this time been convinced that we are to have no war if it can be avoided with honor, or even without — the object of the administration appears to be to treat for the purchase of the Floridas. . . . but not withstanding the pacific temper of our government, there is great reason to expect hostility [with Spain] . . . If these apprehensions should be justified by events, a military force on our part would be requisite and that force must come from your side of the mountains."

To whet Jackson's appetite and to hint that Burr not only had inside information but was in the confidence of Secretary of War Dearborn, Burr told Jackson, "I take the liberty of recommending to you to make out a list of officers . . . for one or two regiments. . . . If you will transmit to me this list, I will, in case troops should be called for, recommend it to the department of war, and I have reason to believe that, on such an occasion, my advice would be listened to." Jackson would briefly turn on Burr, persuaded in December 1806 that Burr had done the one thing Jackson could not abide — lied. But when the trials were over, Jackson would again become Burr's friend.

If Burr had intimated to Jackson in March 1806 that Burr was in the administration's good graces, he had told a whopper. As it happened, two weeks before Burr wrote to Jackson, he visited Jefferson in Washington, D.C., seeking "to engage in something" befitting his high station. According to Jefferson's recollection of the meeting, Burr expressed concern about the negative newspaper reports of his activities. Jefferson cordially reassured Burr that he believed Burr capable and talented. But he offered no help, no office — nothing but bland civilities. Realizing that nothing would come of the meeting, Burr warned Jefferson that he could do the president much harm. Jefferson was not impressed by the threat.

Burr sought Jefferson's patronage because the 1805 tour through the West had not improved the former vice president's finances. From June 6 to 10, 1805, Wilkinson, returning to his post as the governor and military commander of the northern territory of Louisiana, joined Burr at Fort Massac, on the Ohio River at the southern tip of Illinois. There was much talk of projects, but nothing was resolved. Wilkinson, acting governor of the northern Louisiana Territory, a post both military and civil, enjoyed his position and its collateral benefits. As a sometime tradesman, Wilkinson appreciated the opportunities to do some business on the side with the fur traders and other entrepreneurs who came down the river. But no crumbs fell off that table for Burr.

As they parted, Wilkinson embraced Burr as an esteemed friend and offered him a fully equipped barge for the long trip down the Mississippi. Had Burr stumbled into Wilkinson's snare, becoming Wilkinson's tool? Not yet, if ever. Instead, the two talked as equals and promised to keep one another's confidences. Burr would. Wilkinson would not. Had Burr misjudged his new friend? He had the misfortune of trusting men of no character before, as fiscal calamities in New York testified.

On June 25, 1805, Burr landed in New Orleans, the guest of old friend and ally Edward Livingston. James Parton, one of Burr's first biographers, suggested that Burr might have been thinking about practicing law in New Orleans. Though the city was the hub of Mississippi River commerce, it was already overfull with lawyers. Livingston led the pack. Although they were one of the ruling families of New York and New Jersey, the Livingstons could not escape the cycle of debts and bankruptcies that plagued the new nation. Edward had fled debts in New York and found happiness in New Orleans. But he did not ask Burr to join him at the bar. For three weeks, Burr sparkled at public gatherings and in private conversations, but nothing rewarding came of them.

New Orleans simmered with rumors of military adventures and commercial schemes, and Burr's presence added spice to them. Some were new; others were retreads. Many involved Spanish Florida and Spanish Mexico. William Claiborne, the governor of the southern Louisiana Territory, had little use for the Spanish but did not encourage Burr, and Burr did not reveal his plans to anyone.

Burr went north in July, stopping at Natchez on the Mississippi, reconnoitering land speculation opportunities, and again met Wilkinson on September 12, 1805, at Wilkinson's headquarters in St. Louis. Burr still felt that Wilkinson was his ally, while Wilkinson was already hedging his bets. As Burr wrote to Wilkinson at the end of the month, "I never take any sort of liberty with any man's secrets but my own." Wilkinson's conduct was of a different sort. He wrote in his *Memoirs* that the St. Louis conversation shook his confidence in Burr, but at the time Wilkinson seemed, to one subordinate at least, to be leaning toward participation in some secret adventure.

In St. Louis, Burr allegedly spoke of the imbecility of Jefferson's administration. It had not acted to protect Western interests. Wilkinson, according to his later account, replied, "The western people disaffected to the government! They are bigoted to Jefferson." And if Burr believed differently, "no man was ever more mistaken." Oddly, Wilkinson could recall no more of their conversations, though they transpired over the course of an entire week.

For Wilkinson soon knew that the Federalists were already spreading the rumor that Burr intended to sever the union. On August 2, 1805, the Federalist house organ, the *Gazette of the United States*, asked its readers whether Burr planned to raise revolution in the Western states. The Federalists hated Burr, and his travels through the West set off alarm bells for Federalist politicians. The West was Republican territory, and as the country spread west, the Federalists saw the end of their party hopes. One way to attack Western political views was to claim that the section's leaders wanted to sever the union. Bashing Burr allowed the Federalists to express these fears. Supposedly led by Burr, the Western states would plunder the Louisiana Purchase lands, repudiate the payments owed, and declare their independence. The article was widely reprinted in Western newspapers. It may have been that publication that worried Wilkinson.

Burr spent the winter of 1805–1806 in Washington, D.C. Theodosia was having one of her many bouts of illness. The Burr coffers were empty. Burr remained buoyant. He upped his request from Merry to £110,000. The interview with Jefferson went poorly, but Burr had expected as much. He returned to Philadelphia. There Burr cultivated Bollman. The German émigré was a man for all seasons — a medical doctor, engineer, and political activist in Europe, who, like Blennerhassett, had come to America because it seemed to welcome men of adventurous spirit. Bollman would prove a loyal recruit to the Western adventure, particularly when it came to dangerous missions.

In the meantime, Dayton agreed to approach the Spanish with a clever bluff, the object of which was a payoff. The Spanish were interested but never paid a centavo. Burr wrote to and then spent part of a day with Charles Biddle in Philadelphia. To Biddle he revealed that he planned to arm men and post them on the border of the Spanish Empire. They would deter a Spanish incursion (which soon in fact occurred, somewhat south of Burr's planned outpost). Burr also hinted, after some hesitation, that even if there was no war with Spain, its northern colonies were ripe for revolt, and he would be happy to spur it. This was what he meant by "revolutionizing" the West. Biddle would have none of it, but he did not then or later think that Burr intended treason.

In late January 1806, Burr approached General William Eaton, a hero of the Tripoli war disappointed in his treatment by Jefferson and Congress. He should have received a hero's welcome on his return. Instead, he was petitioning for repayment of his expenses. Eaton listened, he later reported, to Burr's increasingly wild-eyed schemes with increasing dismay. He would relate these to Jefferson and to select members of Congress. His affidavit, procured at Jefferson's behest after a series of noncommittal communications between the retired general and the president, would be introduced as evidence against Burr. Burr approached Commodore Thomas Truxton, another disgruntled veteran, with a plan for an invasion of the Spanish Empire. Truxton thought the idea neither criminal nor dishonorable, but he wanted no part of it.

Burr renewed his friendship with Albert Gallatin, Jefferson's secretary of the treasury, and asked Gallatin if he knew how Burr might gain title to the 400,000 acres of Mississippi delta farmland that Felipe Neri, Baron Bastrop, had owned but not improved. It was to have been a colony for Dutch Protestants in Spanish Louisiana, but the project had come to naught. Bastrop sold it to Abraham Morehouse, who deeded it back to Bastrop a year later, in 1800. Bastrop went bankrupt and Morehouse again claimed the land, but he had to fend off rival claimants and creditors. Edward Livingston had invested in the deal as well, but nothing was settled in law or on the ground when Burr decided that he would take part. He raised the money to pay for a share of the grant sometime in the late summer of 1806 and paid for part of it in October.

Burr paid with drafts (a promise to pay) drawn on friends and a small cash deposit, and by assuming as his own part of the debt that Edward Livingston owed for his purchase. The house-of-cards payment scheme was typical of land deals, and like so many speculations, depended on the buyer's credit standing. Burr's credit was none too secure, but then, Bastrop's original title to the vast parcel was no more dependable.

That summer, Burr was on the move again. He laid out his itinerary in vaguely and ominously worded posts to his collaborators. To Blennerhassett he wrote that "the business, however, depends, in some degree, on contingencies, now within my control, and will not commence, before December or January, if ever." At the end of July, he wrote and consigned to Swartwout and Bollman letters for Wilkinson. Swartwout encoded the letter and was to carry it overland. Bollman would travel with it by sea to New Orleans. But as Swartwout later testified, before he could depart, Peter Ogden brought him another letter, sealed, that supposedly came from Burr. It was that letter, in Jonathan Dayton's handwriting, not Swartwout's or Burr's, that Wilkinson received in November 1806.

The awkward prose of the Wilkinson letter suggests that it was originally in the cipher that Wilkinson prepared. A copy went to the Court in *Ex Parte Bollman* (1807), the dress rehearsal for *U.S. v. Burr* (1807), in Wilkinson's hand, not Burr's. Wilkinson admitted in open court, during cross-examination, that he had made "certain alterations" in the decoding of the letter, but that admission came late in September 1807, after Burr was acquitted of the treason charges. Another copy was published by Wilkinson in the course of his attempts to exonerate himself in 1811 and 1816. But before he received the letters from Burr, on August 13, 1806, Wilkinson had written to Burr, "I am ready." Curiouser and curiouser.

It is entirely possible that the Ogden substitute letter was not from Burr at all. Milton Lomask, a leading Burr biographer, notes that the Wilkinson version of the letter said that Theodosia and Burr's grandson would accompany him, but she was sick and his grandson was sicker. The letter mentioned Alston, but Swartwout later swore that the original did not mention Alston. The letter said that the English navy would help in the invasion of Mexico — something that Burr and Wilkinson both knew was out of the question. When Burr finally saw the letter he was supposed to have written, he was astonished. On his deathbed, he regarded it, and the surmises based on it, as madness.

While Burr's confederates left to find Wilkinson, their chief decamped for his second tour through the West. Leaving Theodosia in the healthful hills of western Pennsylvania, he traveled to Pittsburgh, then to Blennerhassett Island, to discuss in "private communication" what Burr had refused to consign to the post. For some reason, along the way, the usually secretive Burr confided some version of his plans to George Morgan, another Revolutionary War veteran. Morgan was astounded, or so he told Jefferson when he reported Burr's conversation a month later. Jefferson was grateful for Morgan's account, received on September 15, which "coincides . . . with what has been learned from other quarters."

The "other quarters" were the letters from third parties reporting a "Burr fever" among Westerners eager to drive Spain from the continent, and repeating Eaton's account of a Burr offer to him to lead an army into Mexico. But the most often repeated of these warning missives arrived from federal attorney Joseph Daveiss in Kentucky. He was a holdover from the Adams administration, and according to Jefferson "a partisan troublemaker."

The first Daveiss letter had arrived at the White House on December 1, 1805, and they kept coming. "We have traitors among us," Daveiss insisted. In a February 13, 1806, report to Jefferson, Daveiss detailed the Republicans intriguing with Burr. They included Jefferson's close friend John Breckinridge, the attorney general of the United States, Senator Samuel Smith of Maryland, and Andrew Jackson, among others. When Daveiss started naming Republicans, Jefferson's initial ardor for more information cooled. Put off by Jefferson, Daveiss stuck off Breckinridge's name. Cut off from access to the president, Daveiss turned to the pages of the Federalist *Western World* to denounce Burr. The July 1806 number of the paper featured the warning: "The project of Colonel Burr is doubtless of the most extensive nature, and if accomplished will not only affect the interests of the Western country, but of the known world." Burr was nothing less than a would-be Napoleon of the West. John Brown was so upset by reading his name in the *Western World*'s account of the Burr conspiracy that he wrote Jefferson on July 25, "the charges exhibited are false and without foundation."

Burr must have smiled to himself when he read the editorials, but he was too busy to reply. He stopped at Blennerhassett Island on August 27 to pay his respects to his hosts and to arrange for boats and supplies for the recruits he expected his lieutenants to send to the island. He contracted for fifteen boats, capable of carrying five hundred men, as well as for provisions. He left the next day, and a week later, he arrived in Cincinnati to confer with John Smith. Smith's two sons would join Burr in his travels. Then the growing Burr party was off to Frankfort, Kentucky, for a visit with John Brown. On September 24, Burr again enjoyed Andrew Jackson's hospitality in Nashville. Burr commissioned the purchase of six more boats. The armada would travel down the Mississippi to the portion of the Bastrop grant that Burr was in the process of purchasing.

One aside: recent scholarship has portrayed the "opening" of the lands on either side of the Mississippi as the great mission of Southern slaveholders. By so doing, they would diffuse the slave population (and thereby reduce the risk of slave insurrections in the Carolinas and Virginia), obtain rich bottomlands for the cultivation of the new cash crop of cotton, and protect slavery from federal intrusion by bringing new slave states into the union. Burr had a slave, a longtime personal servant, but opposed slavery, the slave trade, and the expansion of slavery. If slaveholders looked to the delta as fertile ground for their "peculiar institution," Burr did not share that vision.

But Burr was still playing the war-with-Spain card. He convinced Jackson that war was inevitable and wrote to William Henry Harrison, governor of the Indiana Territory, that "all reflecting men consider a war with Spain to be inevitable." Harrison was dubious. In any case, by this time, Burr had involved so many men of such importance in the Republican Party that Jefferson, until now slow to act, had to bestir himself.

On October 22, Jefferson had called one of his infrequent full cabinet meetings. Its subject was Burr. As Jefferson later wrote, Burr seemed a "a crooked gun . . . whose aim or shot you could never be sure of." But no action was taken. On October 24, after another meeting with his cabinet, he ordered that letters go to the governors of the Western states and the territory of Mississippi warning of unrest, and the next day he sent John Graham, secretary of the southern Louisiana Territory, to dog Burr's steps. Graham would thereafter replace Wilkinson as civil governor of northern Louisiana — a reward for prospective services.

A month later, a fast rider had arrived from Wilkinson's headquarters, reporting the contents of the letter that Swartwout had delivered, and warning of Burr's (alleged) army's descent on New Orleans. On November 25, the president once again summoned his cabinet. This time Jefferson was prevented from precipitate action by James Madison. Asked whether U.S. troops could be used against Burr, Madison had replied that they were not to be used to quell a domestic disturbance.

Jefferson persisted: what about the invasion of another nation's lands? On November 27, he issued a proclamation. "Sundry persons, citizens of the U.S. or resident within the same, are conspiring and confederating together to begin and set on foot . . . a military expedition . . . against the dominions of Spain." Such an enterprise was "criminal," and all who joined in it must either "withdraw from the same without delay" or face the consequences. He did not name Burr, supposedly the chief conspirator, or Wilkinson, who had denounced the plot.

Jefferson was not the only one watching Burr's movements with increasing concern. His motives and conversation were still unknown, which provoked the press to the most outrageous speculation. James Cheetham's Republican paper, the *New York American Citizen*, feasted on Burr rumors. On November 18, the paper reported that suspicions of Burr's criminal activities "swarm around us" and demand "vigilance." Cheetham had long made Burr a target. Even Jefferson conceded as much, though he brushed off the newspaper campaign against Burr. "That as to the attack excited against him in the newspapers, I had noticed it but as the passing wind." But the wind grew stronger. Three days later that vigilance paid off: the newspaper reported that known Federalists were consorting with Burr. While Republican papers decried a Federalist plot, Federalist papers denounced Burr and revealed that his coconspirators were all Republicans.

With Wilkinson's report and the newspaper speculation in hand, Jefferson revealed the chief plotter's identity. On December 20, 1806, the president ordered his secretary of the navy, Robert Smith, to warn all ships against entering into any aggressive act against Spanish territory: "Sir: A military expedition formed on the Western waters by Colonel Burr will soon proceed down the Mississippi, and by the time you receive this letter will probably be near New Orleans. You will, by all the means in your power, aid the army and militia in suppressing this enterprise." Jefferson was not entirely sure what Burr had in mind. In April, Jefferson had written to James Bowdoin in Spain that Burr wanted to attack Mexico. In July 1807, on the eve of the Burr trial, Jefferson would relate to the Marquis de Lafayette that Burr wanted to sever the union.

Daveiss sprang into action without Jefferson's approval. Kentucky was a hotbed of rumor and politicking. Burr's allies included newly chosen Senator Adair and former senator Brown. They lived in Frankfort, the capital. Both, along with Harry Innes, the federal district court judge for Kentucky, were friends of Wilkinson. So were the judges of the Kentucky state court of appeals. Burr had detractors, too, including former senator Humphrey Marshall, a federalist and ally of Daveiss.

With Daveiss gathering information — mostly the same rumors that the *Western World* printed — he approached Innes on November 5 and sought an arrest warrant for Burr. He wanted to prevent Burr from his supposed invasion, so he said. Innes declined to issue the warrant. Daveiss then asked that a federal grand jury be assembled so he could indict Burr for trial in the federal circuit court for Kentucky. Innes acceded to the request, and Daveiss set about gathering his witnesses.

Daveiss not only had to prove that Burr had gathered supplies and men, but that the purpose of the gathering was illegal. Burr heard of the proceedings, writing to Blennerhassett on November 6 that "villains enough may have been found to encounter all the perjuries which may be thought necessary to gratify malice" and support the "absurd and ridiculous" charges. But Burr rushed from Lexington to Frankfort, where he engaged for his defense a rising young attorney named Henry Clay. With key witnesses unavailable, Daveiss could not proceed, and he asked that the grand jury be dismissed. Burr went off to complete his round of Kentucky errands. Clay would go on to a distinguished career in Congress.

By the beginning of December, Daveiss found his witnesses and reconvened the grand jury. Burr satisfied Clay that there was no plot and no armed band, and Clay continued to represent Burr. After grand jury hearings from December 2 to 4, the grand jurors found "no bill" against Burr on the treason charges. There was no probable cause to bind him over for trial. The next day, he convinced the grand jury that he had not violated the Neutrality Act. "The grand jury are happy to inform the court that no violent disturbance of the public tranquility or breach of the laws has come to their knowledge. . . . There has been no testimony before us which does in the smallest degree criminate the conduct of [Burr]."

While Daveiss stumbled about, Graham was making progress. In Marietta, he bumped into Blennerhassett and learned that Burr had plans for some project, but no present interest in acting. Graham concluded that Blennerhassett had not told him the entire truth, and that action of an illegal sort was imminent. Armed with Jefferson's letter to the governors, on December 1, Graham raced to meet Governor Edward Tiffin of Ohio at his home in Chillicothe. He asked the governor to call out the militia and seize the boats and men on Blennerhassett Island. The governor sent a message to the state legislature: boats full of armed Frenchmen were slithering down the Ohio; caches of arms had already arrived on the island; masses of men, perhaps 1,300, maybe 4,000 or more, were hurrying to the rendezvous. A militia troop arrived on the island on December 9 and seized eleven boats and two hundred barrels of provisions. They found no armed band. Perhaps thirty had left on December 5. Seven young men, most of good families, were sailing from Pittsburgh, some of them lawyers. Apparently no conspiracy was complete without a corps of attorneys. Rumors multiplied these few into an army and their flatboats into an armada. Graham was, if not the source of this misinformation, certainly its willing reporter.

What really happened on December 9, 1806, on Blennerhassett Island? Burr could not have told anyone, for he was two hundred miles away. Was an armed body of men climbing into riverboats to "revolutionize" the West? Testimony about the motives of the men would later conflict, but the conflict would mean everything to Burr, for in the end, this was the only overt act of "levying war" that the government's prosecutors could allege in their treason indictment.

Burr left Frankfort and spurred to Nashville, arriving on December 13. Jackson, warned by now that Burr was not a confidant of the administration, covered his back by firing off letters to Jefferson offering to command a force to arrest Burr. But a late-night meeting with Burr convinced Jackson that the ex–vice president was Jefferson's agent. Not waiting for Jackson to change his mind again, Burr set off before Christmas for the Cumberland River. There he launched his flotilla of two flatboats. His party consisted of a few hardy companions and some horses. He met Blennerhassett a little below the mouth of the Wabash on the Ohio, where the party signed "articles of agreement" to settle the Bastrop grant and fight the Spanish. By the end of December, the fleet had ten boats, filled with family and friends, perhaps five dozen men in all, and turned west and south, to the Mississippi.

Burr only now learned that peace with Spain was inevitable: Wilkinson had met a Spanish raiding party at the Sabine River, and a truce was concluded. From that moment, Burr's journey down river was a voyage to nowhere, a winter vacation junket of former government officials, adventurers, speculators, and a few armed men. Tying up the boats and going ashore a few miles above Natchez, on January 10, 1807, Burr learned that Wilkinson had ordered his arrest. He should have expected as much, but witnesses said that Burr was surprised.

Meanwhile, New Orleans newspaper reports preceded Burr's arrival. James L. Donaldson recalled in a later affidavit that he was in New Orleans from the middle of October to December 10, 1806, and that "during the latter part of this time he was frequently in the company of general James Wilkinson." All Donaldson knew about Burr came from Wilkinson. Wilkinson spoke and acted as if Burr's plans were a complete surprise to him until Swartwout and Bollman arrived with the coded letters. Donaldson: "Wilkinson had received a letter from Burr holding forth great inducements to him to become a party, of which he showed me the original in cypher, and another written paper purporting to be a decyphered copy of the letter." Wilkinson "expressed great indignation at the plot, and surprise that one so well acquainted with him as Burr should dare to make to him so degrading a proposal, and declared his determination of defeating the enterprise, or perishing in the attempt." Presumably all the city then learned "That the general had undoubted and indisputable evidence of a treasonable design formed by Aaron Burr and others to dismember the union, by a separation of the Western states and territories from the Atlantic states; that New-Orleans was in immediate danger." For this reason (and not because Jefferson had so instructed, or because he was in the Spanish pay) Wilkinson "had concluded a hasty compromise with the Spaniards, so as to be able to withdraw his troops instantly" to New Orleans, Burr's "immediate object of attack and great vulnerable point."

Wilkinson was already building the case against Burr's accomplices Bollman and Swartwout, and other coconspirators in the city. "Wilkinson observed in addition that there were many agents of Mr. Burr then in the town, who had already been assiduous in their visits, and towards whom he was determined to act with cautious ambiguity, so as at the same time to become possessed of the whole extent of the plan." Wilkinson asked Donaldson to copy "certain papers and documents, and prepar[e] certain dispatches for the general government." The more Wilkinson could vanish into a sea of busy functionaries, the better he could conceal his own guilt.

Donaldson recalled that when he left for Washington, D.C., "the inhabitants of [New Orleans] were in a state of great alarm, and apprehended a serious attack from Mr. Burr and his confederates." Here was the ultimate irony. The newspaper campaign had turned rumor into report. Wilkinson simply gave the rumor mill a fast and strong turn, and out of it came a warning of an imminent invasion. Wilkinson had created the alarm, in part to hide his own complicity, in part to declare martial law and so control the legal process, and in part to prevent Burr from making his case should he arrive. Donaldson "understood that mercantile business was much embarrassed, and great fears were entertained of considerable commercial failures in consequence of the embargo which had been imposed; that general Wilkinson was taking strong measures of defence, and that 400 persons were then actually engaged in the fortifications of the city."

Lieutenant W. Wilson picked up the story. "I left New-Orleans on my way to this city [Washington, D.C.] on the 15th of December last: at that time, and for some time preceding, the strongest apprehensions and belief universally prevailed among the inhabitants of that city, that Aaron Burr and his confederates had prepared an armed force, and were advancing to attack and plunder the city." To counter the false alarm he had spread, Wilkinson turned the city upside down. "The greatest alarms prevailed." Wilkinson seized supplies and building materials without paying for them, and occupied himself "in the most active military preparations for the defence of the place; repairing the forts, mounting cannon, collecting ammunition, &c."

Wilkinson was covering his tracks, telling all who would listen of his "firm persuasion and belief that such an attack was meditated, and about very speedily to take place, by the said Burr." And the proof that Wilkinson was not a culprit but a patriot was that he told Wilson of his accurate "information, that the said Burr and his confederates were advancing with an armed force against this place." When Wilkinson learned that Burr and his small party had reached Natchez, he sent a detachment of 275 men to arrest Burr and any who traveled with him. The agents had no warrants, no charges, and no legal authority — but they had guns.

Back in Natchez, federal judge Thomas Rodney wrote to Caesar, his son, that Burr was to be indicted before a territorial grand jury. Burr insisted that he was there to settle the lands that he bought. He needed armed men because the Indians and the Spanish presented dangers. He had with him the same sixty men, no store of military ordnance (only the muskets such an enterprise would normally carry), and no ill will for the civil authorities. On January 16, he surrendered to them and readied himself for another grand jury hearing.

Burr had already made friends in the territorial legislature. Territorial governor Cowles Mead found the former vice president both a gentleman and, perhaps, even innocent. The result was that Burr negotiated with Mead a pledge "to protect the said A. Burr during his stay in the territory . . . that in the meantime there shall be no restraint of his person, no violence or molestation to his boats or his people." More rumors of the arrival of the rest of the Burr party — hundreds of men armed to the teeth — failed to stir much concern. Graham finally caught up with Burr on January 30, and the two spent a pleasant and uneventful evening discussing Burr's intentions. At Washington, Mississippi, the territorial capital, Judge Rodney, a Republican and a Jefferson appointee, summoned a grand jury to hear charges against Burr. On February 4, it found Burr innocent on all the counts and then added that he had been mistreated by the territorial government.

There would be no trial in Mississippi, but Rodney refused to allow Burr to go free. He was waiting for Wilkinson's armed men to arrive. Burr knew, or at least suspected, that Wilkinson had plans for him that did not include a grand jury hearing or a trial at law. A fatal accident, or a failed escape attempt ending in Burr's death, would be best. On February 5, he forfeited his bail and fled.

After a month of hard riding eastward, away from Wilkinson but toward Washington and Philadelphia, on February 19, 1807, Burr was discovered and recaptured near the Tombigbee River in Alabama. The captors were an army lieutenant from Virginia named Edmund Gaines and an ambitious young lawyer named Nicholas Perkins. Both knew about Burr's flight. Both wanted Jefferson's patronage, and both would profit for their exertions. Burr was a dangerous prisoner, not because he posed the threat of violence to his captors, but because, given the opportunity, he charmed everyone he met. Under guard, he was taken to Fort Stoddard, where the local citizenry were soon roused to sign a petition on his behalf. Wilkinson told Gaines to get a move on, and Burr was hustled from the fort to the Oconee River in northeast

Georgia and thence to South Carolina. For a brief moment, Burr eluded his captors and pled for assistance. Did he mention his son-in-law's name? Alston was a powerful and much-respected man. He would serve as governor from 1812 to 1814. No matter; restrained, he was once more set on the road to Richmond — and trial. His offenses were high treason and high misdemeanor, the latter for violating the Neutrality Act of 1794.

CHAPTER 3

What Is a Little Treason among Revolutionaries?

By the time of his capture and rendition, Burr had twice faced charges of treason. Every government in western history passed laws against this offense. But this most heinous of crimes, from the perspective of the government, was also the most controversial of them in the new nation, in part because the Revolution was in one sense treason on the grandest scale. The framers of the Constitution and the members of the first Congresses had thus a double task. The first was to protect the new federal government and the nation against domestic insurrections. The second was to prevent those in government from using a charge of treason to punish those who merely opposed the current regime.

The law of treason in the Anglo-American world had a long and controversial history before 1787. It is the capital offense most susceptible to political animus and yet the most diffuse and broad in scope. The English Statute of Treasons of 1351 laid out the understanding of the crown, and the legislation underscored the broad discretion the crown gave to its own courts and prosecutors in determining who fell under the shadow of the offense.

Treason in old English law might not entail an act but merely the discussion of an act. This was because the key element of the crime was the protection of the crown and the succession to the crown, not the security of the nation per se. "If a man makes war against our said lord the king in his kingdom, or is an adherent of enemies to our lord the king in the kingdom, giving them aid or comfort in his kingdom or elsewhere," then the charge was treason. The levying of war must be within the kingdom, or the charge of treason could be laid against any prisoner of war or captive anywhere that England fought. Anyone who "slays the chancellor, treasurer, or justice of our lord the king . . . while [such official is] in his place and attending to his office" was a traitor, for these officials were corporeal extensions of royal power.

Finally, and perhaps most importantly, "If a man compasses or imagines the death of our lord the king, of our lady his consort, or of their eldest son and heir; or if a man violates the king's consort, the king's eldest daughter being as yet unmarried, or the consort of the king's eldest son and heir," it was treason. *To compass* was to grasp an idea or to contrive and implied mental acts only.

The overbroad and vague statute allowed the crown to prosecute its most vocal opponents as traitors, to seize their property, and to silence their followers. For imagining and compassing the death of the king implied that any conspiracy to achieve these goals, no matter how lightly undertaken or how abortive, was treasonous. Giving comfort to the king's enemies at home might entail providing a night's bed and board. Words of comfort or complicity were sufficient to comprise the offense, as were thoughts expressed out loud.

Attached to the treason law in England was a *salvo*, a savings or exception clause; the king or the legislature might add offenses to the list as needed. Parliament would make criticism of the crown or seeking to sway the sentiments of the kings' subjects against him into one of these "constructive treasons." The salvo broadened an already Falstaffian statute to cover just about any form of politically inapposite behavior, thought, or utterance. For example, in the treason trial of Sir John Perrot (1592), the prosecution argued, "the original of his Treasons proceeded from the imagination of his heart; which imagination was in itself High-Treason, albeit the same proceeded not to any overt fact: and the heart being possessed with the abundance of his traitorous imagination, and not being able so to contain itself, burst forth in vile and traitorous Speeches."

Even speech that was not directly critical or incendiary came under the purview of the treason statute. In 1535, Henry VIII arranged for his former friend and chancellor Thomas More to be tried for high treason. Although More would have been aghast at any act encompassing the death of King Henry, much less ravishing the king's consort, he refused to accede to Henry's desire to make himself head of the English church. There was no act of treason, only the allegation of words of opposition (and prosecution witnesses to these likely bribed to perjure themselves).

At his examination, More conceded that he was conscience bound to oppose the king, but he was enough of a lawyer to understand he must not act against the king. "He would say no more than that the Statute was like a two-edged Sword, for if he spoke against it, he should be the Cause of the Death of his Body; and if he assented to it, he should purchase the Death of his Soul."

During the trial More was allowed to speak, because all the king really wanted was More's contrition and obedience. More offered neither, but his defense is worth recalling because it touched on all the elements (or essentials) of the offense. "As to the first Crime objected against me, that I have been an Enemy out of stubbornness of Mind to the King's second Marriage; I confess, I always told his Majesty my Opinion of it, according to the Dictates of my Conscience, which I neither ever would, nor ought to have concealed." The good advisor always told the king the truth.

To the next charge, of violating the Act of Supremacy making Henry VIII the head of the state church, More assayed a little sophistry. "The second Charge against me is, That . . . I would not, [because] of a malignant, perfidious, obstinate and traitorous Mind, tell them my Opinion, whether the King was Supreme Head of the Church or not." But More had "nothing to do with that Act, as to the Justice or Injustice of it, because I had no Benefice [office] in the Church." As an officer of the crown, "I had never said nor done any thing against it; neither can any one Word or Action of mine be alleged, or produced, to make me culpable." Opinions kept to oneself were not treason; actions were treason.

More's answer to the third charge revolved around the law of evidence, a subject of great importance in all treason trials. In the "third principal Article in my Indictment . . . I am accused of malicious Attempts, traitorous Endeavours, and perfidious Practices against that Statute [of Supremacy]." This is what was called a general charge, a grab bag of miscellaneous acts and words. In the general charge, the crown did not have to detail every criminal act. Among More's "Traitorous endeavors and perfidious practices" was his writing "diverse Packets of Letters to Bishop Fisher; whereby I exhorted him to violate the same Law and encouraged him in the like Obstinacy" while More was imprisoned in the Tower of London.

More raised an objection to this evidence. "I do insist that these Letters, be produced and read in Court, by which I may be either acquitted or convinced of a Lye; but because you say the Bishop burnt them all, I will here tell you the whole truth of the matter." Written evidence produced and verified in court might have incriminated More, but testimony about documentary evidence had far less weight when the physical evidence could not be produced. For now, the truth depended on whom one believed, and an impartial jury, regarding the defendant as innocent until proven guilty, might presume that the burden of proof in such contests lay with the prosecution.

In More's, it did not. It took a jury hand picked to ensure conviction but an hour to reach the foregone verdict. For the court was the king's, the offense was defined by the king to protect his interest, and nothing, certainly not a jury, could stand between him and his object.

In 1603, Sir Walter Raleigh's loyalty to the late Queen Elizabeth festered in the mind of successor, James Stuart, crowned James I, and Raleigh had to stand trial for allegedly encompassing the death of his sovereign. The prosecution rested on the confession of an alleged confederate of Raleigh in the plot, but when the author of that confession could not be produced in court, the prosecutors fell back on hearsay. A boat pilot overheard another man say that Raleigh planned to depose King James.

Raleigh, who conducted his own defense (no defense counsel was allowed in treason trials until 1695), protested against hearsay evidence: "This is the saying of some wild Jesuit or beggarly Priest; but what proof is it against me?" Edward Coke (later chief justice and still later a victim of James's enmity himself) replied that the rumor "must perforce arise out of some preceding intelligence and shews that your treason had wings." Raleigh languished in the Tower of London because that is where James wanted Raleigh.

Thomas Wentworth, the first earl of Strafford, a leading figure in Charles I's employ, was impeached in Parliament for high treason in the winter of 1640–1641. His offense was the general charge that his actions tended to the destruction of the law and the liberties of the people. Strafford, a notably arrogant man, had been a high-handed military governor in Ireland, a tyrannous commander in the war against the Scots, and an unpopular political figure in England. But did the twenty-eight charges laid against him amount to a treason against the king? Surely not, for he had the king's permission for everything he did. One should note that the lawyers who led the prosecution for parliament argued for the broadest and most vague definition of treason, while Strafford, who previously loathed lawyers now surrounded himself with them, argued for the narrowest, most legalistic definition of the offense. He was convicted and beheaded.

The abuses of the treason law came full circle when Charles I was tried and convicted of high treason in 1648, on a charge of being a "Tyrant, a Traitor, a Murderer, and a public Enemy to the Commonwealth of England." To which the king, powerless and without legal counsel himself, replied "Ha . . . Let me see a legal Authority warranted by the Word of God, the Scriptures, or warranted by the Constitutions of the Kingdom, and I will answer." Adjudged guilty, he was beheaded. Was his attempt to regain his kingdom by force a treason, when the only definition of treason on the books was levying war against the king? Parliament amended the treason statute in 1695 to permit "all just and equal Means for Defence of . . . Innocencies in such Cases," which meant that defense counsel could examine and cross-examine witnesses and could compel the production of evidence. It did not make treason an offense against the realm, however. The object was still to protect the person and the succession of the ruling prince.

Although in the eighteenth century, after counsel was permitted defendants in treason trials, and rules for the admissibility of evidence tightened, the English experience proved that treason charges were yet potent government weapons, particularly when joined to two other offenses. First, treason might entail conspiracy. Even if the conspirators were not successful, even if there was no overt act on their part, merely whispering treasonous plans was treason. Conspiracy remains to this day an open-ended offense in itself, a weapon against alleged criminals that state and federal prosecutors frequently use.

As it happened, there was an analogous offense to the English notion of constructive treason in the Anglo-American colonies. A conspiracy among slaves to harm their masters, called *petty treason*, was punishable by death even if the conspirators did nothing to further the plan. Most of the colonies and, after independence, all of the Southern states kept this offense on the books. A conspiracy of this sort (a capital offense) was simply a gathering of slaves at which a crime against their masters was discussed. No attempt to carry out the plot by any of the slaves was necessary to institute the prosecution. All the slaves present (passive as well as active participants in the conversation) were equally liable under the law. This offense was as broadly defined and as impervious to defense argument as was constructive treason against the crown. The crime need not come to fruition, nor the conspiracy involve more than words. Although the analogy may seem a little far-fetched, it is worth more than passing notice. Just as the constructive conspiracy charge was a perfect way for an oppressive government to control dissidents, so the slave conspiracy charge was a perfect way for the master class to control unruly slaves.

The second offense that touched treason was seditious libel. Any libel of the government, no matter its truth, was actionable. Colonial law incorporated this offense. The charge of seditious libel—a written "censure of public men" for their official conduct—could be laid against anyone who published criticism of a royal governor. In *Zenger's Case* (1735), a New York newspaper editor who criticized governor William Cosby only escaped conviction when the editor's counsel convinced the jury that truth was a defense to the law. (In fact, as the chief justice of the colonial court instructed the jury, it was not a defense.)

In the new nation, the seditious libel provisions of the Sedition Act of 1798 punished any person who might "write, print, utter or publish . . . any false, scandalous and malicious writing or writings against the government of the United States, or either house of the Congress . . . or the President . . . with intent to defame . . . or to bring them, or either of them, into contempt or disrepute; or to excite against them, or either or any of them, the hatred of the good people of the United States." The Jeffersonian Republicans hated the act not only because it was aimed at them, but also because the judges of the federal courts at the time were all Federalists, the federal marshals who chose the juries were all Federalists, and one could expect the jurymen to be all Federalists. Jefferson pardoned all those convicted under the act, and Congress, after the act expired in 1801, repaid the fines.

There were a few colonial cases in which rebels were accused of treason—for example, in New England after King Philip's War and in Virginia after Bacon's rebellion—but these cases were not uppermost in American revolutionaries' minds when they contemplated resistance to the crown. Instead, the long shadow of the English law of treason, the English paranoia about conspiracies, and the severe punishments of the seditious libel laws darkened the Revolutionary crisis. On August 23, 1775, King George III, whose subjects the American colonists were in law and long usage, proclaimed:

> Whereas many of our subjects in divers parts of our Colonies and Plantations in North America, misled by dangerous and ill designing men, and forgetting the allegiance which they owe to the power that has protected and supported them . . . have at length proceeded to open and avowed rebellion, by arraying themselves in a hostile manner, to withstand the execution of the law, and traitorously preparing, ordering and levying war against us . . . we have thought fit, by and with the advice of our Privy Council, to issue our Royal Proclamation, hereby declaring . . . that all our subjects of this Realm, and the dominions thereunto belonging, are bound by law to be aiding and assisting in the suppression of such rebellion, and to disclose and make known all traitorous conspiracies and attempts against us.

While the king was warning the revolutionaries against treason, the revolutionaries were warning the loyalists. The Second Continental Congress resolved, in 1775, "That all persons abiding within any of the United Colonies . . . owe, during the same time, allegiance thereto. That all persons, members of, or owing allegiance to any of the United Colonies . . . who shall levy war against any of the said colonies within the same, or be adherent to the king of Great Britain, or others the enemies of the said colonies . . . giving to him or them aid and comfort, are guilty of treason against such colony." Although the language seemed to be a mirror image of the king's proclamation, Congress did require that offenders perform some overt act of treason. The word *conspiracy* was not used. These departures from the English law heralded an American law of treason far more constrained that its progenitor.

With the king and the revolutionaries hurling treason charges against one another, the notion of treason became a centerpiece of Revolutionary legal thinking, and a serious concern. Was treason simply a matter of perspective? Could the winners in battle simply punish the losers as traitors? Was the definition of the offense merely a matter of proclaiming that one's enemies were traitors? If so, then the revolutionaries would have welcomed into their laws the very arbitrariness and brutality of the common law against which they had fought. Even though loyalist bands carried on bloody guerilla warfare against citizens of New Jersey, South Carolina, and Georgia during the Revolutionary War, there were comparatively few trials of loyalists for treason, and in all of them, the defendants were clearly levying war. As Jefferson himself wrote when secretary of state, in 1792, "Treason . . . when real, merits the highest punishment. But most codes extend their definition of treason to acts not really against one's country. They do not distinguish between acts against the government and acts against the oppressions of the government; the latter are virtues; yet they have furnished more victims to the executioner than the former; because real treasons are rare; oppressions frequent. The unsuccessful strugglers against tyranny, have been the chief martyrs of treason laws in all countries."

The ambiguity about what was and what was not treason continued to beset the founders of the new nation in the Confederation period, from 1781 to 1788. In Massachusetts, the hard times following the War for Independence had left many Western farmers without the money to pay their mortgages or their taxes. Banking interests in Boston and Salem demanded that the legislature help them collect debts owed them. Dominated by the creditors, the legislature obliged. Resistance to foreclosure on farm mortgages for failure to pay led farmers in western Massachusetts to armed insurrection, led by one Daniel Shays, a Revolutionary War hero. After two affrays, a mercenary troop raised by governor John Bowdoin routed the rebels. Not only had the governor used mercenaries to quell the rebellion, a step that was entirely foreign to Revolutionary thinking, but he had also asked the legislature to suspend of the writ of habeas corpus — the means by which anyone in government custody could seek a court hearing on the reasons for the imprisonment. The legislature complied.

The rebels had certainly given effect to their views. The treason was action, not thought or dissent. Still, the rebellion in western Massachusetts, and the means that Bowdoin had used to quash it, gave politicians all over the new United States pause. Although only two of the many insurrectionists who followed Daniel Shays were executed, it was plain that the streak of stiff-necked New England resistance to central authority that had fed the Revolutionary fervor had not died with the end of the war. Shays' Rebellion was one of the reasons why so many of the states (save Rhode Island) sent delegates to the Constitutional Convention in Philadelphia the next year. A stronger national government than the congress under the Articles of Confederation was necessary if such rebellions were not to spread from state to state. And the rebellion induced the framers of the Constitution to write a definition of treason into their new government's fundamental law.

Part of the effort to insure "domestic tranquillity," as the preamble to the Constitution would read, was to include provisions for the suppression of rebellions and the punishment of treason in the federal Constitution. According to the records of the Constitutional Convention, the first try at including a definition of treason in the nascent federal constitution came as part of the work of the "committee of detail." The committee met for a long stretch during the dog days of summer in 1787, and Edmund Randolph, a member of the committee, proposed that treason, so open an offense to prosecutorial discretion in England, was to be closely cabined in the new document. A draft document in Randolph's hand limited the offense to "levying war" against the United States or adhering to its enemies in time of war.

The Randolph draft, with additions by other committee members, was debated in the convention on August 20, 1787, and the convention added the "aid and comfort" and "two witnesses to" the same "overt act" to its language. Although the debate demonstrated that some delegates simply wanted to import the language of the English statute, overall the members of the convention preferred to limit the definition. No one argued that constructive treasons should be included or were included in the definition by implication. The final version, inserted at the end of Article III on the courts, read: "Treason against the United States, shall consist only in levying War against them, or in adhering to their Enemies, giving them Aid and Comfort. No Person shall be convicted of Treason unless on the Testimony of two Witnesses to the same overt Act, or on Confession in open Court. The Congress shall have power to declare the Punishment of Treason, but no Attainder of Treason shall work Corruption of Blood, or Forfeiture except during the Life of the Person attainted."

James Wilson, also a member of the committee of detail and one of the first justices of the new United States Supreme Court, was particularly pleased with the limitations on the definition of treason. If the two-witness rule made prosecution difficult, the likelihood of party prejudice, perjury, and prosecutorial misconduct required some kind of constraint on the prosecution. Too loose a definition of treason gave too much power to a government and led to untrammeled despotism.

Wilson told a Philadelphia audience in 1791 that "Treason is unquestionably a crime most dangerous to the society, and most repugnant to the first principles of the social compact. It must, however, be observed, that as the crime itself is dangerous and hostile to the state, so the imputation of it has been and may be dangerous and oppressive to the citizens." The members of the convention recognized the danger that treason posed to public order, that partisan treason accusations had posed to liberty, and had to balance the two. "To secure the state, and at the same time to secure the citizens — and, according to our principles . . . the law of treason should possess the two following qualities. 1. It should be determinate. 2. It should be stable."

Insofar as party, interest, or immediate passions might rule the government at a given time, a charge of treason might be entirely partisan, "to harass the independent citizen, and the faithful . . . by prosecutions for treasons, constructive, capricious, and oppressive." The English law, given in the past to such flimsy and partisan prosecutions, "was grossly deficient." The definition of treason was "uncertain and ambiguous; and its denomination and penalties were wastefully communicated to offences of a different and inferiour kind." Wilson's not-so-subtle reference to the treason indictments against the leading revolutionaries could not have been missed by his audience, many of whom had feared they too might be hanged if Britain had won the war.

But victory had brought the opportunity to reform the law of treason, to make it republican. "Admonished by the history of such times and transactions as these, when legislators are tyrants or tools of tyrants . . . the people of the United States have wisely and humanely" written safeguards into the law. The result was that "Little of this [English] statute, however, demands our minute attention now; as the great changes in our constitutions have superceded all its monarchical parts." With a single stroke, Wilson swept away the English cases and commentaries on the subject, or tried to, but in fact the old law books would remain on the lawyers' shelves, and the English cases and commentaries would find their way into American prosecutions soon enough.

By arguing that the precedents set in English cases no longer applied to American treason law, Wilson raised the importance of the precise language of the Constitution. As he understood that language, only citizens of this country could commit treason against it. Levying war was when the suspects were "arrayed in a warlike manner. As where people are assembled in great numbers, armed with offensive weapons, or weapons of war, if they march thus armed in a body . . . If they have no military arms, nor march or continue together in the posture of war; they may be great rioters, but their conduct does not always amount to a levying of war . . . So an actual insurrection or rebellion is a levying of war, and by that name must be expressed in the indictment."

What was more, war must be levied against the United States, not against a particular person, even if that person held high office. "A rising to maintain a private claim of right; to break prisons for the release of particular persons . . . this is not a levying of war against the United States. . . . The line of division between this species of treason and an aggravated riot is sometimes very fine and difficult to be distinguished. In such instances, it is safest and most prudent to consider the case in question as lying on the side of the inferiour crime."

Did the salvo on constructive treason arrive, under the radar, and attach itself to the constitutional language? Wilson thought not, but he did not have the final word on the matter. In 1798, U.S. Supreme Court Chief Justice Oliver Ellsworth, riding circuit (the Supreme Court justices sat with district court judges to hold federal circuit courts until 1891), charged a grand jury that their purview included "all offences against the United States. . . . Those offences are chiefly defined in the statutes . . . the residue are . . . acts manifestly subversive of the national government, or of some of its powers specified in the constitution." The last phrase sounded ominously like a constructive treason. Ellsworth sailed even closer to that port in his next words: "An offence consists in transgressing the sovereign will, whether that will be expressed, or obviously implied. Conduct therefore, clearly destructive of a government, or its powers, which the people have ordained to exist, must be criminal."

What were these offenses, if not spelled out in the statutes? Ellsworth found them in the very place that Wilson said one should not look: the common law of England. "It is not necessary to particularize the facts falling within this description, because they are readily perceived, and are ascertained by known and established rules; I mean the maxims and principles of the common law of our land. This law, as brought from the country of our ancestors, with here and there an accommodating exception, in nature of local customs, was the law of every part of the union at the formation of the national compact; and did, of course, attach upon or apply to it, for the purposes of exposition and enforcement." Did this apply to the treason provisions?

Ellsworth's reading of the law was a minority view. Supreme Court Justice James Iredell, sitting on a circuit court in a case of treason, had considered that point and rejected it. In a treason case coming to court in 1800, he opined, "a mere act of [the U.S.] Congress . . . could not interpret the meaning" of the treason clause. "In this we differ from the practice of England, from whence we received our jurisprudential system in general; for they having no constitution to bind them, the parliament have an unlimited power to pass any act of whatever nature they please; and they, consequently, cannot infringe upon the constitution." Although the treason statute of Edward III gave parliament this power, "Because other like cases of treason may happen in time to come, which cannot be thought or declared at present, it is thought that, if any such does happen, the judges should not try them without first going to the king and parliament, where it ought to be judged treason, or otherwise felony," Congress was forbidden to add to the types of treason or the requirements to prove it by the strict language of the constitutional provisions on treason.

Setting aside the question of whether Congress could add to the constitutional definition of treason, federal judges could ask what constituted a levying of war. Two major rebellions in the 1790s forced the new federal courts to decide whether they would, by interpreting the constitutional definition broadly, return treason to its common-law breadth. The first real test for the courts came after the suppression of the Whiskey Rebellion in 1793–1794. Farmers in western Pennsylvania and other wheat-growing regions in the western portion of the nation objected to the excise taxes that Congress, at Hamilton's behest, passed on distilled liquors. It was customary for farmers to distill grains that could not be transported to market. The excise tax fell particularly heavily on these farmers. While in other states farmers simply evaded the taxes, in Pennsylvania they threatened the excise tax collectors, closed the courts, and armed themselves to resist federal authority.

In reply, on August 7, 1794, President Washington issued a proclamation against those "combinations to defeat the execution of the laws . . . in some of the western parts of Pennsylvania . . . proceeding in a manner subversive equally of the just authority of government and of the rights of individuals." The rest of the proclamation sounded remarkably like King George's in 1775. The rebels had "effected their dangerous and criminal purpose by the influence of certain irregular meetings . . . by endeavors to deter those who might be so disposed from accepting offices . . . through fear of public resentment and of injury to person and property, and [by] compel[ling] those who had accepted such offices by actual violence to surrender or forbear the execution of them." The revolutionaries had done all of the above, and more, in violation of the laws and their sacred oaths to the crown.

Washington surely was aware of the similarities, but "by intercepting the public officers on the highways, abusing, assaulting, and otherwise ill treating them; by going into their houses in the night, gaining admittance by force, taking away their papers, and committing other outrages, employing for these unwarrantable purposes the agency of armed banditti disguised in such manner as for the most part to escape discovery," the Whiskey rebels were engaging in an insurrection "which I am advised amount[s] to treason, being overt acts of levying war against the United States."

Governor Thomas Mifflin, a conservative Republican, refused to call out the militia, recognizing that many militiamen were among the rioters. He wanted the federal courts to handle the problem. But the federal circuit judge, Supreme Court Justice Wilson, signified to the president that "in the counties of Washington and Allegheny, in Pennsylvania, laws of the United States are opposed and the execution thereof obstructed by combinations too powerful to be suppressed by the ordinary course of judicial proceedings or by the powers vested in the marshal of that district." Consequently, Washington ordered "all persons, being insurgents, as aforesaid, and all others whom it may concern, on or before the 1st day of September next to disperse and retire peaceably to their respective abodes. And I do moreover warn all persons whomsoever against aiding, abetting, or comforting the perpetrators of the aforesaid treasonable acts all in arms to lay them down."

Setting aside the disturbing similarity between 1794 and 1775, could a president define for himself what treason was? Was the president the final authority on the meaning of the Constitution? Although the point of precisely defining the scope of treason in the Constitution was (according to Wilson) to deny Congress the power to politicize treasons, nothing he said related to the power of the president.

Washington marched an army toward the area in rebellion, and the rebels surrendered. Hamilton, along as second in command, hoped that the ringleaders of the mob would include prominent western Pennsylvania antifederalists, but he was disappointed. A net cast so wide only dragged in twenty ordinary men. Left to languish in Philadelphia's new jail (brick instead of wood, and harder to escape), only two of the twenty actually came to trial. Nevertheless, at these trials, federal circuit court judges had the opportunity to decide whether the executive or the judicial branch had the final say on the meaning of the Constitution. In the end, only two of the thousands of protesters were convicted, and Washington, mindful of the Revolutionary echoes of the protest, pardoned both men.

In *U.S. v. Vigol* (1795), the single recorded case, Justice William Paterson, presiding over the circuit court trial of one of the armed conspirators, gave a three-paragraph opinion that did not deal with the law. Instead, it summarized the evidence and offered a gloss on the defense tactics. Paterson concluded, "With respect to the evidence, the current runs one way. It harmonizes in all its parts. It proves that the prisoner was a member of the party who went to [tax collector] Reigan's house, and, afterwards, to the house of [tax collector] Wells, in arms, marshalled and arrayed; and who, at each place, committed acts of violence and devastation." This was an act of war against the United States, not just against the two federal tax collectors. There were many witnesses to the act. The only question was whether Vigol feared for himself in committing the atrocity. "If, indeed, such circumstances could avail, it would be in the power of every crafty leader of tumults and rebellion to indemnify his followers by uttering previous menaces; an avenue would be forever open for the escape of unsuccessful guilt, and the whole fabric of society must, inevitably, be laid prostrate."

The sole case out of the rebellion that came to the High Court—the court whose interpretation of the Constitution governed proceedings in all the federal circuit and district courts—was *U.S. v. Hamilton* (1795), and in that case, the High Court did not redefine the constitutional provisions or deal with Washington's proclamation. In 1795, the courts faced the question of whether they could, or should, read the treason clause of Article III loosely or strictly. They consistently elected to read the language in its narrowest, strictest sense. Bearing in mind that the judges were all Federalists and that the culprits were not, one sees in the treason cases not party politics but a stern and self-denying fidelity to the rule of law.

Another antitax riot erupted in Pennsylvania in 1799, led (like Shays' Rebellion) by a Revolutionary War hero, John Fries. The tax on houses to support the anticipated war against France was so hated in Pennsylvania that Fries and others not only protested, but they also broke other protesters out of jail. John Adams issued a similar proclamation to Washington's: "I . . . command all persons being insurgents as aforesaid, and all others whom it may concern . . . to disperse and retire peaceably to their respective abodes: and I do, moreover, warn all persons whomsoever, against aiding, abetting or comforting the perpetrators of the aforesaid treasonable acts." The end result was the capture of Fries and two others and their trials for treason for forcibly rescuing other rioters from custody. Whether or not the direct tax Congress levied on homes was constitutional, armed resistance to the tax and its collectors was surely an offense—but what offense?

Iredell delivered a charge to the grand jury and summed up the evidence to the trial jury in Fries's first trial. The justice spent much of his time defending the Federalist Congress, warning about the impending war with France, and explaining why the Sedition Act was constitutional. "Such incessant calumnies have been poured against the government for supposed breaches of the constitution, that an insurrection has lately begun for a cause where no breach of the constitution is or can be pretended. The grievance is the land tax act, an act which the public exigencies rendered unavoidable, and is framed with particular anxiety to avoid its falling oppressively on the poor, and in effect the greatest part of it must fall on rich people only."

Was violent opposition to the act tantamount to treason? Iredell addressed the grand jury: "The only species of treason likely to come before you is that of levying war against the United States. There have been various opinions, and different determinations on the import of those words . . . if, in the case of the insurgents . . . the intention was to prevent by force of arms the execution of any act of the Congress of the United States altogether (as for instance the land tax act, the object of their opposition), any forcible opposition calculated to carry that intention into effect, was a levying of war against the United States, and of course an act of treason. But if the intention was merely to defeat its operation in a particular instance, or through the agency of a particular officer, from some private or personal motive . . . it did not amount to the crime of treason."

Iredell continued: There must be two witnesses to the same overt act. Conspiracy to undermine the government, punishable under the Sedition Act, did not by analogy or loose construction make conspiracy to levy war against the government treasonous, for treason required overt acts. Congress could not enlarge the definition of treason. Trial could be held where the federal court sat, and not (as would be true in a state criminal proceeding) in the county where the offense occurred. There must be a treasonable intention as well as the overt act of levying war. There must be force, but its extent may only be minimal. (It was not necessary to harm, merely to threaten harm.) But this case ended in a mistrial when evidence presented to Iredell convinced him that one of the jurors had prejudged the case. The juror was alleged to have said "Fries should hang" before the prosecution opened its case.

Iredell died before the second trial convened, and Justice Samuel Chase presided at it. Chase had summarized the law to the jury in terms similar to Iredell's. "A combination, or conspiracy to levy war against the United States is not treason, unless combined with an attempt to carry such combination, or conspiracy, into execution; some actual force, or violence, must be used, in pursuance of such design to levy war." Fries was convicted, although with "with great concern and reluctance" Chase noted. At the sentencing hearing two weeks later, Chase then lectured the defendant, and the country. Fries had no grounds for his conduct. The government under the Federalists was mild; the sentences of the Whiskey rebels had been commuted; Fries and his cohort should have learned from the events of 1794 what would happen to insurrectionaries; Congress's tax on homes to pay for the anticipated war with France was wholly constitutional; and capital punishment (under the 1790 Act punishing treason) was necessary as "a severe example to deter others." Chase then commended Fries to the mercy of a forgiving Christ, for Fries would find no forgiveness on earth.

Chase was mistaken. John Adams pardoned Fries in 1800. "I must take on myself alone the responsibility," he wrote, "of one more appeal to the humane and generous natures of the American people." In 1809, Adams wrote to a friend that the pardon gave him "great satisfaction." In 1815, Adams returned to the subject, somewhat less sympathetically. "What good, what example would have been exhibited to the nation by the execution of three or four obscure, miserable Germans." The fact remains that at the time, Hamilton complained that "temporisings like these, in times of fermentation and commotion" cost "men at the head of affairs to lose the respect of both friends and foes." It was one of Hamilton's many grievances against Adams, all rehearsed in the pamphlet Hamilton printed during the campaign. The publication widened the split in the Federalist Party, doomed Hamilton's political prospects, and prevented Adams from gaining reelection.

The treason trials had grown out of popular resistance to Federalist fiscal measures. Hamilton, at the center of these controversies, was also the indirect author of the second charge laid against Burr. The Neutrality Act of 1794, proposed in Washington's address to Congress on December 3, 1793, was drafted by Hamilton and passed on June 4, 1794. It punished those who waged wars against nations with whom the United States was at peace. "Every person who, within the limits of the United States, fits out and arms, or attempts to fit out and arm, or procures to be fitted out and armed, or knowingly is concerned in the furnishing, fitting out, or arming, of any vessel with intent that such vessel shall be employed in the service of any foreign prince or state . . . to cruise or commit hostilities against the subjects, citizens, or property of any foreign prince or state, or of any colony . . . with whom the United States are at peace . . . shall be deemed guilty of a high misdemeanor, and shall be fined not more than ten thousand dollars, and imprisoned not more than three years."

The purpose of the statute was generally to maintain American neutrality in the wars engulfing Europe. In particular, it barred Americans from outfitting vessels to aid the French. As such, the Federalists pushed it and the Republicans opposed it, because France, a military ally under the treaty of 1778, had called on the United States to honor its commitment to mutual defense. The federal government unilaterally renounced that obligation in the spring of 1793, when President Washington issued his Neutrality Proclamation. That decision sent Secretary of State Jefferson out the door, to return to Monticello and temporary retirement, and put Hamilton even closer to the levers of power.

Hamilton, dead by Burr's hand, had in spectral form twice struck against his ancient enemy. If the arming of men and the procurement of the riverboats was intended for an invasion of Spanish possessions, Burr and his men would have been guilty of a high misdemeanor under the statute. For this reason, when Burr came to trial, the prosecution lodged two charges against him, one for violation of the statute and the other for high treason.

The evidence for both charges came principally from Eaton, Wilkinson, and Thomas Jefferson, and was rehearsed before the U.S. Supreme Court and the nation while Burr was under close guard. On its face, that evidence seemed damning.

The Great Conspiracy Revealed

On January 27, 1807, Erick Bollman and John Swartwout arrived in Washington, D.C. Wilkinson had sent them, under guard, along with his affidavit, a copy of the decoded letter, and a cover letter. In the preceding week, Jefferson had addressed Congress, calling for the swift and public trial of Burr. The president also solicited an affidavit from Eaton. These three pieces of evidence — the Eaton account, the Wilkinson letters and affidavit, and Jefferson's summary view of the events — seemed to reveal a great conspiracy, nipped in the bud through the courage of Wilkinson and the wisdom of Jefferson.

William Eaton, a former army general, had confidential talks with Burr in the early winter of 1806. "Early last winter, col. Aaron Burr ... signified to me ... that, under the authority of the general government, he was organizing a secret expedition against the Spanish provinces on our south-western borders ... in which he was authorised to invite me to take the command of a division." This confirmed what Bollman had told Jefferson in a private conversation after Bollman was brought to Washington, in January 1807. Burr intended a filibustering expedition against the vulnerable Spanish provinces. This was illegal under the 1794 statute so long as the country was at peace with Spain, but not treasonous. Eaton, however, was eager to tell a fuller story. As much to ingratiate himself with Jefferson as to denounce Burr, Eaton went on at length. "I had never before been made personally acquainted with col. Burr; and, having for many years been employed in foreign service, I knew but little about the estimation this gentleman now held in the opinion of his countrymen and his government." Eaton, apparently innocent of all taint of conspiracy, had "no right to suspect [Burr's] patriotism. I knew him a soldier. In case of a war with the Spanish nation, which from the tenor of the president's message to both houses of Congress seemed probable, I should have thought it my duty to obey so honourable a call of my country; and, under that impression, I did engage to embark in the expedition."

In fact, Eaton was a proud man, and a disappointed one. His country had never honored him (or properly paid him) for his services abroad. He had no love for Jefferson and less for the Spanish. "I had frequent interviews with col. Burr in this city — and, for a considerable time, his object seemed to be to instruct me by maps, and other information, the feasibility of penetrating to Mexico — always carrying forward the idea that the measure was authorised by government."

Eaton reported that Burr then revealed another plot hidden beneath the first. "At length, some time in February [1806], he began by degrees to unveil himself. He reproached the government with want of character, want of gratitude, and want of justice." Burr knew Eaton had been lobbying in vain for back pay. "He seemed desirous of irritating resentment in my breast, by dilating on certain injuries . . . I had suffered . . . and from the delays of government in adjusting my claims for disbursements."

There was nothing in the foregoing, however, that would lead to the suspicion of treason. Eaton nevertheless "began to entertain a suspicion that Mr. Burr was projecting an unauthorised military expedition." Eaton now became the subtle interrogator, drawing Burr out by pretending to go along with him. "Desirous to draw an explanation from him, I suffered him to suppose me resigned to his counsel." It was the same role that Wilkinson would claim he adopted with Swartwout and Bollman.

Burr, a man of exquisite secrecy, supposedly now told Eaton, a man of bilious indiscreetness, a full and frank account of his plan to separate the West from the East. "He now laid open his project of revolutionising the western country, separating it from the union, establishing a monarchy there, of which he was to be the sovereign, and New-Orleans to be his capital; organising a force on the waters of the Mississippi, and extending conquest to Mexico."

Eaton had to pitch his story carefully, for he did not want to appear a collaborator only recently turned informant. "I suggested a number of impediments to his scheme — such as the republican habits of the citizens of that country, and their affection towards our present administration of government; the want of funds; the resistance he would meet from the regular army of the United States on those frontiers." All of these were obvious obstacles, in fact insuperable ones. Burr knew all of them.

But Burr refused to regard any of them, or Eaton, as a bar to the realization of his grandiose scheme. "Mr. Burr found no difficulty in removing these obstacles — he said he had, the preceding season, made a tour through that country, and had secured the attachment of the principal citizens of Kentucky, Tennessee, and Louisiana, to his person and his measures." Actually, Burr had done no such thing. He met with a handful of old and new friends and discussed a filibustering expedition, should war be declared. Supposedly, Burr also told Eaton that "he had inexhaustible resources." In fact, he was borrowing.

Finally, Burr "assured me the regular army would act with him, and would be reinforced by ten or twelve thousand men from the above mentioned states and territory, and from other parts of the union." By this time, surely Eaton knew (as Burr knew) that the likelihood of a reinforcement of ten or twelve thousand men was small. The regular army only had a little over three thousand men, but most of these were assigned to Wilkinson. The likelihood that the regular army (a tiny force) would rally to Burr was zero — about the same odds that he could defeat the loyal detachments on the Mississippi with a handful of filibusterers.

According to Eaton, Burr "now proposed to give me the second command in his army. I asked him who should have the chief command? He said, General Wilkinson." This revelation posed a serious problem for Eaton, not so much at the time that Burr allegedly revealed the Wilkinson side of the story, as a year later, when Eaton was framing his account for public consumption and the attention of the D.C. Court. By that time, Jefferson had already praised Wilkinson's honesty, honor, and patriotism in the message to Congress. So Eaton, who intimated in the affidavit that Wilkinson's career included some fast and loose conduct, told the D.C. Court, "I observed it was singular that he should count on general Wilkinson; the elevated rank and high trust he now held as commander in chief of our army and governor of a province, he would hardly put at hazard for any precarious prospects of aggrandizement." Burr replied not to worry — Wilkinson was in on the plan.

By implication, Eaton's account allowed Burr to impeach the patriotism and truthfulness of Wilkinson. "I asked Mr. Burr if he knew general Wilkinson? He answered yes, and echoed the question. I said I knew him well. 'What do you know of him?' said Mr. Burr. I know, I replied, that general Wilkinson will act as lieutenant to no man in existence." Eaton concluded that Wilkinson could only have been "seduced" into the conspiracy by Burr's "artful argument," though that same argument had failed to move Eaton one inch.

"At length," Eaton "discovered that [Burr's] ambition was not bounded by the waters of the Mississippi and Mexico, but that he meditated overthrowing the present government of our country." Burr would "gain over the marine corps, and secure the naval commanders, Truxton . . . and others, he would turn Congress neck and heels out of doors, assassinate the President, seize on the treasury and the navy, and declare himself the Protector of an energetic government." No one ever before accused Burr of such excesses of ambition, or oratory. On his deathbed, asked whether he had intended such a scheme, Burr answered that it would have been sheer madness. Eaton must have thought so as well. But all this "colonel Burr proposed confiding to me."

Eaton's account did not end with this revelation. Instead, he made himself the center of the next segment of the story. "Shocked at this proposition, I dropped the mask, and exclaimed against his views." Eaton's wounded honor spurred his protests. "I told colonel Burr he deceived himself in presuming that he, or any other man, could excite a party in this country who would countenance him in such a plot of desperation, murder and treason." Thus far, the two men had engaged in a heated but private political conversation, with some overheated posturing. But "I told him one solitary word would destroy him. He asked, what word? I answered, Usurper!" But Eaton still hesitated to pronounce that word. "Though wild and extravagant Mr. Burr's last project, and though fraught with premeditated slaughter, I felt very easy on the subject, because its defeat he had deposited in my own hands. I did not feel so secure concerning that of disjointing the union."

Eaton nevertheless weighed his next step. "The very interesting and embarrassing situation in which his communications placed me, left me, I confess, at a stand to know how to conduct myself with propriety." Eaton, no lawyer, still knew that Burr had committed "no overt act of aggression against law." Eaton chose to "expose myself to all consequences by a disclosure of his intentions. Accordingly, I waited on the President of the United States; and after some desultory conversation, in which I aimed to draw his view to the westward, I used the freedom to say to the President I thought Mr. Burr should be sent out of this country, and gave for reason that I believed him dangerous in it."

Of all the courses of action open to Eaton, telling Jefferson what Burr had said was surely the most extreme. Eaton could have threatened Burr with disclosure, told Burr's friends that he had gone off the tracks, denounced Burr anonymously, or spoken directly to Wilkinson to warn him, or warn him off. Instead, Eaton went to the one man whom Eaton knew despised and distrusted Burr, and who had the power to make Burr's life miserable. In all likelihood, Eaton went to Jefferson to curry favor with the president and to help his own cause: getting repaid for expenses he incurred in the Tripoli war.

Jefferson was either uninterested or himself played the innocent. "The President asked where [Burr] should be sent? I mentioned London and Cadiz. The President thought the trust too important, and seemed to entertain a doubt of Mr. Burr's integrity." Asking Jefferson to do something for Burr was almost as unbelievable as Burr asking the president for preferment. Both ended in failure. "I perceived the subject was disagreeable to the President; and to give it the shortest course to the point, declared my concern that if Mr. Burr were not in some way disposed of, we should, within eighteen months, have an insurrection, if not a revolution, on the waters of the Mississippi. The President answered, that he had too much confidence in the information, the integrity, and the attachment to the union, of the citizens of that country, to admit an apprehension of the kind."

Having just denounced Burr to the president and been embarrassed by the conversation, one would imagine that Eaton would not mention it to any one else. "But I detailed, about the same time, the whole projects of Mr. Burr to certain members of Congress. They believed colonel Burr capable of any thing, and agreed that the fellow ought to be hanged." At least Eaton would deny his hospitality to the "usurper" entirely, having just accused Burr of the most heinous of plans. Instead, "Mr. Burr's visits to me became less frequent, and his conversation less familiar. He appeared to have abandoned the idea of a general revolution, but seemed determined on that [against the Spanish on the] Mississippi." What was more, "I could perceive symptoms of distrust in him towards me." Distrust? Whispering in the Washington political community was like shouting into the microphone at a rock concert. Everyone heard everything. Burr must have been unhinged or at least deaf if Eaton's conversations with the president and members of Congress only raised "symptoms of distrust." The denouement came in the fall: "I now spoke publicly of the fact . . . and about the same time forwarded, through the hands of the post-master general, to the President of the United States, a statement in substance of what is here above detailed concerning the Mississippi conspiracy."

Jefferson took Wilkinson's warnings more seriously than Eaton's. Indeed, the only grounds the administration had to defend Wilkinson's extraordinary exercise of power in New Orleans, circumventing and then ignoring the civil authorities, was Wilkinson's insistence that Burr's treason could only be averted by swift and summary action. But Wilkinson's affidavit demonstrated that Bollman and Swartwout arrived and presented the coded message to him in November, over a month before he had them arrested.

Plainly, Wilkinson had some explaining of his own to do, and his affidavit had to be carefully crafted to shield him while striking at Burr. "On the sixth day of November last, when in command at Natchitoches, I received by the hands of a Frenchman, a stranger to me, a letter from doctor Erick Bollman, of which the following is a correct copy." The Bollman cover letter to Wilkinson allegedly said, "I have the honour to forward to your excellency the enclosed letters." The letter Bollman supposedly conveyed was "a communication in cypher from colonel Aaron Burr, of which the following is substantially as fair an interpretation as I have heretofore been able to make, the original of which I hold in my possession."

The enclosure was a copy, not the original. If Wilkinson were a court clerk or a judge, the copy might have been admitted into evidence without much ado. But Wilkinson may have been a party to the conspiracy, and if so, his "copy" might not be entirely accurate. Why not send the original and make a copy for security's sake? The answer is that the original, allegedly from Burr detailing the plot, was not in Burr's handwriting, and for any student of Burr's prose, it did not resemble Burr's writing at all. One way to disguise this embarrassing fact was to send a copy in Wilkinson's hand.

Baron Gilbert and all subsequent English authorities on the "best evidence rule" said that a copy, particularly one made by a party at interest, was not as good as the original. Wilkinson should have sent the original. Worse, he decoded it. That deciphering itself was questionable if he were a party to the conspiracy, for he would have every reason to slant the decoding to blacken Burr's reputation and protect himself.

Wilkinson's translation hinted at a different and more sinister purpose in Burr's preparations than Bollman had reported to Jefferson, and Burr had told others, including Smith, Brown, Adair, Biddle, and Truxton:

I (Aaron Burr) have obtained funds, and have actually commenced the enterprise. Detachments from different points and under different pretences, will rendezvous on the Ohio, 1st November. Every thing internal and external favours views; protection of England is secured. T. [Truxton] is gone to Jamaica to arrange with the admiral on that station, and will meet at the Mississippi England — navy of the United States are ready to join, and final orders are given to my friends and followers; it will be an host of choice spirits. Wilkinson shall be second to Burr only; Wilkinson shall dictate the rank and promotion of his officers. Burr will proceed westward 1st August, never to return; with him go his daughter; the husband will follow in October with a corps of worthies; send forth with an intelligent and confidential friend, with whom Burr may confer; he shall return immediately with further interesting details: this is essential to concert and harmony of movement; send a list of all persons known to Wilkinson west of the mountains, who could be useful, with a note delineating their characters. By your messenger send me four or five of the commissions of your officers, which you can borrow under any pretence you please; they shall be returned faithfully: already are orders to the contractor given to forward six months' provisions to points Wilkinson may name: this shall not be used until the last moment, and then under proper injunctions: the project is brought to the point so long desired: Burr guaranties the result with his life and honour, the lives, the honour, and fortunes of hundreds, the best blood of our country: Burr's plan of operations is to move down rapidly from the falls on the fifteenth of November, with the first five hundred or one thousand men, in light boats, now constructing for that purpose; to be at Natchez between the fifth and fifteenth of December, then to meet Wilkinson; then to determine whether it will be expedient in the first instance to seize on or pass by Baton Rouge: on receipt of this send Burr an answer; draw on Burr for all expenses, &c. The people of the country to which we are going are prepared to receive us: their agents now with Burr say, that if we will protect their religion, and will not subject them to a foreign power, that in three weeks all will be settled. The Gods invite to glory and fortune: it remains to be seen, whether we deserve the boon: the bearer of this goes express to you; he will hand a formal letter of introduction to you from Burr, a copy of which is hereunto subjoined: he is a man of inviolable honour and perfect discretion; formed to execute rather than to project; capable of relating facts with fidelity, and incapable of relating them otherwise: he is thoroughly informed of the plans and intentions of [blank] and will disclose to you as far as you inquire, and no further: he has imbibed a reverence for your character, and may be embarrassed in your presence; put him at ease and he will satisfy you: doctor Bollman, equally confidential, better informed on the subject, and more intelligent, will hand this duplicate. 29th July. [1806]

Swartwout, the man of "inviolable honour," arrived at Natchitoches. Less experienced in intrigues than Bollman, Swartwout appeared to the wily Wilkinson as a soft touch. He could be duped into revealing the true nature of Burr's plot. Swartwout had "followed me down the Mississippi to Fort Adams, and from thence set out for Natchitoches . . . under the pretense of a disposition to take part in the campaign against the Spaniards." Swartwout allegedly confided to Wilkinson "that colonel Burr with the support of a powerful association, extending from New-York to New-Orleans, was levying an armed body of 7,000 men from the state of New-York and the western states and territories, with a view to carry an expedition against the Mexican provinces."

Had Wilkinson not suspected much more of Burr, his conversation with Swartwout would have ended here. Burr thought he could take advantage of a war with Spain. Wilkinson would prevent that war, and the business would be at an end. An objective observer may note that either Swartwout had a remarkable facility for summoning up large bodies of men, or Wilkinson was remarkably gullible. But Wilkinson, according to his affidavit, was not convinced that Swartwout had told the whole story. "I inquired what would be their course?" Swartwout allegedly replied, "this territory would be revolutionized, where the people were ready to join them, and that there would be some seizing, he supposed, at New-Orleans; that they expected to be ready to embark about the first of February, and intended to land at Vera Cruz, and to march from thence to Mexico."

Why would it have been necessary to "revolutionize" New Orleans to take ship to go to Vera Cruz? Did Burr, already supposedly gathering supplies, need to further arm his men by ransacking New Orleans? Surely that would not further the goal of invading Mexico. Perhaps Burr's aim was to raise more troops. Taking him at his word, however Wilkinson interpreted Swartwout's comments, there was no obvious plan for treason against the United States. Instead, like Bollman's later report to Jefferson, the only conclusion one could reach from it was that Burr planned a filibustering expedition to Mexico whose object was the despoiling of the Spanish colony.

Wilkinson had more imagination that Swartwout, however, and supplied the gaps in the younger man's story. "I observed that there were several millions of dollars in the bank of this place; to which he replied, 'We know it full well;' and on remarking that they certainly did not mean to violate private property, he said they 'merely meant to borrow, and would return it; that they must equip themselves in New-Orleans.'"

The rest of the affidavit was pure invention. Wilkinson reported that Swartwout, whose only job was to deliver a message, now adopted the voice and manner of political observer and revolutionary leader. Swartwout supposedly said that "disgusts prevailed throughout the western country, where the people were zealous in favour of the enterprise." This was an amazingly full account of Western sentiment from someone who had just dashed from Philadelphia to meet Wilkinson.

Wilkinson now duplicated Eaton's ruse. "Though determined to deceive him if possible, I could not refrain telling Mr. Swartwout it was impossible that I could ever dishonour my commission," and then, in a complete about-face, Wilkinson related, "and I believe I duped him by my admiration of the plan." Setting aside the improbability of this convoluted part of the tale, why did Wilkinson have to dupe Swartwout? He had already condemned himself and his distant master. What was more, he was in Wilkinson's power.

And why dissemble a moment longer? But this is exactly what Wilkinson did. For a month after "the moment I had decyphered the letter," Wilkinson waited to inform his commander in chief, Jefferson, of the character of the plot. Then, and only then, "I immediately employed lieutenant T. A. Smith to convey the information, in substance, to the President, without the commitment of names."

Swartwout stayed with Wilkinson for eight days, from October 4 through 12. After Swartwout left (the exact date was the subject of a later acrimonious dispute between the two men), Wilkinson delayed, deciding where his best interests lay. On October 21, he sent a report to Jefferson detailing the imminent arrival of some ten thousand men in New Orleans, but did not name Burr.

Wilkinson had in his hands proof positive, or so it seemed to him, that Burr was preparing an assault on New Orleans, and good soldier that Wilkinson was, he "immediately" informed his commander in chief. But he left out Burr's name. "For, from the extraordinary nature of the project, and the more extraordinary appeal to me, I could not but doubt its reality." More likely, Wilkinson was covering his bases. If Burr persisted, Wilkinson would protect himself by denouncing Burr to Jefferson. If Burr stopped, Wilkinson had to protect himself against whatever Burr might say. Better, then, not to name Burr.

In fact, Wilkinson only acted decisively after the Sabine River truce with the Spanish was concluded and it became apparent that Burr was on his way. Wilkinson knew how persuasive Burr could be. "Mr. Swartwout informed me he was under engagements to meet colonel Burr at Nashville the 20th of November." But Burr's imminent arrival made Wilkinson's problem acute. To distance himself from the evidence of his own misconduct while providing enough evidence to drown Burr, Wilkinson became a marvel of activity. He rushed to the Sabine to confront the Spanish troops and negotiated a truce. The threat of war over, "After my return from the Sabine, I crossed the country to Natchez." Wilkinson had made up his mind. Time to pull Burr's fangs.

Wilkinson ran into Swartwout and Peter V. Ogden, another Burr associate, in Natchez. They were surveying the Washita lands, but Wilkinson (so he said) regarded them as the advance guard of a massive force of armed men. Then off to New Orleans where Wilkinson received Bollman with false bonhomie. He listened as Bollman boasted that "(colonel Burr) had numerous and powerful friends in the United States, who stood pledged to support him with their fortunes, and that he must succeed." Wilkinson kept Bollman close by. On December 5, "I called on [Bollman] the second time. The mail having arrived the day before, I asked him whether he had received any intelligence from colonel Burr; he informed me that he had seen a letter from colonel Burr, of the 30th October, in which he (colonel Burr) gave assurances that he should be at Natchez with 2,000 men on the 20th December . . . that he would be followed by 4,000 men more, and that he (colonel Burr) if he had chosen, could have raised or got 12,000 as easily as 6,000, but that he did not think that number necessary."

Now Wilkinson threw off his disguise as a conspirator and donned the mantle of patriot. "Confiding fully in this information, I became indifferent about further disguise. I then told the doctor that I should most certainly oppose colonel Burr if he came this way." There was no evidence that Burr had obtained munitions (he had not) from New York or anywhere else, or that two thousand armed and grim-faced rebels, much less ten thousand, were descending the Mississippi heading for New Orleans. Again, what had stirred Wilkinson was not the imminence of a threat, but the imminent arrival of Burr himself. With Burr at hand, Wilkinson had no more wiggle room. If he welcomed Burr, Wilkinson would be suspected of complicity in Burr's affairs. (Fair enough, he was.) But if he acted swiftly to arrest Bollman and Swartwout and then Burr (or order Burr's capture as he approached), he could maintain the disguise of the clever inquisitor.

On December 14, 1806, on his own authority as governor-general, Wilkinson ceased to be the host and became the jailer. "From the documents in my possession and the several communications, verbal as well as written, from the said doctor Erick Bollman, on this subject, I feel no hesitation in declaring under the solemn obligation of an oath, that he has committed misprision of treason against the government of the United States." Bollman, Swartwout, and other Burr associates were rounded up and imprisoned.

{ *Chapter 4* }

On January 5, Wilkinson declared martial law in New Orleans. The judge who would have heard any case that Wilkinson mounted against Burr was John Bartow Prevost, Burr's stepson. The federal attorney who would have prosecuted Burr was James Brown, whose brother, Kentucky U.S. Senator John Brown, had been a Burr confidant. The most important lawyer in the city was Edward Livingston, Burr's good friend. When Wilkinson tried to persuade James Brown to indict Burr, Brown thought the evidence, including the deciphered letter, inconclusive.

Claiborne, whom Wilkinson approached next, refused to declare martial law because there was no clear and present danger to civil order. Claiborne did not trust the general, and what business did he have in New Orleans, where Claiborne represented civil authority? Wilkinson ignored Clairborne and arrested James Alexander, Burr's lawyer in the city, joined him with Bollman and Swartwout, added the missives and the enclosures, and sent the entire package to Jefferson by sea.

In the process, Wilkinson ignored the civil courts' issuance of habeas corpus writs for Bollman and Swartwout. More important, though not to the imperious general, the summary proceeding at gunpoint ignored the Sixth Amendment to the United States Constitution: "In all criminal prosecutions, the accused shall enjoy the right to a speedy and public trial, by an impartial jury of the State and district wherein the crime shall have been committed, which district shall have been previously ascertained by law, and to be informed of the nature and cause of the accusation; to be confronted with the witnesses against him; to have compulsory process for obtaining witnesses in his favor, and to have the assistance of counsel for his defence." Wilkinson's high-handed actions denied to all three men every one of these Bill of Rights protections. Shaking with fever, unable to communicate with counsel, much less with Burr, bundled onto a boat in the dark, Swartwout cried in despair, "you mean to murder me!"

Jefferson's message to Congress on January 22, 1807, ignored all of these nice points of law, telling a story of a nation in dire peril from Burr's tiny band. Jefferson prepared that story not only to cap the public campaign of vilification against Burr, but to prepare Congress for Republican Senate leader William Branch Giles's motion to suspend the writ of habeas corpus. This was the legal process by which individual prisoners held in custody could force the government to explain why they were confined. Wilkinson had already done as much. The Constitution provided that Congress could suspend the writ, but only "when in cases of rebellion or invasion the public safety may require it." The framers of the Constitution debated the clause only briefly, with some arguing that there should never be a suspension. Judges were free to refuse to "return" the writ, and presumably would refuse when the occasion demanded.

At the Philadelphia Constitutional Convention, Luther Martin of Maryland voted against the suspension power, arguing that "a citizen of Georgia may be bastilled [the Bastille was an infamous prison in Paris] in the furthest part of New Hampshire . . . cut off from their family and friends, and their every connection" if the writ was suspended. Patrick Henry, speaking against the Constitution at the Virginia ratification convention, worried that the power to suspend the writ might be abused because the definition of invasion and rebellion lay in the same hands as the power to suspend the writ.

When Bollman and Swartwout reached Washington, Giles moved for the suspension of the writ. The Senate voted to do so, with one dissent. A weekend intervened, and the House voted 113 to 19 against suspension. It was the first blow to the president's plan to punish Burr.

Although not offered to the Court in evidence, Jefferson's message was on the judges' desks. His report of Burr's motives and doings were intertwined with Wilkinson's, for Jefferson had depended on the general's communications. The House of Representatives had asked about the particulars of the alleged plot on January 16, and Jefferson used that request to tell the nation about Burr's perfidy and Wilkinson's heroic efforts to save the West. This was "information received touching an illegal combination of private individuals against the peace and safety of the Union, and a military expedition planned by them against the territories of a power in amity with the United States, with the measures I have pursued for suppressing the same."

If such a major campaign had been underway for any length of time, Jefferson had some explaining to do of his own. Why had he been inactive? "I had for some time been in the constant expectation of receiving such further information as would have enabled me to lay before the legislature the termination as well as the beginning and progress of this scene of depravity." With the culprits in hand, it was time to inform Congress and the nation. "The delay was indulged the rather, because no circumstance had yet made it necessary to call in the aid of the legislative functions. Information now recently communicated has brought us nearly to the period contemplated."

The evidence for these arrests did not yet "constitute formal and legal evidence. It is chiefly in the form of letters, often containing such a mixture of rumors, conjectures, and suspicions, as render it difficult to sift out the real facts." But Jefferson already knew and now told Congress about the "general outlines, strengthened by concurrent information." Everything depended on the "credibility of the relater." Although Jefferson no doubt knew that Wilkinson was not the most reliable or candid of correspondents (his delay in writing to Jefferson was sufficient proof of this), the president had to rely on his local commander.

Just as Wilkinson had apologized to Jefferson for not immediately naming Burr, so Jefferson related to Congress, "In this state of the evidence, delivered sometimes too under the restriction of private confidence, neither safety nor justice will permit the exposing names, except that of the principal actor, whose guilt is placed beyond question." As a legal opinion, Jefferson's account made no sense. If the evidence from Wilkinson was too slender to name Bollman or Swartwout, why was the same source of evidence sufficient to name Burr? After all, it was the same kind of evidence — hearsay, rumor, affidavits from interested parties.

The answer was that Jefferson did not need the October 22 letter from Wilkinson to know that Burr was up to something. "Some time in the latter part of September, I received intimations that designs were in agitation in the western country, unlawful and unfriendly to the peace of the Union; and that the prime mover in these was Aaron Burr." Jefferson, not entirely candid about these intimations, left out Daveiss's and Eaton's earlier warnings. "The grounds of these intimations being inconclusive, the objects uncertain, and the fidelity of that country known to be firm, the only measure taken was to urge the informants to use their best endeavors to get further insight into the designs and proceedings of the suspected persons." In other words, Jefferson was either inattentive or thought the entire Burr plan nonsense. "It was not until the latter part of October, that the objects of the conspiracy began to be perceived." Presumably, this was the first

Wilkinson letter, but it was vaguer than what Jefferson already knew and named no one when Jefferson had already heard Burr's name many times.

Why had not Jefferson acted to find out for himself what Burr planned? "In this state of uncertainty as to the crime contemplated, the acts done, and the legal course to be pursued, I thought it best to send to the scene where these things were principally in transaction, a person, in whose integrity, understanding, and discretion, entire confidence could be reposed, with instructions to investigate the plots." John Graham, the super sleuth, would discover with precision what was happening. In fact, Graham's job was less to find out the secrets of the conspiracy than "to enter into conference (for which he had sufficient credentials) with the governors and all other officers, civil and military, and with their aid to do on the spot whatever should be necessary to discover the designs of the conspirators, arrest their means, bring their persons to punishment." Why did Jefferson not communicate with these states' governors himself? Why not direct one of the federal attorneys general to detain Burr and convene a special grand jury, as Daveiss finally did in December?

In the end, the information Jefferson gathered came from self-interested parties, gossip, newspaper innuendo, and his own agents' surmise rather than civil and military officers — save Wilkinson. "By this time it was known that many boats were under preparation, stores of provisions collecting, and an unusual number of suspicious characters in motion on the Ohio and its waters." The Ohio River was the main turnpike for settlers and merchants supplying the West. On it traveled wild-eyed adventurers, river pirates, criminals fleeing sheriffs, and a host of suspicious characters. Slave traders and secret agents drank and dined alongside one another on flatboats. Among such as these, Burr would pass for an angel.

"Besides despatching the confidential agent to that quarter, orders were at the same time sent to the [territorial] governors of the Orleans and Mississippi territories, and to the commanders of the land and naval forces there, to be on their guard against surprise, and in constant readiness to resist any enterprise which might be attempted on the vessels, posts, or other objects under their care." Without naming Burr, such orders were superfluous. The whole of the lower Mississippi was overrun with brigands, Indian war parties, and Spanish troops. Any and all of these men might try to destroy federal property.

The most important and the most candid statement in the message to Congress was that on November 8, Jefferson ordered Wilkinson to "hasten an accommodation with the Spanish commander on the Sabine, and as soon as that was effected, to fall back with his principal force to the hither bank of the Mississippi, for the defence of the intersecting points on that river." That order told Wilkinson that the filibuster he and Burr had planned was not to be. Wilkinson had better make his peace with Jefferson. For his own part, Jefferson, having to choose between a clumsy and self-important Wilkinson and a Burr whose secrets might be embarrassing, told Congress that Wilkinson, "with the honor of a soldier and fidelity of a good citizen," was about to "enter on measures for opposing the projected enterprise."

Jefferson conceded that Burr's plan might be any one of three. "One of these was the severance of the Union of these States by the Allegheny mountains; the other, an attack on Mexico. A third object was provided, merely ostensible, to wit: the settlement of a pretended purchase of a tract of country on the Washita, claimed by a Baron Bastrop." Jefferson, on no more evidence than Wilkinson's letter, judged the last option "the pretext for all his preparations, an allurement for such followers as really wished to acquire settlements in that country, and a cover under which to retreat in the event of final discomfiture of both branches of his real design."

Jefferson happily reported that "the attachment of the western country to the present Union was not to be shaken." When Burr found he could not dismember the union, he had instead "determined to seize on New Orleans, plunder the bank there, possess himself of the military and naval stores, and proceed on his expedition to Mexico." The only evidence for this was Wilkinson's interrogation of Swartwout, assuming that Swartwout was naively truthful and Wilkinson thoroughly trustworthy.

The farther that Jefferson went into such surmises, the more he became dependent on Wilkinson. This is akin to a person buying a fake Rembrandt. The more it costs, the more insistent that the buyer will be that the painting is genuine. So Jefferson plunged on. Burr "collected from all the quarters where himself or his agents possessed influence, all the ardent, restless, desperate, and disaffected persons who were ready for any enterprise analogous to their characters." These numbered at most about a hundred men, as it happened. "He seduced good and well-meaning citizens"—a necessary concession if a significant portion of the United States Senate was not to be indicted for their part in the plot.

The November proclamation exhibited the same ambivalence as Jefferson's previous actions. Some step was necessary, but it was just as necessary not to inflame the situation or to further distance the administration from disaffected Westerners, Jefferson had concluded. "The proclamation of November 27, two days after the receipt of General Wilkinson's information, was now issued." Some kind of proclamation was needed for the government to "seize on all the boats and stores provided for the enterprise, to arrest the persons concerned, and to suppress effectually the further progress of the enterprise." After all, Washington had called out the militia at the height of the Whiskey Rebellion in 1794, and Adams summoned armed forces and supplied to quell John Fries's Rebellion in 1799. Jefferson thanked Ohio Governor Tiffin for "promptitude, an energy, and patriotic zeal."

When similar accusations against Burr were put to the test before actual grand juries, they failed to persuade. Jefferson dismissed these hearings. "In Kentucky, a premature attempt to bring Burr to justice, without sufficient evidence for his conviction, had produced a popular impression in his favor, and a general disbelief of his guilt." Against this finding, Jefferson offered no more contrary evidence than his own preparations. "The arrival of the proclamation and orders, and the application and information of our confidential agent, at length awakened the authorities of that State [of Kentucky] to the truth, and then produced the same promptitude and energy of which the neighboring State had set the example." Long after Burr departed, the Kentucky militia, most of whose men would gladly have followed Burr into Mexico, "was instantly ordered to different important points, and measures taken for doing whatever could yet be done."

What of the Burr armada? Here Jefferson had to give some credit to fact. "Some boats (accounts vary from five to double or treble that number) and persons (differently estimated from one to three hundred) had in the meantime passed the falls of the Ohio, to rendezvous at the mouth of the Cumberland, with others expected down that river." Instead of proof of an army on the march or a navy deploying for battle, Jefferson offered a travelogue. "On the 22d of December, Mr. Burr descended the Cumberland with two boats merely of accommodation, carrying with him from that State no quota toward his unlawful enterprise."

Jefferson looked for the great flotilla of flatboats filled with armed men and found neither. So he substituted further evidence of his own preparations against Burr's expedition. "By the same express of December nineteenth, orders were sent to the governors of New Orleans and Mississippi, supplementary to those which had been given on the twenty-fifth of November, to hold the militia of their territories in readiness to co-operate for their defence, with the regular troops and armed vessels then under command of General Wilkinson." Jefferson's conclusion from all the foregoing was a remarkable twisting of facts and causes. "Great alarm, indeed, was excited at New Orleans by the exaggerated accounts of Mr. Burr, disseminated through his emissaries, of the armies and navies he was to assemble there." Exaggerated by whom, one might ask? Perhaps by the president's own proclamation? Or Wilkinson's exertions?

At first, Jefferson had accused Burr of acting in secret, a true conspirator. Now Burr was the head of a marching band announcing to all in his path his plans. Jefferson obliquely conceded that Wilkinson, not Burr, created the great alarm in Washington and New Orleans. "General Wilkinson had arrived [in New Orleans] himself on the 24th of November and had immediately put into activity the resources of the place for the purpose of its defense." Contrary to what Donaldson and Wilson reported about the merchants' dismay at the confiscations, Jefferson added a dramatic and entirely creative touch to the end of the story. "Great zeal was shown by the inhabitants generally, the merchants of the place readily agreeing to the most laudable exertions and sacrifices for manning the armed vessels with their seamen, and the other citizens manifesting unequivocal fidelity to the Union, and a spirit of determined resistance to their expected assailants."

The impact of Jefferson's announcement was electric. It gave reliable confirmation to "so much agitation in the public mind" of Burr's "attempt to rear in the very bosom" of the nation "the standard of insurrection and rebellion." Republican members of Congress like Representative George W. Campbell now happily reported to their constituents that "the active and energetic measures of the Executive of the United States" had Burr "reduced to perfect submission."

Jefferson had made himself sole judge of Burr's motives as well as his actions in advance of the trial. He had usurped the place of the criminal courts, redefined the nature of the offense, and took as fact the allegations of those whose interest (not to say whose veracity) should have been more carefully weighed. He then gave the verdict: guilty.

CHAPTER 5

Dress Rehearsal
Ex Parte Bollman I and II

On January 27, the day that Bollman and Swartwout were brought to jail in the capital, Bollman agreed to a private meeting with Jefferson. Madison was present. Jefferson insisted the Bollman could walk away from the affair if he testified that Burr intended to sever the union. Bollman insisted that Burr only wanted to invade Mexico if the United States went to war with Spain. Jefferson pressed Bollman, but he would not budge.

Instead, Bollman and Swartwout sought a court hearing on the charges and their continued incarceration by petitioning the circuit court for the District of Columbia for a writ of habeas corpus. By a 2-to-1 vote (the one dissenter was Federalist district judge William Cranch, reporter of the Supreme Court), the circuit court denied the request. The vote was along party lines, with the two Jefferson appointees agreeing that the writ could not be issued.

The Constitution provided for the "great writ" of habeas corpus, except when Congress itself should suspend the writ "in Cases of Rebellion or Invasion the public Safety may require it." The Judiciary Act of 1789 filled in the missing space in Article III by giving to all the federal courts, and all federal judges sitting when the courts were not in session, the power to issue the writ. Habeas corpus protected, at least in theory, against illegal and arbitrary imprisonment, or imprisonment without adequate cause. Anyone held in custody might sue for the writ. Its relief was not confined to citizens.

Historians interested in Burr's case have naturally focused on the Burr trial itself, with its fulsome and sustained bouts of oratory and Marshall's remarkable ruling on the admissibility of Wilkinson's evidence. That trial came to a sudden end precisely because the legal issues involved, particularly the key questions of the admissibility of evidence and the definition of treason, had already had a hearing in the U.S. Supreme Court of Bollman's and Swartwout's appeal from the D.C. Court ruling. To maintain that Burr's emissaries should not gain the Court's ear through habeas corpus, the government's lawyers provided the High Court in January with essentially the same evidence of a great conspiracy the circuit trial court would hear in August. The ruling of the Supreme Court on the motions in February touched on all of the legal issues that the trial court would face six months later.

Perhaps even more important, Burr's trial was in circuit court; the U.S. Supreme Court decided *Ex Parte Bollman* and *Ex Parte Swartwout* (1807). The Burr precedent applied only to its facts, though later courts could cite it if they chose. *Bollman* (although the facts in the two cases were slightly different, the reasoning and outcome in *Swartwout* was the same as *Bollman*) I and II applied to all cases of treason in federal courts because the Supreme Court is the highest appeals court in the federal system, and when the Court's majority agrees to an opinion, that opinion becomes law (although later courts could distinguish a case they were hearing from *Bollman* if they did not want to use it as precedent).

Jefferson, recognizing that Bollman and Swartwout's motion to the High Court for a habeas corpus hearing was a trial run for Burr, caused a thousand copies of his January 22 message to be printed and distributed. The Republican newspapers added it to the backlog of editorials and reports they had published on Burr's alleged misdeeds for the past six months. The political pressure on the Court was almost unbearable.

Members of the High Court, then in session, had been the center of political controversy from the moment that the Republican Congress convened in December 1801. All but one of the justices were Federalists. Threatened with impeachment by Republican majorities in the House of Representatives, these justices knew how politically explosive and potentially damaging to the court this case could be. Chase had already been targeted for removal by Jefferson and Congress. He barely escaped when the Republicans failed to obtain the two-thirds vote necessary to convict him in the Senate. Chase's health was failing, but he was a more virulent Federalist than Marshall. Justice Bushrod Washington, the former president's nephew, was another Virginia gentleman, like Marshall, known for his polite and civil manner. He almost invariably followed Marshall's lead. Brockholst Livingston, appointed by Jefferson and confirmed in January 1807, was a

Republican in name only. His views and his background were more Federalist than Jeffersonian. He knew the Jeffersonians might shift their guns on him if he came down the wrong way. Only William Johnson of South Carolina could be counted on politically by the Jeffersonians, but the Court had its own politics, and Johnson very often fell in line behind Marshall.

Chase "wished the motion [for habeas corpus] might lay over to the next day. He was not prepared to give an opinion. He doubted the jurisdiction of this court to issue a habeas corpus in any case." Johnson also "doubted whether the power given by the act of Congress, of issuing the writ of habeas corpus, was not intended as a mere auxiliary power to enable courts to exercise some other jurisdiction given by law." Prospects looked bleak for Burr's two messengers.

Marshall thought the question important enough for a full hearing of opposing counsel, although from his later opinion it is clear that he knew how he would vote before oral argument had begun. With Chase wavering and Johnson plainly opposed to allowing the writ, Marshall's deliberateness allowed counsel to develop their arguments, and perhaps equally important, gave him time to sway the Court. "It is the wish of the court to have the motion made in a more solemn manner tomorrow, when [counsel] may come prepared to take up the whole ground." He wished no suggestion that his actions or his views were dictated by party or by animus against Jefferson — though in fact he thought Jefferson "totally . . . unfit" to be president.

On February 9, 1807, the Court met in the damp and cramped basement of the new Capitol building. The justices complained of the mildew and the drafts. They had no offices and no reading or robing rooms, and the arched, low roof of the courtroom caused the voices of the counsel and the justices to bounce all over. Oral argument on *Bollman* would take days. There was no time limit as there is today, and long-winded oratory was a hallmark of the early national legal profession. Lawyers did not have to submit written briefs, so the justices had to listen carefully. Marshall took notes, as did the self-appointed reporter of the cases, Judge William Cranch, along with counsel for the government and the prisoners. What we know of the opinions was a reconstruction, in part from notes, and in part from the papers of the principles, as assembled and published by Cranch after more than a year's delay.

Charles Lee, representing Swartwout, knew his way around the new capitol. A scion of one of the first families of Virginia, Lee was fifty-one years old when he appeared for Swartwout. Lee was educated at the College of New Jersey, a tie to Burr, and like Burr had read law. He was admitted to the bar in 1780, after which he served in the Continental Congress and his state assembly. In December 1795, he was appointed attorney general of the United States by President Washington. Burr was in the Senate at the time, and Lee would have known Burr. Lee remained in the post until Johns Adams lost the election of 1800, and with Adams, he left office in February 1801. As attorney general, he performed the roles of advisor to the president on legal matters and arguing suits to which the United States was a party (the role now performed by the solicitor general). He determined the pay scale for federal judges, and he advised Congress in the first impeachment inquiry of a federal judge.

Lee was a believer in the rule of law. When a newspaper editor insulted a foreign emissary in print, Lee advised Adams that the courts, not the president, should determine the meaning of the First Amendment's provisions on free speech. In 1803 Lee represented William Marbury in *Marbury v. Madison*, arguing that the High Court must deliver the commission to Marbury. He lost. But he won when it counted — as Justice Chase well knew. In 1804, the Republicans in the House of Representatives impeached Chase for his virulently anti-Republican charges to federal grant juries, and a variety of other plainly political acts and words. Burr presided at the impeachment trial in the Senate. Lee defended Chase and got him off.

The next day Robert Goodloe Harper made a habeas corpus motion on behalf of Bollman. Harper, a representative from South Carolina and later a senator from Maryland, was born near Fredericksburg, Virginia, in January 1765. He moved with his parents to Granville, North Carolina, in about 1769. He received his early education at home and later attended grammar school. When only fifteen he joined a volunteer corps of cavalry and served in the Revolutionary army. He graduated from the College of New Jersey in 1785, then studied law in Charleston, South Carolina, where the next year he was admitted to the bar. He was a state assemblyman, and then served in the U.S. House of Representatives from February 1795 to March 1801. He was one of the managers appointed by the House of Representatives in 1798 to conduct the impeachment proceedings against William Blount. A good marriage to a daughter of one of the leading families of Maryland brought a move to Baltimore, and there a resumption of his legal practice. Harper was renowned for his ability to argue cases for hours, even days, on end. Like Lee, Harper was a Federalist, and the two men knew one another, and Burr. Both had urged Burr to seek the presidency when he and Jefferson found themselves tied in electoral votes.

The third and fourth lawyers appearing for Burr's emissaries, Francis Scott Key and Luther Martin, were for the present silent, but when the question of the two emissaries' freedom was heard, on February 16 and 17, both would speak. It was not by accident that the same four men had defended Chase at his impeachment trial, but their presence in court could not have surprised the justices. They were the elite of the Federalist bar. Martin would go on to represent Burr at his own trial.

Lee based his case on precedent and the letter of the law. Both are parts of the common-law tradition in which lawyers like Lee were trained. In common law, the decision of the appropriate appeals court on an issue becomes part of the law. These precedents go beyond the decision in the case, for in common-law appeals courts, the judges or justices often write opinions explaining their decision.

The United States Supreme Court, though still in its relative youth in 1807, had already rendered such opinions. In particular, Marshall's opinion for the unanimous Court in *Marbury v. Madison* (1803) had established the authority of the Court to determine the meaning of the Constitution and overturn legislation that contravened that meaning. The Court also had the power to reverse the decisions of lower federal courts and state courts. As it performed these functions, its opinions added to the growing store of constitutional law.

Lee also relied on the texts of law for authority. Although the highest interpretative authority was the Supreme Court, much law came from the legislative branch of government. Acts of Congress were law and must be obeyed. The most important of these in the present matter were the Judiciary Act of 1789 and the Process Act of 1789. These two acts of Congress were necessary because Article III allowed — in fact called upon — Congress to supply the appellate jurisdiction and procedure for all federal courts.

The Judiciary Act of 1789 gave to the federal district, circuit, and supreme courts the authority to issue writs, including habeas corpus. Section 14 of the act provided "that all the before mentioned courts of the United States," including the Supreme Court, "shall have power to issue writs of scire facias, habeas corpus, and all other writs," etc., "And that either of the justices of the supreme court, as well as judges of the district courts, shall have power to grant writs of habeas corpus, for the purpose of an inquiry into the cause of commitment."

Lee began with precedents. He had two on point—that is, directly related to the case at hand. In both *U.S. v. Hamilton* (1795) and *U.S. v. Burford* (1806), the circuit courts allowed hearings on habeas corpus writs. Burford's case should have disposed of the first issue in *Bollman*. John Burford was an Alexandria, Virginia, shopkeeper who refused to post bond for his good behavior. When jailed, he sought review of the case by the circuit court and release until the review on the writ of habeas corpus. Marshall, riding circuit in Virginia, opined, "There is some obscurity in the [Judiciary] act of Congress, and some doubts were entertained by the court as to the construction of the Constitution. The court, however, in favor of liberty, was willing to grant the habeas corpus." Even more definitive was *United States v. Hamilton* (1795). "It was there determined that this [Supreme] court could grant a habeas corpus; therefore, let the writ issue, returnable immediately, together with a certiorari, as prayed."

In times of genuine national emergency, the executive branch of the federal government has acted without congressional approval to suspend habeas corpus. In 1861, President Abraham Lincoln ordered the arrest and military trial of a confederate sympathizer named John Merryman and at first refused to honor a habeas corpus that Chief Justice Roger Taney granted. In *Ex Parte Merryman* (1861), Taney, on circuit, reminded Lincoln that only Congress could suspend the writ. Merryman was in fact levying war against the United States, and could, without much of a stretch, have been indicted in the federal courts for the offense. The next year, ignoring *Merryman*, Lincoln ordered the arrest of a group of Confederate conspirators in Illinois. The military tribunal found them guilty and ordered their execution. In *Ex Parte Milligan* (1866), the High Court found that this procedure violated the Constitution. None of the men was executed. In 1942, eight German saboteurs captured on American soil were not tried by a civil court, but under orders from President Franklin D. Roosevelt they were bound over to a military tribunal hastily and secretly convened for the sole purpose of the trial. Before the Supreme Court could publish their opinion in *Ex Parte Quirin*, six of the eight had been executed, though the Court had already found that the trials were constitutional. After the terrorist attacks of September 11, 2001, American citizens accused of dealing with Al Qaeda or other foreign terrorist groups were summarily arrested, held without bail or trial, or even for a time access to counsel at the command of President George W. Bush, until the High Court found that procedure violated the Constitution in *Hamdi v. Rumsfeld*, *Rasul v. Bush*, and *Al Odah v. United States* (2004). Jefferson did not go as far as Lincoln, Roosevelt, and Bush.

Lee now turned to black-letter law. "By the Constitution of the United States . . . the grant of jurisdiction to the courts of the United States is general, and extends to all cases arising under the laws of the United States . . . The appellate jurisdiction given by the Constitution to this court includes criminal as well as civil cases, and no act of Congress has taken it away." What kind of appeal was habeas corpus? Not an appeal at all, but the refusal to grant the writ might come to the High Court on appeal from a lower court decision. It had in *Bollman*. "If it be said that the writ can only issue where it is in exercise of appellate jurisdiction, we say it is appellate jurisdiction which we call upon this court to exercise. The court below has made an illegal and erroneous order, and we appeal in this way, and pray this court to correct the error."

What if the case was not regarded as an appeal at all? "By the judiciary act . . . 'All the beforementioned courts [and the Supreme Court was the court last mentioned in the preceding section] shall have power to issue writs of scire facias, habeas corpus, and all other writs not specially provided for by statute.'" Open and shut. Either way, the Court should issue the writ.

Caesar A. Rodney, the attorney general, declined to argue the point on behalf of the United States. He expressed no objection to the Court issuing the writ. Rodney (not to be confused with his older kinsman who signed the Declaration of Independence) was a Delaware lawyer, legislator, and ardent Jeffersonian who became attorney general in 1807, just in time to argue the case against Bollman and Swartwout.

He served briefly in the House of Representatives and there distinguished himself in the campaign to impeach Federalist judges. He would serve in James Madison's and James Monroe's administration after Jefferson left office. Rodney was the consummate professional, a lawyer's lawyer, and he knew that he had a losing case. Rodney's colleague, George Hay, signaled his agreement by his silence.

Harper thus could have let the matter rest where Lee had ended. Bollman's situation was the same as Swartwout's. Rodney all but conceded the point. But Harper wanted to use the occasion for another purpose, a political one, and on February 11, he got his chance. Unlike Lee, Harper had served in the Federalist congressional majority that enacted the Sedition Act, and he saw this opportunity to defend it.

The gist of Harper's argument was that the Court had the power to issue the habeas corpus because the Court had, like all federal courts, all the powers that the common-law courts of England had. In other words, the Constitution had imported the English common law—which made the Sedition Act of 1798, which was based on common law, constitutional. "Every court possesses necessarily certain incidental powers as a court. . . . If this court possessed no powers but those given by statute, it could not protect itself from insult and outrage. . . . It could not imprison for contempts in its presence. It could nor compel the attendance of a witness, nor oblige him to testify. It could not compel the attendance of jurors, in cases where it has original cognizance, nor punish them for improper conduct. These powers are not given by the constitution, nor by statute, but flow from the common law." This was exactly the same argument that the Federalists had made in defense of the Sedition Act.

But the argument was double-edged. If the English law of treason, with its salvo, was similarly incorporated, then Burr's activities, and Bollman and Swartwout's part in those activities, might fall under the category of constructive treason. Harper knew he was treading dangerous ground. To make a political point, he might be sacrificing his client's interest. He had to step lively. "This question is not connected with another, much agitated in this country, but little understood, viz. whether the courts of the United States have a common law jurisdiction to punish common law offences against the government of the United States."

The common-law-based power to issue the writ was procedural.

The English law of treason was substantive. The federal courts had to have common-law procedural powers. The substance of common law was another matter. The distinction between procedure (or "adjectival law") and content ("substantive law") is one easier to make in the abstract than in practice. Habeas corpus and other motions were procedural — they went to the operation of courts, their jurisdiction, the standing of parties to bring suits, and other initial legal matters. But was a favorable ruling on the writ not a substantive victory too? If the habeas corpus writ was properly brought, then the High Court could immediately hear argument on the law of treason — the underlying charge against Burr's two emissaries. A successful argument for habeas corpus would then flow into the substantive question of what constituted treason, and the line between the procedural and the substantive become paper thin.

Why would Harper, whose job that day was to get a hearing for Bollman, and at that hearing get Bollman off, open a door to the importation of the very doctrine that could get Bollman hanged? Given Harper's bilious and partisan character, it is most likely that he simply wanted to lecture the Jeffersonians on the prosecution side of the courtroom. "It being clear then that incidental [procedural] powers belong to this in common with every other court, where can we look for the definition, enumeration and extent of those powers, but to the common law; to that code from whence we derive all our legal definitions, terms and ideas, and which forms the substratum of all our juridical systems, of all our legislative and constitutional provisions." With a flourish, Harper had defended his party and its signature contribution to constitutional law. "The common law, in short, forms an essential part of all our ideas." By implication, then, it was the Federalist Party that protected the rights of Americans, not the Republicans.

Harper's message was one part legal and nine parts political. Indeed, Harper's oratory was better suited to a congressional debate than a court hearing. In that vein, Harper praised the justices sitting in front of him as "a tribunal, for such purposes, raised by its rank in the government, by its independence, by the character of those who compose it, above the dread of power, above the seductions of hope and the influence of fear, above the sphere of party passions, factious views, and popular delusion." They were "exempted, from all those sinister influences that blind and swerve the judgments of men" and decided questions "from their own consciences and . . . the awful judgment of posterity." Unlike Jefferson, his administration, and Giles and the Republicans in Congress, Marshall and the Court would not be swayed by personal animus and party advantage. "It is in the hands of such a tribunal alone, that in times of faction or oppression, the liberty of the citizen can be safe."

Such judges could be trusted to know when the common law was not so safe a haven for liberty. "There have, indeed, been instances where precedents destructive to liberty, and shocking to reason and humanity, established in arbitrary and factious times" had led to injustices. But "when in times of quiet, and in cases calculated to excite no improper feelings, precedents have been established in favor of liberty and humanity, the [common-law precedents] become the most sacred as well as the most valuable parts of the law, the firmest bulwark for the rights of the citizens, and the surest guardian for the consciences and the reputation of judges."

Whether or not Harper had sidestepped the yawning gap in his argument, the fact remained that the circuit court had not allowed the habeas corpus. The reason, Harper hinted, was that the Republican appointees to the federal courts were perverting the law to harass the Federalists. Harper and the Federalists were greatly disappointed when the Republicans repealed the Judiciary Act of 1801. It had created intermediate courts of appeal and staffed them with Federalists. The repeal gave to the Jeffersonians a chance to start appointing federal judges when Federalists stepped down. Harper referred to these events when he blasted, "the servile tools of those in power for the moment. Can any thing like independence or integrity be expected from such judges? Will they not act continually under the influence, not merely of their own party passions and prejudices, but of hope and of fear, those great perverters of the human mind?"

This kind of oratory was campaign-trail bluster and would not have any effect on the justices or the outcome of *Bollman*, but Harper knew that the arguments of counsel would be published, and he wanted his countrymen to read all about the perfidy of the Republicans: "how ready, how terrible, and how irresistible an engine of oppression is placed in the hands of a dominant party, flushed with victory, and irritated by a recent conflict; or struggling to keep down an opposing party which it hates and fears." Harper did not note that the Republicans had written just as inflammatory words about the Federalists in 1798.

On February 13, 1807, Marshall read the opinion of the Court on whether the Court could issue the writs. He had taken time to write his opinion and secure the assent of two of his fellow justices. (Only four were sitting to hear the case.) Why he had insisted on such a full hearing, and why his decision was so meticulous remains a matter of conjecture, but a careful parsing of his opinion suggests an ulterior motive.

The ongoing drumfire of criticism of his opinion in *Marbury* was on his mind. The Republicans could do nothing to challenge *Marbury* directly because the Court had denied that it had the power to order Jefferson to give William Marbury the office he sought. But the Republicans denounced both Marshall and the Court for asserting that "It is emphatically the province and duty of the judicial department to say what the law is. Those who apply the rule to particular cases, must of necessity expound and interpret that rule."

Just as Harper took the occasion to denounce the Republicans, so Marshall availed himself of the opportunity to defend his Court. He did it with his customary delicacy, by denying that the Court would ever think of going beyond its constitutional bounds. "As preliminary to any investigation of the merits of this motion, this court deems it proper to declare that it disclaims all jurisdiction not given by the Constitution, or by the laws of the United States." The Court had no intention of intruding on the proper functions of the other branches. What was more, Marshall needed to protect himself and the Court from the charge of partisanship hanging over its head after *Marbury*, in particular because the Federalists had so assiduously courted Burr in 1801. Most of the same Federalists condemned Burr for the duel, but the Republicans could still charge the High Court with partiality.

Marshall knew that Jefferson had already prejudged the case, taken testimony from Bollman, and ordered the capture and return of Burr. Marshall knew that Jefferson would love to find some reason to embarrass him. The two men were already enemies. So Marshall piled layers of argument atop one another, iced the cake with copious citations, and served it to the administration.

On the one hand, he denied that his Court received the common law. "Courts which originate in the common law possess a jurisdiction which must be regulated by their common law, until some statute shall change their established principles; but courts which are created by written law, and whose jurisdiction is defined by written law, cannot transcend that jurisdiction." The Court owed its existence to the federal Constitution and its jurisdiction to Article III and the Judiciary Act of 1789. "In relation to . . . the meaning of the term habeas corpus, resort may unquestionably be had to the common law; but the power to award the writ by any of the courts of the United States, must be given by written law."

So far, Marshall duplicated the arguments that Republicans made against the Sedition Act in 1798 and 1799. He had opposed the act himself, though he did not enter Congress in time to vote on it. Did he demur from the general proposition that the common law of England was incorporated by the federal Constitution? Maybe not, but it was still good in the states unless they renounced it. As he wrote in 1800 to Virginia jurist St. George Tucker, "My own opinion is that our ancestors brought with them the laws of England both statute & common law as existing at the settlement of each colony, so far as they were applicable to our situation. That on our revolution the preexisting law of each state remained so far as it was not changed either expressly or necessarily by the nature of the governments which we adopted. That on adopting the existing Constitution of the United States the common & statute law of each state remained as before & that the principles of the common law of the state would apply themselves to magistrates of the general as well as to magistrates of the particular government."

In *U.S. v. Hudson and Goodwin* (1812), all the justices joined in an opinion by William Johnson, a Jefferson appointee, that there was no federal common law of crimes. "The only question which this case presents is, whether the Circuit Courts of the United States can exercise a common law jurisdiction in criminal cases. . . . Although this question is brought up now for the first time to be decided by this Court, we consider it as having been long since settled in public opinion. In no other case for many years has this jurisdiction been asserted; and the general acquiescence of legal men shews the prevalence of opinion in favor of the negative of the proposition."

Johnson's reading of precedent might have been correct, but his history was poor. Chief Justice John Jay had not been one of these "legal men," nor had Ellsworth, and nor had Justice Joseph Story, who later wrote that excepting Judge Chase, "every Judge that ever sat on the Supreme Court Bench, from the adoption of the Constitution until 1804," thought that the circuit courts could hear a prosecution based on English common law. Maeva Marcus, the leading modern student of the first Supreme Courts, agrees with Story. Excepting Chase among the first circuit court judges, "no federal judge actually denied the existence of a general federal common law jurisdiction." Johnson concluded that federal courts could only prosecute crimes that Congress defined by statute. (Treason was the exception, because it was defined in the Constitution.) No one dissented at the time, including Marshall.

But Marshall did not need to discourse on the incorporation or reception or influence of English common law on federal court because the issue before him was far simpler. How federal courts gained the power "over their own officers, [and] to protect themselves, and their members, from being disturbed in the exercise of their functions" might come from common law, natural law, common sense, or the Judiciary and Process Acts, but the case at hand "extends only to the power of taking cognizance of any question between individuals, or between the government and individuals."

Cleverly Marshall was doing in *Bollman* what he had done in *Marbury:* take a case about a narrow issue and use it to lecture on the power that courts had and would always have to protect themselves and the independence of their rulings. Once again, characteristically, he wrote as if that power were not controversial at all, but rested on easily understood "written law."

The only question was whether the habeas corpus powers given to the federal courts in the Judiciary Act and the Process Act violated the Constitution. "The 14th section of the judicial act has been considered as containing a substantive grant of this power. . . . That all the before mentioned courts of the United States shall have power to issue writs of scire facias, habeas corpus, and all other writs, not specially provided for by statute, which may be necessary for the exercise of their respective jurisdictions, and agreeable to the principles and usages of law."

A clear and simple reading of the statute offered no problem to the Court—or did it? In *Marbury*, William Marbury approached the

High Court first, rather than the circuit court, because the Judiciary Act had added to the High Court's "original jurisdiction" the power to issue a writ of mandamus. This old writ commanded an officer of the government to do something (in *Marbury*, to issue William Marbury his commission as a justice of the peace). But Article III spelled out the original jurisdiction of the High Court, and it did not include the writ of mandamus. Marshall had ruled in *Marbury* that Congress could not add to the original jurisdiction of the Court because that would alter the Constitution.

Marshall could distinguish *Bollman* from *Marbury* easily by saying that Bollman was appealing the lower court's denial of the writ to the High Court. Had Marshall stopped here, the Republicans might smart from his implied criticism, but they would not be able to pin him down. Instead, like Harper, Marshall started lecturing Jefferson and Giles. This part of the opinion may be labeled *dictum* — that is, it was not necessary to settle the issue. "It may be worthy of remark, that this [Judiciary] act [of 1789] was passed by the first Congress of the United States, sitting under a Constitution which had declared 'that the privilege of the writ of habeas corpus should not be suspended, unless when, in cases of rebellion or invasion, the public safety might require it.'" In other words, the framers did not want the writ suspended lightly — not as lightly as the Jeffersonian Republicans had proposed a week earlier. "Acting under the immediate influence of this injunction, they must have felt, with peculiar force, the obligation of providing efficient means by which this great constitutional privilege should receive life and activity."

Having struck his blow against the president and his party poking their noses into judicial business, Marshall returned to the Judiciary Act. "The section proceeds to say, that 'either of the justices of the supreme court, as well as judges of the district courts, shall have power to grant writs of habeas corpus for the purpose of an inquiry into the cause of commitment.'" At one point in the oral argument, George Hay, federal attorney for Virginia, had insisted that "Congress could never intend to give a power of this kind" to the Court sitting in session. Marshall lifted up the claim for all to see: "There is certainly much force in this argument"; then dashed it: "and it receives additional strength from the consideration, that if the power be denied to this court, it is denied to every other court of the United States. . . . It would be strange if the judge, sitting on the bench, should be unable to hear a motion for this writ where it might be openly made, and openly discussed, and might yet retire to his chamber, and in private receive and decide upon the motion." Finally, Marshall blew away the little pieces of Hay's argument. "Whatever motives might induce the legislature to withhold from the Supreme Court the power to award the great writ of habeas corpus, there could be none which would induce them to withhold it from every court in the United States."

Now Marshall came to the gist of the matter: "it remains to inquire whether this be a case in which the writ ought to be granted." The writ was not to be confused with bail, a privilege that did not apply to treason. "It has been demonstrated at the bar [that is, by the briefs of counsel], that the question brought forward on a habeas corpus, is always distinct from that which is involved in the cause itself." Marshall knew that the Supreme Court did not have jurisdiction over the treason charge; that was for the federal circuit court, a trial court, to handle (though the law applied in the trial court might be appealed to the Supreme Court). The Court granted the petition for the writs of habeas corpus and ordered a hearing on the confinement of Bollman and Swartwout.

Justice William Johnson dissented. The case seemed to Johnson to shift the balance of power from state to federal government, and from state courts to the High Court. Johnson was only a reluctant nationalist. Appointed in 1804 at the height of the Republican-Federalist Party wars, Johnson's youth (he was thirty-two when appointed), his eccentricity and contrariness and his early advocacy of states' rights should have made him the odd man out on the Marshall Court. But Marshall's attention to the younger man seemed to quiet his bilious disposition. After all, Marshall was a fellow Southerner and a man of such geniality and amity that it would have been hard for even so temperamental, stubborn, and impatient a man as Johnson to stay mad at Marshall.

Thus Johnson: "In this case I have the misfortune to dissent from the majority of my brethren. As it is a case of much interest, I feel it incumbent upon me to assign the reasons upon which I adopt the opinion, that this court has not authority to issue the writ of habeas corpus now moved for." Attorney general Rodney had not objected, but Johnson still had qualms. They arose from his reading of *Marbury*.

Could the Court as a whole issue the writ? Not under its original jurisdiction as spelled out in Article III. "In all other cases within the judicial powers of the union, it can exercise only an appellate jurisdiction."

But that appellate jurisdiction was also limited. "Without a violation of the Constitution, that division of our jurisdiction can neither be restricted or extended." No one argued that the commitment of Bollman and Swartwout violated their constitutional rights (though one could have found habeas corpus in the body of the Constitution). The majority needed "to prove that the issuing of this writ is an act within the power of this court in its original jurisdiction, or that, in its appellate capacity, the power is expressly given by the laws of Congress." This defense counsel "attempted to do, by the fourteenth and thirty-third sections of the Judiciary Act, and the cases of Hamilton and Burford, which occurred in this court, the former in 1795, the latter in 1806."

But they erred. "The claim of the prisoners, as founded on precedent, stands thus. The case of Hamilton was strikingly similar to the present. The prisoner had been committed by order of the district judge on a charge of high treason. A writ of habeas corpus was issued by the supreme court, and the prisoner bailed by their order. The case of Burford was also strictly parallel to the present; but the writ in the latter case having been issued expressly on the authority of the former, it is presumed that it gives no additional force to the claim of the prisoners, but must rest on the strength of the case upon which the court acted." But the Court had read the *Hamilton* precedent wrongly. According to *Marbury*, as Johnson, who took no part in the case, read it, "Congress could not vest in the supreme court any original powers beyond those to which this court is restricted by the Constitution. That an act of Congress vesting in this court the power to issue a writ of mandamus [the power that Marshall had denied the Court had in *Marbury*] in a case not within their original jurisdiction, and in which they were not called upon to exercise an appellate jurisdiction, was unconstitutional and void."

Now it is clear why Marshall went to such lengths in his opinion on the writ. Johnson was waving Marshall's own opinion in *Marbury* in the chief justice's face. If the Court could find the assignment of mandamus an unconstitutional congressional addition to the original jurisdiction of the Court, so should the Court have found the assignment of habeas corpus. "It is necessary to premise that the case of treason is one in which this court possesses neither original nor appellate jurisdiction."

Johnson thought that the Court should abjure the power to issue these writs, just as it did the writ of mandamus in *Marbury*. "On considering this act it cannot be denied that if it vests any power at all, it is an original power. 'It is the essential criterion of appellate jurisdiction, that it revises and corrects the proceedings in a cause already instituted.' I quote the words of the court in the case of *Marbury v. Madison*."

One may conclude that Johnson was not particularly concerned about Bollman and Swartwout, or indeed about habeas corpus. He was instead exercising the time-honored function of justices who disagree with a prior decision (to be sure one handed down before Jefferson had a chance to appoint Republicans to the High Court). He was using a later case as the occasion to berate the Court for an earlier opinion. "Should we perform an act which according to our own principle we cannot be vested with power to perform, what obligation would any other court or judge be under to respect that act?"

Common sense dictated that all the justices were also judges, and Johnson conceded that "We may in our individual capacities, or in our circuit courts, be susceptible of powers merely ministerial, and not inconsistent with our judicial characters, for on that point the Constitution has left much to construction; and on such an application the only doubt that could be entertained would be, whether we can exercise any power beyond the limits of our respective circuits."

Johnson, a prickly man, had one more burr to pluck from Marshall's opinion. He had disagreed with the granting of the habeas corpus in *Burford*. But at the time he had not dissented. Why not then? The time was not ripe, and the politics of that case were not appropriate. At that time, "No popular observations on the necessity of protecting the citizen from executive oppression, no animated address calculated to enlist the passions or prejudices of an audience in defense of his motion, imposed on me the necessity of vindicating my opinion. I submitted in silent deference to the decision of my brethren." Harper's partisanship, not Lee's technical craftsmanship, stoked Johnson's fires.

After Marshall had delivered the opinion of the Court on its competence to issue the writs of habeas corpus, he turned to the petition of counsel to hold the two men over for trial. *Bollman* I was simple, for the Court's authority to issue the writ could hardly be questioned. *Bollman* II was complicated. In effect, without the benefit of a trial record and the matters of fact established by such a record, the High Court must decide whether Bollman and Swartwout could be held on a charge of treason. Bear in mind that, except for its original jurisdiction, the High Court was an appeals court. It determined law, not facts. What was more, the long shadow of what would become *U.S. v. Burr* touched *Bollman* II, for surely the government would try to indict Burr for treason. Whatever Marshall said with respect to the law of treason in *Bollman* would affect *Burr.*

As taxing as *Bollman* II was for Marshall and the Court, it was a boon to the counselors. It gave both sides the chance to try out arguments about Burr before they had to face the real Burr trial. From February 16 to 19, the Court heard argument on this matter. Rodney wanted to base Bollman's and Swartwout's continued confinement on the crisis that Wilkinson depicted. "The affidavit of General Wilkinson is sufficiently authenticated. The justices of peace in the territory of Orleans are officers of the United States — they are appointed by the governor of the territory, who is appointed by the President of the United States; and the secretary of the territory is bound by law to transmit copies of all the executive proceedings of the governor of the territory every six months to the President of the United States. All the officers of the United States are bound to take notice of each other." The High Court should defer to the inferior courts and their officers.

Rodney made some concessions. "It is true that none of the evidence now offered would be competent on the trial; nor even if it appeared in a proper shape, would it be sufficient to convict the prisoners. But the question is whether, in this incipient stage of the prosecution, it is not sufficient to show probable cause." Rodney knew that the Supreme Court hearing was not a grand jury proceeding, and probable cause was not the measure the Court must use. "The expedition against Mexico would not be treason, unless it was to be accomplished by means which in themselves would amount to treason." This was a concession fatal to the prosecution.

"But if the constituted authorities of the United States should be suppressed but for one hour, and the territory of Orleans revolution- ized but for a moment, it would be treason." What did *revolutionize* mean? It meant overthrowing a government and establishing a new one in its place. If the purpose of the prospective Burr raid on New Orleans was only to empty its banks, that was robbery, not treason. The actual offense would be robbery.

Whatever Burr may have planned, how did Burr's alleged plan lead to the constraint on Bollman's and Swartwout's freedom? Rodney now introduced the argument that the government would replay through- out the prosecution of Burr. "In treason all are principals. There are no accessories." If Bollman and Swartwout were culpable, even though they did no more than carry letters, then Burr was culpable, even though he never made it to New Orleans — and vice versa.

This doctrine was a common-law fixture but was not part of the constitutional definition of treason. One had to perform a treasonous act, not be a party to a plan to perform such an act. Rodney had com- pleted the flip-flop that Harper began. The Republicans, heretofore enemies of loose construction, had become its proponents, adding by interpretation the notion of conspiracy to the constitutional defini- tion of treason. The Federalists, experts at loose construction, were now decrying it. It was an ironic turnabout, and potentially deadly for Burr.

Rodney did not have much American law on his side. But he wanted a trial jury to decide whether treason included conspiracy. No doubt the plan for the trial was to introduce every prejudicial rumor and alleged conversation that Burr had and prepare the jury to believe that a vast conspiracy existed. "It has been argued, (and the respectable authority of Judge [St. George] Tucker is cited) that none are princi- pals but those present at the treasonable act. The argument may have some weight, but it is a point at least doubtful, and therefore ought to be left to be decided on the trial."

When was a jury competent to decide a matter of law? William Nelson and other legal historians have found evidence that early national juries claimed, or were allowed to claim, the right to inter- pret law as well as find facts. Judges in civil and criminal cases some- times instructed the jury in the relevant law, but not always. They made rulings, particularly about the admissibility of evidence and whether witnesses would be allowed to testify, but judges often let the testimony and evidence in, and told the jury to use its "conscience" to decide what to believe. One must bear in mind that these early national juries were elite men. They were the top tenth of colonial society in wealth, education, experience, and status. Some were office-holders themselves.

Whether or not colonial juries and early national juries claimed, and judges conceded, their right to determine law as well as fact, some early national judges believed that to have been the case. In a case of alleged treason arising out of the War of 1812, *U.S. v. John Hodges* (1815), Supreme Court Justice Gabriel Duvall, sitting on a circuit court, did not think that Hodges's cooperation with the British was coerced. But he told the jury that "The jury are not bound to conform to [his reading of the law of treason] because they have the right, in all criminal cases, to decide on the law and the facts." The federal district judge on the bench with Duvall, James Houston, agreed that the jury could decide on the law and the facts. The jury acquitted Hodges.

A more appropriate authority, not least because it preceded *Bollman*, was St. George Tucker's *Commentaries on Blackstone with Notes of Reference to the Constitution and Laws of the Federal Government of the United States and of the Commonwealth of Virginia* (1803). The fourth volume of this five-volume recapitulation of Blackstone's commentaries, with notes and references to federal and Virginia law and procedure, touched on the question of jury law finding. Virginia judges did not as a rule instruct juries on the law, although, as Tucker wrote, there were "numberless niceties and distinctions of what is or is not, legal evidence to a jury," and those distinctions arose from judicial rulings.

It was clear to Tucker that "It is the province of a jury, alone, to judge of the truth of facts, and the credibility of witnesses, and the party cannot, by a demurrer to evidence, or any other means, take that province from them." According to the Judiciary Act of 1789, federal courts were to use the procedural law of the state in which the court sat. But the High Court was not bound by this portion of the Judiciary Act, and no jury sat to hear and determine facts in *Bollman* II.

The fate of Bollman and Swartwout did not rest with a jury at all— not yet. It rested with the highest appeals court in the land. So Rodney had to argue law, not facts. And the constitutional definition of treason required the levying of war, not participation in a conspiracy. Rodney found himself backed into a corner. He could not argue law, for the law required what he could not prove, and he could not argue facts, for "we cannot at present say exactly when and where the overt act of levying war was committed, but from the affidavits we think it fair to infer that an army has been actually levied and arrayed." Inference from what source? "The declaration of one of the prisoners was, that Col. Burr 'was levying an armed body of 7,000 men.'" That was Bollman, but Bollman speaking through Wilkinson's affidavit. The High Court could not call Bollman to confirm or deny what Wilkinson had said, nor could it call Wilkinson to be examined and cross-examined because the High Court was not a trial court (except in its original jurisdiction, and that door was closed and nailed shut in *Bollman* I).

Rodney was clearly uneasy. No one could say from eyewitness testimony "that any men have been seen collected in military array." There was only a chain of inference based on rumor based on fear, and Wilkinson's affidavit about what Bollman said. "If Col. Burr was actually levying an armed body of men, if he expected to be at Natchez on the 20th of December with 2,000, and calculated upon being followed by 4,000 more, and if he found it so easy to raise troops, is there not a moral certainty that some troops at least have been raised and embodied?" Shades of Edward Coke's prosecution of Walter Raleigh! But where was enough evidence of Burr's levying of war to indict Bollman and Swartwout for carrying off their part of the alleged conspiracy?

Rodney knew that Wilkinson's reputation, should it be tested in court, might not hold up. "It may be admitted that General Wilkinson was interested to make the worst of the story, but the declarations of the prisoners themselves are sufficient." The prosecution conceded that "It has been insinuated that General Wilkinson is to be considered as *particeps criminis* [a partner in the crime]. If that were the case, it would be no disqualification of his testimony." Why not? If testimony is "against interest" or an admitted partner in crime testifies about his accomplices, then the testimony does not violate the "hearsay" rule, but neither was true of Wilkinson's testimony.

The modern rules on hearsay are complex but fairly clear. Hearsay is testimony by a person about what that person heard from another person. "I heard him say he took the car," the witness says. Hearsay, literally secondhand oral testimony, is not admissible when the original speaker can be present in court. But the rules are a little more complicated. Certain kinds of secondhand testimony are not hearsay. For example, a statement made in court by an alleged coconspirator about what another member of the conspiracy said during the course of the conspiracy is not hearsay. Nor is it hearsay to introduce into trial as evidence earlier recorded and documented statements by a defendant.

Wary of relying solely on Wilkinson's affidavit about what Burr's messengers allegedly said to Wilkinson, Rodney threw Jefferson's message into the pot to raise the stakes. Harper lifted it out with tongs and examined it the way an exterminator would examine the corpse of a rat. Harper reminded the Court that it was highly unusual for "executive messages . . . to be received as evidence in a criminal prosecution." The prosecutors feebly rejoined that "The sole purpose for which we introduced the president's message, was to show that the assemblage of a military force by Colonel Burr was a matter of notoriety. We did not attempt or wish to introduce it as direct evidence." Was not *notoriety* a synonym for hearsay?

Jefferson's message relied on Wilkinson's information, and Wilkinson's information relied on his translation and interpretation of the July 22 letter from Burr. Harper: "We object to the translation of the ciphered letter contained in General Wilkinson's affidavits, being admitted as evidence, because General Wilkinson has not sworn that it is a true translation, nor sent the original, with the key, so that the court can have a correct translation made. Nor is it proved that the original was written by Colonel Burr, or by his direction, nor that the prisoners were acquainted with its contents."

Although the rules of evidence were not in 1807 as well developed as they are today, for the previous century, English and American jurists had given serious thought to what kinds of evidence could be admitted in a hearing before a court, what kinds of evidence were most probative, and what kinds — for example, secondhand stories — were unreliable.

In 1754, Geoffrey, Baron Gilbert's *The Law of Evidence* appeared. This text, although primarily concerned with written evidence, also covered oral testimony. The value of evidence admitted at trial was to allow the jury to reach the correct verdict of fact. Excluded was evidence that might sway a jury's feelings or sentiments against the facts. Gilbert also ranked different types of evidence in order of their probative value — that is, how trustworthy they were. Certain individuals' testimony could not be trusted and should not be heard by the jury. These included individuals with a personal interest in the outcome of the case and individuals who had been convicted or were accused of certain crimes.

Gilbert did not trust hearsay, and witnesses were to testify only to what they knew from their own senses, not what they had heard from others. Above all, in civil cases, written proofs were preferred over oral ones, and the best written proofs were the original documents rather than copies. These rules were not particularly helpful at criminal trials, where evidence was overwhelmingly oral and testimony of coconspirators had to be admitted, a large exception to the hearsay limitation.

Within fifty years of Gilbert's treatise, the distinction between direct proof and circumstantial proof (inference from the smoking gun in the hand and the dead body at the feet of the suspect, when no one saw the defendant fire the shot) had established itself. The list of exceptions to the hearsay rule was growing to include the admission of third-party evidence on reputation and prior criminal activity, evidence from a person who had died before trial, statements that the witness had overheard while present, and admissions by the party himself. Most important, oral evidence had gained equal stature with documentary evidence. The right of the defendant to testify under oath (forbidden in old English law), the presence of skilled legal counsel to conduct direct and cross-examination, and the requirement of an impartial jury (rather than a jury of people who knew about the offense) supposedly ensured that the jury could weigh oral testimony for its veracity.

Luther Martin, until now silent, joined Harper to exploit the evidentiary breaches in the prosecution case. Martin could be intemperate (indeed, he was often inebriated), but his grasp of legal issues was superb. He was also notable for the passion of his advocacy. Jefferson cordially hated Martin, in part for Martin's acerbic political diatribes. Martin was another graduate of the College of New Jersey, like Harper and Burr, and moved to Maryland, then Virginia. He was a staunch advocate of independence, and became attorney general of the new state of Maryland in 1778, in which capacity he served until 1805. This did not deter him from engaging in one of the country's most active and remunerative private practices. Like Burr and Hamilton, Martin did not regard public office as a deterrent to private gain. Though he attended the Constitutional Convention in 1787, he was a notable antifederalist. But he found himself attracted to other Federalists, and by the end of the 1790s, he was a stalwart of that party.

For the present, Martin trimmed his sails, sensing that the Court did not need to hear a flowery oration to free his clients. In any case, he needed to make a technical point. "The act of Congress [passed in 1790] for the punishment of certain crimes [permitting summary arrest and confinement] does not apply to crimes committed in any territory of the United States in which there are courts of the United States having cognizance of the offence." Given that "the courts of the United States erected in the territory of Orleans are competent to try the offence of treason against the United States committed within that territory," Bollman and Swartwout should never have been brought to Washington.

But warming to the task, and seeing the opportunity to swipe at Jefferson (whose hatred he readily returned), Martin concluded, "It was therefore a wanton and unnecessary exertion of arbitrary power to send the prisoners here, where they cannot be tried. If there is any probability that a crime was committed by the prisoners, it is equally probable that it was committed in the territory of Orleans. It is at all events certain that it was not committed here."

Marshall had some questions for counsel. He requested that they return the next day to clarify whether Wilkinson's affidavit could be read as evidence, given the problems surrounding it and its contents, and whether the copy of the letter from Burr that Wilkinson enclosed was admissible. The very same question would become the turning point at the Burr trial.

When the Court reassembled, Rodney had nothing to add, but a fourth member of the legal team for Bollman and Swartwout, Francis Scott Key, had used the day's respite to study his lawbooks. He found that English precedents and treatises agreed: "that, as General Wilkinson did not apply to justices [of the peace in New Orleans] for a warrant to arrest Dr. Bollman and Mr. Swartwout, and as he did not make the affidavit for the purpose of obtaining from [justices of the peace] such warrants, the whole proceedings before those justices were extrajudicial. The affidavits are not such as would support an indictment, if false. . . . If it be not a judicial proceeding, it is not evidence."

Rodney, awakened to the danger that the charges against the prisoners, temporarily free on bail, would be dismissed, interjected, "The first [Wilkinson] affidavit would be sufficient, unless disproved or explained by the prisoner on his examination." The letter was not necessary. Harper countered that only dire necessity could displace due process, and once Bollman and Swartwout were in custody in New Orleans, there was no dire necessity to deny them their legal rights there, including the right to a public and speedy trial and counsel.

On February 21, after more questions in court and some arm-twisting among the brethren at the inn where the justices lived, Marshall delivered the second of the Court's rulings on Bollman and Swartwout. Chase, Bushrod Washington, and William Johnson sat on the bench with Marshall.

In *Bollman* II, Marshall announced that "the question to be determined is, whether the accused shall be discharged or held to trial; and if the latter, in what place they are to be tried, and whether they shall be confined or admitted to bail." They were free to go if "upon this inquiry it manifestly appears that no such crime has been committed, or that the suspicion entertained of the prisoners was wholly groundless."

The two were charged with "levying war against the United States," one of the two constitutional definitions of treason. They were not charged with any of the other offenses that might constitute the offense. Although this was not the first occasion for the Court to consider a rebellion, it was the first time that the Supreme Court explored the nature of treason. "To constitute that specific crime for which the prisoners now before the court have been committed, war must be actually levied against the United States. However flagitious may be the crime of conspiring to subvert by force the government of our country, such conspiracy is not treason. To conspire to levy war, and actually to levy war, are distinct offences."

The evidence from Wilkinson that Bollman and Swartwout were part of a conspiracy to sever the union by force had no weight because it did not prove — even if it was true and admissible — that the two men levied war. Then Marshall added in a curious afterthought: "It is not the intention of the court to say that no individual can be guilty of this crime who has not appeared in arms against his country. On the contrary, if war be actually levied, that is, if a body of men be actually assembled for the purpose of effecting by force a treasonable purpose, all those who perform any part, however minute, or however remote from the scene of action, and who are actually leagued in the general conspiracy, are to be considered as traitors." This closing remark was a dictum — a statement not necessary to settle the matter of Bollman and Swartwout's petition for freedom.

What was Marshall up to? Why go beyond what was necessary to settle the case before the Court? The answer must lie in inference: Marshall had agreed to the language to gain a majority for his opinion. It sailed close to the English idea of a constructive treason — "Crimes so atrocious as those which have for their object the subversion by violence of those laws and those institutions which have been ordained in order to secure the peace and happiness of society, are not to escape punishment because they have not ripened into treason." Did "not ripened" amount or equate to merely planned or plotted, something like the furtherance of a conspiracy rather than an overt act of violence against the laws? Was Marshall giving back with one hand what his earlier words had taken away?

Marshall always chose his words carefully. He had made the concession to Justice Johnson and perhaps to Justice Chase, but he did not want to open a door to convictions for conspiracy. "The framers of our Constitution . . . not only defined and limited the crime [of treason], but with jealous circumspection attempted to protect their limitation by providing that no person should be convicted of it, unless on the testimony of two witnesses to the same overt act, or on confession in open court." What was more, "It is therefore more safe as well as more consonant to the principles of our Constitution, that the crime of treason should not be extended by construction to doubtful cases."

There is another hint that a deal was struck among the justices that led to Marshall's hedged reference to "ripened." As authority for the overt act of levying war, Marshall added, "Judge Chase, in the trial of Fries, was more explicit. He stated the opinion of the [circuit] court to be, 'that if a body of people conspire and meditate an insurrection to resist or oppose the execution of any statute of the United States by force, they are only guilty of a high misdemeanor; but if they proceed to carry such intention into execution by force, that they are guilty of the treason of levying war . . . some actual force or violence must be used in pursuance of such design to levy war.' "

The evidence against Bollman and Swartwout came from the same sources as the evidence against Burr. To resolve the former case, Marshall laid down principles that would apply to reading evidence in the latter case, should Burr be indicted. Nothing in Wilkinson's correspondence with the courts showed that Bollman and Swartwout had levied war against the United States, or engaged in anything that came close. Marshall went through the Wilkinson letter and the affidavit with a fine-tooth comb, sentence by sentence, and concluded, "There certainly is not in the letter delivered to Gen. Wilkinson, so far as that letter is laid before the court, one syllable which has a necessary or a natural reference to an enterprise against any territory of the United States." What was more, Swartwout himself had said that "their object [was] to be, 'to carry an expedition into the Mexican provinces.' "

Other crimes there might be, and other grounds for indictment and trial. But "the words used by the prisoner in reference to seizing at New-Orleans, and borrowing perhaps by force from the bank, though indicating a design to rob, and consequently importing a high offence, do not designate the specific crime of levying war against the United States." Swartwout was free to go. "Against Erick Bollman there is still less testimony. Nothing has been said by him to support the charge that the enterprize in which he was engaged had any other object than was stated in the letter of Colonel Burr. Against him, therefore, there is no evidence to support a charge of treason." Perhaps the Neutrality Act was a more appropriate avenue for the prosecution to seek an indictment, for "crimes not clearly within the constitutional definition, should receive such punishment as the legislature in its wisdom may provide."

A flourish closed the opinion: "That both of the prisoners were engaged in a most culpable enterprize against the dominions of a power at peace with the United States, those who admit the affidavit of General Wilkinson cannot doubt. But that no part of this crime was committed in the District of Columbia is apparent. It is therefore the unanimous opinion of the court that they cannot be tried in this district."

Marshall's dictum about treason by remote control would come back to haunt him. It was a mischievous addendum, not necessary to resolve the cases before him, and it traversed the very precedents that Marshall cited. It cracked open a door for prosecutions based on this theory. And through that door Burr's prosecutors hastened.

CHAPTER 6

Waiting for Wilkinson

The day after the March 30, 1807, meeting with Burr at the Eagle Tavern, Virginia federal district attorney George Hay moved for Burr's imprisonment to await trial. Burr must not be bailed. He was too dangerous. Still, if Hay had not yet formulated the indictment for treason, could he ask that Burr be held in custody on what amounted to mere suspicion of Burr's incendiary purposes?

Hay was well regarded by Jefferson, and no neophyte. At forty-one, he was a close friend of those in Jefferson's inner circle and in constant contact with Jefferson. He was Jefferson's trusted representative at all the trials, and in time he would be rewarded for his loyalty with a federal judgeship.

Hay was eager for the grand jury proceedings to begin, at which he could present an indictment for treason, but he was hamstrung in his efforts. His star witness for the grand jury, James Wilkinson, had not yet arrived. Until Wilkinson appeared, Hay had to tread water. Deluged with almost daily instructions from an increasingly impatient Jefferson, facing what he knew was an unsympathetic bench and a superb defense team, Hay coped well. Indeed, historians have not given him the credit he deserves for his conduct of the prosecution.

Marshall was there to conduct a hearing on Burr's motion for bail. The circuit court of which he was the senior judge would not be in session until May 22, at which time the grand jury would be summoned and indictments presented to it. Judge Griffin would then join Marshall on the bench to constitute the circuit court. If the grand jury handed down indictments, trial would begin in the court. For now, however, the issue remained Burr's freedom on bail.

Hay's problem was keeping hold of Burr without having presented formal charges. His burden was far greater than the defense team's. For in fact Burr was captured, held incommunicado, transported from the scenes of his alleged crimes to Washington, D.C., diverted to Richmond, and remained in close confinement without an arrest warrant, an indictment, or any of the other usual accompaniments of due process in a criminal case.

Although the attorneys understood what was at stake, such fine distinctions were lost on many of the throng of gawkers, visitors, thrill seekers, and residents who jammed the streets to see the principals and share gossip. When Marshall convened the bail hearing on April 1 on the top (courtroom) floor of the Virginia statehouse, so many came to watch that the court adjourned to the House of Delegates (assembly) hall below. It was to be the longest and perhaps the most luminous bail hearing in American legal history.

Jefferson had designed and ordered the construction of the neoclassic capitol when he was governor and the capital moved to Richmond from Williamsburg. The legislators moved into the building in 1788 and it is still in use as a museum; the lower house now sits in a wing added in 1904. To get to the hall, delegates passed under the rotunda and through a lobby featuring a classically posed full-body statue of George Washington. The lower house chamber hall was not grand, though its open rectangular design accommodated all the parties at the Burr hearing, and later his trial. The floor was covered with sawdust, and the acoustics were terrible. Marshall sat on a raised platform that the presiding officer of the house of delegates normally occupied. The hall was divided along its center aisle, counsel for the defense and the government sitting behind benches facing the judges. The rest of the seats, the gallery, the hallway, and the surrounding streets were full of spectators.

Jefferson was watching the proceedings from afar, in the presidential mansion in Washington, D.C. On April 1, he wrote to Giles: "That there should be anxiety & doubt in the public mind, in the present defective state of the proof, is not wonderful; and this has been sedulously encouraged by the tricks of the judges to force trials before it is possible to collect the evidence, dispersed through a line of 2000 miles from Maine to Orleans. The Federalists, too, give all their aid, making Burr's cause their own, mortified only that he did not separate the Union or overturn the government, & proving, that had he had a little dawn of success, they would have joined him to introduce his object, their favorite monarchy, as they would any other enemy, foreign or domestic, who could rid them of this hateful republic for any other government in exchange."

Jefferson's anger extended to Marshall, who had, in what amounted to an aside, asked why the government had not yet provided proofs of the overt act: "But a moment's calculation will shew that this evidence cannot be collected under 4 months, probably 5, from the moment of deciding when & where the trial shall be. I desired Mr. Rodney expressly to inform the Chief Justice of this, inofficially." Jefferson suspected that Marshall would not be friendly to the prosecution. "All this, however, will work well. The nation will judge both the offender & judges for themselves." A dire warning worthy of an Olympian deity, but Jefferson, unlike Zeus, did not have any thunderbolts to hurl down at the judges in Richmond.

Hay's argument for a commitment order was opposed by Burr's counsel, John Wickham and Randolph. Wickham was a local attorney and would do most of the heavy lifting for the defense. He spoke to every prosecution motion, sometimes for hours. Randolph, privately embarrassed and publicly dismissed by Jefferson, had personal reasons to join the Burr team. He did not like Burr, but he liked Jefferson less. A man of singular honesty and public spirit, he had borne the calumny of both parties, though he stood above party himself. Ill much of the time, stricken by palsy, he still had star power. He spoke rarely, and always with grave politeness. Luther Martin and Charles Lee would arrive a week later. The long conversation began that day and continued in one form or another until October 20, 1807, when it ended with a whimper.

But it began with a bang. Hay opened. Burr was guilty of "High Misdemeanor" (under the Neutrality Act, the equivalent of a felony) for preparing to war with Spain. Worse, Burr engaged in treason, assembling an armed force with a design to seize the city of New Orleans, to revolutionize the territory attached to it, and to separate the Western from the Atlantic states. Hay treated the evidence against Bollman and Swartwout as common knowledge, but Hay did not present any evidence.

Wickham responded that there was no evidence of treason, no overt act. He too treated the cipher letter as common knowledge. But the letter to Wilkinson was not written by Burr, delivered by Burr, or in his handwriting, and even if the court admitted the letter as evidence, all that it showed was preparation for warring on Spanish possessions should the country go to war with Spain.

Randolph added that there was no evidence of any criminal act, and the alleged conspiracy was neither proven nor a crime. It was Wilkinson who had caused the disorder with a false alarm, to conceal his "arbitrary and violent proceedings." Burr's men could hardly be called an armed force capable of violating the Neutrality Act, for they had neither arms nor ammunition.

Burr spoke ably in his own defense, as he would throughout all of his trials. Of all the lawyers present in the room, the cream of the early national bar, he was the most astute. He was certain of his own innocence under the law, and as he wrote to William Van Ness later in April, "it is not possible that I can be convicted of any crime unless by the agency of the most horrible prejudice or by the most barefaced assertion of partiality and party spirit." From the first grand jury hearing, Burr claimed that there was no cause for alarm, other than the false trail laid by Wilkinson.

Burr insisted that his movements were not dictated by a plot or by the desire to avoid prosecution. Every time he heard that he was indicted in the regular course of law, he "invited inquiry" and made himself available for it. When he fled at last, he "abandoned a country where the laws ceased to be the sovereign power." Over the course of the month, when he was dragged from the Tombigbee in Alabama to Richmond, he was never allowed a pen or paper, the right to counsel, or any of the other elements of due process. He was a prisoner of a military escort though charged with a civil crime, and he was carried from the alleged vicinity of that crime to a distant court.

Attorney general Rodney explained why Burr was treated so arbitrarily. "Public anxiety, so strongly excited," had necessitated close confinement and removal of Burr to Richmond, far from the scenes of his alleged conspiracy. Rodney's explanation would use the same theme every time: the government had perceived a national emergency and thus had curtailed due process rights. The justification was national security, although in retrospect some element of political partisanship revealed itself. Seen in this light, Jefferson's campaign against Burr was the mildest form of tyranny. Burr had his day in court. Not every suspected traitor or terrorist gets his.

On April 1, 1807, Marshall ruled on the question whether the government had presented enough evidence to hold Burr for trial. It was the first of many rulings he made in *U.S. v. Burr*. "On an application of this kind [from the prosecution] I certainly should not require that proof which would be necessary to convict the person to be committed, on a trial in chief . . . nor should I even require, that which should absolutely convince my own mind of the guilt of the accused."

The prosecution had made two charges against Burr, first for violating the Neutrality statute, second for high treason. The first, the statutory offense, rested on the affidavit Wilkinson sent and the letter enclosed. Were the enclosed letter absent, "nothing remains in the testimony which can in the most remote degree affect Colonel Burr." Marshall had heard all this before and was tempted to throw out the entire matter. But "I could not in this stage of the prosecution absolutely discredit the affidavit, because the material facts alleged may very well be within the knowledge of the witness."

For an indictment for treason, the evidence would have to persuade Marshall that the overt act of levying war had already occurred. Intent, if proved, was not enough to encompass the crime of treason, though it was necessary. The "communications" enclosed in the affidavit were not sufficient to show that the plan, if such there be, had been consummated, or that Burr had taken part in any such act. In support of this reading of the evidence, Marshall cited his own opinion in *Bollman* II.

At trial, Swartwout might give further proof that Burr's design was against the United States rather than a foreign power. On the other hand, could Swartwout testify to the overt act—the assembling of men—in which Burr had taken part? If Swartwout could say that Burr was gathering armed men for a treasonous purpose, and if that purpose had ripened (the key element Marshall required for the crime, as expressed in *Bollman* II), the probable cause to try Burr certainly existed.

Marshall had not repudiated the language of *Bollman* II, and he saw no need to qualify it. Nothing in his application of the *Bollman* II test for ripening crossed over into a constructive treason. According to the Constitution, the act had to be "a visible transaction," and "numbers must witness it." But why, Marshall asked, after five weeks had the prosecution still not produced evidence of the act? "If in November or December last a body of troops had been assembled on the

Ohio, it is impossible to suppose that affidavits establishing the fact could not have been obtained by the last of March."

Marshall slyly dug at Jefferson's efforts to find evidence: "I ought not to believe, and I do not believe that there has been any remissness on the part of those who prosecute." Indeed, there had not been any remissness. Jefferson had sent Graham to gain evidence, had promised a pardon to Bollman, and had assembled 140 witnesses, paying out of funds in the treasury for them to be conveyed, housed, and fed in Richmond. Marshall instructed the prosecution not to present the charge of high treason until such evidence of an overt act could be produced. Until then, Burr was free on $10,000 bail.

The government prosecution team now had to find such an overt act or compose one from the bits and pieces of Burr's words and travels and embed it in an indictment. To ease the task by spreading the labor, Hay and Rodney were joined by Alexander MacRae, hired counsel and lieutenant governor of the state, and William Wirt.

Wirt was more than just a skilled lawyer. He was a notable orator, essayist, and biographer. Later in life he would serve as attorney general of the United States and run for the presidency. Born in Maryland, educated privately, he read law and joined the Virginia bar in 1792. He was never a legal scholar, but his command of the language made him a superb courtroom debater. His voice, described as melodious, could hold an audience for hours — a useful talent when much argument proceeded in court without written briefs. He married well, and his gregariousness brought him powerful patrons and many friends in Richmond and Williamsburg. Never sure of his income, and his income never quite adequate for his growing family, Wirt preferred private practice to public office. But he was in Richmond and accepted Jefferson's commission to join the prosecution team against Burr. He would represent the government before the High Court on many occasions, and he represented the Cherokee Indians in their attempt to retain their ancestral homelands against the state of Georgia.

One incident at this time (around April 1) set the newspapers aflutter. Wickham had a dinner party at his home in Richmond, and Burr was present. So, by invitation, was John Marshall. Although the entire episode is testimony to the incestuous nature of the Richmond legal community — Wickham's cocounsel Benjamin Botts, Hay, Wirt, and

Marshall all saw one another regularly in court, at the market, in taverns, and at one another's homes—suspicious minds saw Marshall acting out of spite to Jefferson. But Marshall was not sending a message to anyone when he remained at Wickham's table. Gentlemen did not abruptly depart other gentlemen's dinner tables.

On May 22, the circuit court convened. Wilkinson was still absent. Randolph and Wickham were there for Burr, as was Botts, a young but able and well-regarded Richmond lawyer, and John Baker, another Virginia lawyer. Charles Lee sat with the Burr defense team, as did Luther Martin. Rodney had departed. The defense outnumbered the prosecution, but both sides were superbly skilled and well prepared.

Indeed, one must note here how professional and able counsel on both sides of the aisle were. These men were not only respected lawyers, they were also learned and hardworking. In the coming months, all of them would speak for hours, spicing the argument with citations from English and American law. Although the record does not indicate whether they brought the books into court, one can imagine stacks of bound reports of cases and commentary on the desks in front of the lawyers, and perhaps on the judges' bench as well.

The jurors sat through these often complicated and scholarly discourses. No doubt, as was custom at the time, the jurors asked questions themselves. Many of the jurors matched the lawyers in status and education. The jury list reads like a who's who of the Virginia men of parts. They were drawn from the vicinity, but that included all the counties surrounding the capital. The foreman of the grand jury was John Randolph, a member of Congress and one of the leaders of the conservative wing of the Republican Party. He did not like Jefferson or Burr. The foreman of the trial jury was Edward Carrington, like Hamilton and Burr addressed as "colonel" for his service in the Continental army, Chief Justice Marshall's wife's brother-in-law, Mayor of Richmond, and a former federal marshal in the state.

The high tone of the entire proceeding was ensured by the men behind the bench. Federal district court judge Cyrus Griffin was not recorded as saying a word, but surely he did. He was simply overshadowed by his colleague. Marshall listened with patience to the interchanges of the lawyers, interjecting questions to refocus the argument and to cool tempers. Marshall was no scholar, but he took time, often over the evening or a Sunday, to prepare rulings on key motions.

One of these rulings would determine the outcome of the first trial, and a second would determine the outcome of the entire case against Burr.

Marshall knew that the circuit court was bound by the Judiciary Act of 1789 to follow the state's procedures for summoning grand and petit (trial) jurors. The grand jury would have to decide whether there was probable cause for the prosecution to pursue the case. In technical terms, they would find the indictment either a true bill or not. The trial jurors would hear evidence in court on the indictment and render a verdict — guilty or not guilty. The judges might instruct the jurors on the evidence and the law, but both, under Virginia practice, belonged to the jurors.

The federal marshal had brought together twenty-four "freeholders" — that is, voters — to serve on the grand jury. The composition of the grand jury mattered. Insofar as the case was a political one held in Jefferson's backyard — not in Kentucky, or Mississippi, or Ohio, or lower Louisiana Territory, where Burr had friends, but a few miles down the road from Jefferson's aerie in Charlottesville — could Burr expect to find fair-minded grand jurors? Or even grand jurors who were not related to Jefferson or owed him some debt of gratitude?

If the federal marshal, a Jeffersonian appointee, could tap the shoulders of any freeholder who happened to be in court to fill vacancies on the panel (as he could according to state law), or if he could substitute anyone he chose for a juryman who could not attend according to the original summons, he could pack the grand jury panel. The marshal was a Republican, and Burr's legal team objected when he added two grand jurors of his own choosing to the panel.

Not that Burr could not have ingratiated himself with the marshal, given time and the right situation. Burr had proved that in Alabama, when he convinced the sheriff who arrested him, Theodore Brightwell, that the charges were trumped up. But not so today. Hay replied to Wickham that Marshal Joseph Scott could supply vacancies. Botts said this was not so. All three men knew that in state criminal trials, Virginia sheriffs often stepped out of the county courthouse to see if any freeholders were in the courtyard or the tavern next door, and tapped them on the shoulder. He knew who qualified for service on juries and escorted the volunteers inside. Did this apply to a federal criminal trial?

Marshall was perplexed. On the one hand, a federal court sitting in Virginia, according to the Judiciary and Process Acts of 1789, was bound by the state's procedural rules. These were clear in William Hening's *The New Virginia Justice* (1799), a manual that everyone who practiced in the state (including Marshall) owned. Hening reported that a defendant in a Virginia criminal proceeding could challenge the entire array (panel) of a grand jury "in respect of the partiality or default of the sheriff." Or the defendant might challenge the panel for "favor" (partiality). A defendant might also challenge individual members of the panel (called *polls*) simply because he disliked the potential juror. These "peremptory challenges" were limited in number to twenty-four. A "principal challenge" was a challenge of a potential juror for cause—for example, "if the juror hath declared his opinion beforehand, that the party is guilty." If a poll was challenged, it was up to the court to decide whether to replace the potential juror.

There was a case on point as well. In *Commonwealth v. Leath* (1806), a manslaughter case that defendants appealed to the state supreme court, that court opined that "If the said Heartwell and Peter Leath shall make it appear to the said district court that they have by any illegal means whatever been deprived of their right to elect at their trial the persons or either of them returned by the sheriff [to serve on the jury] . . . that the said court ought in such case to set aside the verdict rendered in consequence of such deprivation, and to award a new trial." At the very least, Burr had the right under Virginia law to challenge jurors.

And he did, starting with the grand jury. But when could Burr object to the grand jury selection? Did he have to wait until the entire grand jury was seated, or could he object to individual jurors, as a defendant could to the members of a petit or trial jury? Hay said that Burr must wait until the entire panel was assembled. Wickham rejoined: "if once the [marshal], who holds his commission at the will of the government, were permitted to alter the panel as he pleased, the life of every citizen in this state would be held at his pleasure." Scott interrupted to defend himself against the implication that his choices were politically motivated. Who had he excused illegally? "Name him, sir. I demand his name."

Fortunately, the contretemps did not lead to a duel. Wickham did what a gentleman, even a gentleman of the law defending his client zealously, must do to avoid more serious consequences than a dispute. He apologized. "He meant no imputation upon the sheriff [that is, the marshal] . . . it was only an error in [his] judgment." Then, because he was a lawyer in court as well as a gentleman, Wickham added that he would "not submit to such interruptions."

The brief exchange among the counsel, the marshal, Wickham, and Marshall indicated how swiftly the slightest hint of insult could, if left untended, spiral into a challenge and, as in the Burr-Hamilton episode, a duel. The alternative to self-help was law, and within the courtroom, lawyers could say without fear what out of door might be highly inflammatory. But one still had to be civil.

Marshall cooled the atmosphere. Had the precise issue ever been discussed in the state courts? he asked the senior counsel, Randolph. Randolph thought not. Marshall opined that Scott may have simply excused a juror whose excuse had been compelling. That was perfectly legitimate. But he ruled that the federal marshal could not simply substitute or designate for substitution one individual for another. The issue was settled amicably. As a result, two of the marshal's substitutes had to leave the panel.

Burr then challenged for "favor" William Branch Giles, the very man who in the Senate had proposed the suspension of habeas corpus and who came closest to being Jefferson's right-hand man in that body. Burr averred that Giles had pronounced Burr guilty of treason publicly. Giles replied that he had no objection to telling the Court what he thought, for his "mind was free to receive impressions from judicial evidence." He did not think it proper for the gentleman jurors to be examined by Burr, but for himself, "I have no personal resentments against the accused; and if he has received any information inconsistent with this statement, it is not true."

Perhaps Giles had no intention of being the next target of Burr's dueling pistols, but more likely, Giles was hinting what many in Jefferson's circle believed: Burr was never a gentleman, not as the Virginia planters understood the term. Burr, a true gentleman whatever Giles implied, characteristically refused to return insult for insult. The Hamilton duel would remain the one real exception to Burr's self-control. He replied to Giles's nonapologetic apology, "[Giles] is one of the last men on whom I would wish to cast any reflections. So far from having any animosity against him, he would have been one of those whom I should have ranked my personal friends." Giles voluntarily withdrew.

Burr also objected to Wilson C. Nicholas. Burr did not want to enter into details, save that Nicholas had "entertained a bitter personal animosity against me." Nicholas responded that he did not want to serve and had objected to being placed on the panel because he thought Burr guilty. He was excused. Another juror said that he had read accusations against Burr in the newspapers, and at the time had exclaimed an unfavorable judgment on Burr. He had not yet made up his mind, however. Burr responded that so notorious had the coverage been, no impartial juror on that score could have been found. He was content with grand jurors' professions of open-mindedness.

Once the grand jury was completed, counsel turned to procedural jousting over bail for Burr recalling the oral argument in *Bollman* II. What charges? What evidence was sufficient at this stage for the grand jury? Could the grand jury hear the Wilkinson affidavit? The only notable event was a legally irrelevant bit of bombast from Wirt placed in front of the grand jurors. It resembled less a procedural point than a summation at the end of a trial. He thought that the court had "carried politeness beyond its ordinary pitch" in allowing Burr to slander Wilkinson. The trial was not an "epic," mere dramatic show to amuse the nation. "I recollect nothing in the history of his deportment, which renders it so very incredible, that Aaron Burr would fly from a prosecution." The defense merely "divert[ed] attention" from Burr "to another quarter." They meant to sway "popular prejudices" against Wilkinson. Poor Wilkinson was not there to defend his name. By the time Wirt was done, it was easy to see why he had been added to the prosecution team.

Burr could not let this pass by unanswered. He ignored Wirt and struck at Wirt's master. How could he be charged with treason? "Our president is a lawyer, and a great one too. He certainly ought to know what . . . constitutes a war. Six months ago, he proclaimed that there was a civil war. . . . For six months they have been hunting for it, and still cannot find one spot where it existed." Instead, there was "a terrible war in the newspapers; but no where else."

On May 26, Marshall ruled on whether Burr could be granted bail or must remain in custody. The court had the authority to commit Burr to prison during the trial. It could also allow him freedom on bail because the indictment was for a high misdemeanor. "The commitment is not made for the sole purpose of bringing the accused before a grand jury; it is made for the purpose of subjecting him personally to the judgment of the law, and the grand jury is only the first step towards that judgment."

The charges were another matter. Hay refashioned the treason indictment. Marshall noted that "the government now had . . . testimony for the establishment of the fact" and "an immense crowd of witnesses are attending for the purpose" of proving that Burr had caused an armed body of men to assemble on Blennerhassett Island for the purpose of levying war. In a rare admission that the pressure for an indictment had gotten to Marshall, he admitted, "No man, feeling a correct sense of the importance which ought to be attached by all to a fair and impartial administration of justice, especially in criminal prosecution, can view, without extreme solicitude, any attempt which may be made to prejudice the public judgment, and to try any person, not by the laws of his country and the testimony exhibited against him, but by public feelings." But the defense claim that Burr was being tried in the public press was not going to sway Marshall. "If it is the choice of the prosecutor on the part of the United States to proceed with this motion [to commit Burr while the grand jury deliberated], it is the opinion of the court that he may open his testimony."

Almost immediately, the prosecution ran into the same snag as on April 5. Hay still wanted to start with Wilkinson, but the general was still not present. Thus his affidavit, which Marshall had already ruled inadmissible until Wilkinson arrived, could not be offered in evidence. Instead, Hay had to produce other written evidence, which Marshall again ruled inadmissible because it was not taken under oath. On application of Burr's counsel, the court admitted him to bail. Luther Martin, newly arrived as another of Burr's attorneys, put up half of the $5,000, the court having rejected Hay's request that bail be set at $50,000.

With the court in recess and the grand jury allowed to go home until they were recalled, Burr decided to put the prosecution on the defensive. On June 10, he argued that the October Wilkinson letter to Jefferson, and the answer from Jefferson, "may be material in his defense," and he asked the court to issue a subpoena duces tecum for the documents. He also wanted to see the evidence to which Jefferson alluded in his messages. In a way, the request was spiteful and disrespectful—no doubt Burr getting back the only way he could against his chief accuser. Burr and his team of lawyers knew exactly what information Jefferson had received.

For four days, counsel debated Burr's motion to subpoena the president's office for papers relating to the charge. Luther Martin once again lambasted the president. "The president has undertaken to prejudge my client. . . . He has assumed to himself the knowledge of the Supreme Being. . . . He has let slip the dogs of war, the hell-hounds of persecution, to hunt down my friend." Martin implied that Jefferson would, if he could, withhold information that might exonerate Burr, for the president was guided by "anger, jealousy, and hatred." Wilkinson had marked his correspondence with the president "sacredly confidential," but neither the confidence that Wilkinson reposed in the president nor the inclination of the president to hide the documents should stand in the way of Burr's constitutional rights. MacRae called Martin's speech a "defamation" of the president; he insisted that the papers had nothing to do with the charges, but that was not credible. Jefferson himself had cited the Wilkinson letter in his message to Congress.

Although they had nothing new to say, counsel on both sides seemed unable to let the matter rest. Finally, on June 13, 1807, Marshall ruled on the request for the papers. "The object of the motion now to be decided is to obtain copies of certain orders, understood to have been issued to the land and naval officers of the United States for the apprehension of the accused, and an original letter from General Wilkinson to the president in relation to the accused, with the answer of the president to that letter, which papers are supposed to be material to the defense."

Marshall professed to be hesitant about issuing the subpoena. "When this subject was suddenly introduced, the court felt some doubt concerning the propriety of directing a subpoena to the chief magistrate, and some doubt also concerning the propriety of directing any paper in his possession, not public in its nature, to be exhibited in court." What if Jefferson refused, initiating a major constitutional crisis? But Marshall's hands were tied. "The practice in this country has been, to permit any individual, who was charged with any crime, to prepare for his defense, and to obtain the process of the court, for the purpose of enabling him so to do." The same was true for the production of witnesses, to allow the defense to cross-examine prosecution witnesses (an aside, and a dig, at the prosecution for not having produced Wilkinson).

Marshall was lecturing the prosecution on its dilatory tactics, and by proxy, the president on his great show of energy and its minuscule success. "The genius and character of our laws and usages are friendly, not to condemnation at all events, but to a fair and impartial trial; and they consequently allow to the accused the right of preparing the means to secure such a trial." But was the president subject to such process? Yes. No man was above the law, and the "Constitution and laws of the United States" made plain the president's duty to the court.

In the preceding months, Jefferson had acted in the role of judge, prosecutor, and jury. This was Marshall's opportunity to reassert the supremacy of the judicial branch in matters judicial and to call Jefferson to account. "The Sixth Amendment to the Constitution gives to the accused, 'in all criminal prosecutions, a right to a speedy and public trial, and to compulsory process for obtaining witnesses in his favor.' The right given by this article must be deemed sacred by the courts, and the article should be so construed as to be something more than a dead letter."

Congress could not take away these rights. Even before the ratification of the Sixth Amendment, Congress understood that speedy and fair trials were impossible without access to all relevant evidence. In the very first congressional act spelling out federal offenses, in 1790, the lawmakers provided that "every such person or persons accused or indicted of the crimes aforesaid, [including treason] shall be allowed and admitted in his said defense to make any proof that he or they can produce by lawful witness or witnesses, and shall have the like process of the court where he or they shall be tried, to compel his or their witnesses to appear at his or their trial as is usually granted to compel witnesses to appear on the prosecution against them." The 1790 act placed both sides at trial "on equal ground."

If the president was a witness to a crime, could he be ordered to appear in court? "In the provisions of the Constitution, and of the statute [of 1790], which give to the accused right to the compulsory process of the court, there is no exception whatever." The common law exempted the king of England from subpoenas, but "many points of difference . . . exist between the first magistrate in England and the first magistrate of the United States."

Marshall understood that a president might find it awkward to travel to trial courts all over the vast territory of the United States, "because his duties as chief magistrate demand his whole time for national objects." If such duties prevented his personal appearance, however, they did not prevent the production of documents. True, in an early version of the claim of "executive privilege," President Washington had refused to provide papers to Congress. In 1792, President Washington hesitated to share documents with Congress on General Arthur St. Clair's disastrous invasion of Ohio Indian country in 1791. Washington consulted his cabinet, and they agreed that he could withhold materials whose public disclosure would endanger the public interest. In the end, he gave Congress the documents. Two years later, the Senate requested that the president provide it with documents relating to relations with revolutionary France, then at war with Great Britain. Washington again asked his cabinet how to proceed, and his attorney general, William Bradford, advised that the president could withhold any and all documents that he deemed "unsafe and improper" to share. Washington took this advice. In 1796, Madison and other members of the House of Representatives demanded to see documents regarding the highly controversial treaty that John Jay had concluded with the British. Washington replied that such material had nothing to do with the lower house's role in treaty making and withheld the documents. Over the next two centuries, presidents have tried to retain control over who could and who could not review classified or confidential documents for purposes of a congressional hearing.

But the judicial branch was not a legislative body riven with party feeling, like Congress. A trial was not a congressional debate. Marshall: "A subpoena duces tecum, then, may issue to any person to whom an ordinary subpoena may issue, directing him to bring any paper of which the party praying it has a right to avail himself as testimony." Marshall promised that all such evidence from the president would be handled with the care and decorum that Jefferson's high station required, but he must comply with the subpoena.

Marshall's assertion of the sensitive nature of judicial authority to review documents sought in the course of a criminal trial has been revisited over the years, and found wise. As Chief Justice Warren Burger wrote for a unanimous Court in *U.S. v. Nixon* (1974), *Marbury* established that the Court had the duty of determining what the law was, and that included claims by the other branches of the federal government. Chief Justice Burger continued that "No holding of the Court has defined the scope of judicial power specifically relating to the enforcement of a subpoena for confidential Presidential communications for use in a criminal prosecution, but other exercises of power by the Executive Branch and the Legislative Branch have been found invalid as in conflict with the Constitution." Had the request for the subpoena in *U.S. v. Burr* been appealed to the High Court (in what is termed an interlocutory appeal), Marshall's reasoning would have become part of constitutional law. Burger could then have relied on it, instead of arguing from analogies. But Burger came to the same conclusion in *U.S. v. Nixon* that Marshall reached in *U.S. v. Burr*: "Notwithstanding the deference each branch must accord the others, the 'judicial Power of the United States' vested in the federal courts by Art. III, § 1, of the Constitution can no more be shared with the Executive Branch than the Chief Executive, for example, can share with the Judiciary the veto power, or the Congress share with the Judiciary the power to override a Presidential veto. Any other conclusion would be contrary to the basic concept of separation of powers and the checks and balances that flow from the scheme of a tripartite government." The president had to surrender the documents to the court.

What of the rules for the trial court's handling of the materials sought? Burger dealt with that issue. "In order to require production [of subpoenaed documents] prior to trial, the moving party must show: (1) that the documents are evidentiary and relevant; (2) that they are not otherwise procurable reasonably in advance of trial by exercise of due diligence; (3) that the party cannot properly prepare for trial without such production and inspection in advance of trial and that the failure to obtain such inspection may tend unreasonably to delay the trial; and (4) that the application is made in good faith and is not intended as a general 'fishing expedition.'" Burr's application for the letters and other materials met all of these criteria, as Marshall, with prescience and care, next demonstrated.

"The first paper required is the letter of General Wilkinson, which was referred to in the message of the president to Congress." The prosecution objected because the letter was immaterial to the defense. But the use of a prior statement to impeach the validity of a later statement by a witness was well established in the law of evidence. "The second objection is, that the letter contains matter which ought not to be disclosed." Certainly some government documents' secrecy is so vital to the national defense that their public scrutiny would imperil the nation. "What ought to be done under such circumstances presents a delicate question, the discussion of which, it is hoped, will never be rendered necessary in this country. At present it need only be said that the question does not occur at this time." The prosecution asked that if required, a copy might be substituted for the original. Nonsense, Marshall replied. "The copy would not be superior to the original, and the original itself would not be admitted, if denied, without proof that it was in the handwriting of the witness." This was a pregnant ruling, for it would apply as well to the Wilkinson translation of the Burr letter, were the latter admitted in evidence.

During the prolonged and often acrimoniously political argument of counsel on the subpoena, Marshall had admonished both sides for trying to excite popular prejudices and uttering personal slurs. Now he offered an olive branch: "Much has been said about the disrespect to the chief magistrate, which is implied by this motion. . . . These observations will be very truly answered by the declaration that this court feels many, perhaps, peculiar motives for manifesting as guarded a respect for the chief magistrate of the Union as is compatible with its official duties." In addition, Marshall's own honor was at stake. "Might I be permitted to utter one sentiment, with respect to myself, it would be to deplore, most earnestly, the occasion which should compel me to look back on any part of my official conduct with so much self-reproach as I should feel, could I declare, on the information now possessed, that the accused is not entitled to the letter in question, if it should be really important to him."

Jefferson's reply was frostily formal, but entirely appropriate. Jefferson had developed early in his political career the ability to project one face to the public and another to his intimates. He controlled his fury, and on June 17, 1807, he wrote to Hay, who presented the letter to Marshall: "In answering your [Marshall's] letter . . . I informed you . . . that I had delivered [Wilkinson's letter], with all other papers respecting the charges against Aaron Burr, to the attorney general when he went to Richmond." Jefferson assumed that Rodney would share them with the court, but Rodney was no longer in Richmond, and Jefferson promised to write Rodney "to forward that particular letter without delay." Other material sought by the court Jefferson instructed the heads of his departments to send to Richmond. "I forwarded you copies of two letters from the secretary at war, which appeared to be within the description expressed in your letter." It is not clear from the letter whether this last was addressed to Hay or to Marshall.

Attending the court in person was another matter entirely. "If the defendant suppose there are any facts within the knowledge of the heads of departments or of myself, which can be useful for his defense, from a desire of doing anything our situation will permit in furtherance of justice, we shall be ready to give him the benefit of it, by way of deposition through any persons whom the court shall authorize to take our testimony at this place." The taking of depositions from parties to a suit was well established in Virginia in the colonial period. Jefferson's own law practice included taking evidence in this manner. He continued:

> As to our personal attendance at Richmond, I am persuaded the court is sensible that paramount duties to the nation at large control the obligation of compliance with its summons in this case, as it would should we receive a similar one to attend the trials of Blennerhassett and others in the Mississippi territory, those instituted at St. Louis and other places on the western waters, or at any place other than the seat of government. To comply with such calls would leave the nation without an executive branch. . . . The respect mutually due between the constituted authorities in their official intercourse, as well as sincere dispositions to do for every one what is just, will always insure from the executive, in exercising the duty of discrimination confided to him, the same candor and integrity to which the nation has, in like manner, trusted in the disposal of its judiciary authorities.

The sideshow of the subpoenaed documents did not end with the president's reply, but when the grand jury reconvened on June 14, all eyes turned to the entrance to the Delegates Hall. Wilkinson had arrived in Richmond. Dressed in the uniform of a major general, all gold braid and sashes, Wilkinson was primed and ready. Washington Irving, on his way to becoming one of the nation's first popular essayists and literary critics, was covering the story. He knew Burr, having been one of little Theodosia's tutors. He wrote, "Wilkinson strutted into court . . . stood for a moment swelling like a turkey-cock," and when Burr saw the general, arrayed in his uniform, he "turned his head, looked him full in the face with one of his piercing regards, swept his eye over his whole person from head to foot . . . then coolly resumed his former position." He had dismissed his former coconspirator with a glance. Wilkinson bowed to the bench, then made his exit, slightly less pompously than he had entered.

Jefferson, who did not witness the impact of Wilkinson's brief presence, nevertheless tried to buck up his prime witness: "I received last night yours of the 16th, and sincerely congratulate you on your safe arrival at Richmond, against the impudent surmises & hopes of the band of conspirators, who, because they are as yet permitted to walk abroad, and even to be in the character of witnesses until such a measure of evidence shall be collected as will place them securely at the bar of justice, attempt to cover their crimes under noise and insolence."

In the meantime, Jefferson's letters to Hay, micromanaging the prosecution, became more pointed and impatient as the president learned of each day's deliberations. On May 20: "Dr. Bollman, on his arrival here in custody in Jan[uary], voluntarily offered to make communications to me, which he accordingly did, Mr. Madison, also being present. I previously & subsequently assured him, (without, however, his having requested it,) that they should never be used against himself." Bollman would get a pardon, whether he liked it or not, and would then have to testify against Burr. "The object is as he is to be a witness, that you may know how to examine him, & draw everything from him." Jefferson was also sending a sealed bundle—"other blank pardons are sent on to be filled up at your discretion."

The letters kept coming. On May 26, Hay was admonished to press for the grand jury indictment and to pay witnesses out of the funds Jefferson had provided. Three more blank pardons, bringing the total to six, were enclosed. On June 19: "You ask what is to be done if Bollman finally rejects his pardon, & the Judge decides it to have no effect? Move to commit him immediately for treason or misdemeanor, as you think the evidence will support. . . . As to obscure offenders & repenting ones, let them lie for consideration." On June 20: the executive must not be made the dependent of the judiciary. Burr was up to his old tricks in seeking to worm his way out of the charges by embarrassing the president. June 23: ask Wilkinson for copies of the documents he wrote Jefferson, or rely on his memory to reproduce the correspondence.

What lay behind Jefferson's conduct? Did he truly fear for the nation's security? Was he motivated by party animus? Personal spite? There are actually two questions about motive. The first is what motivated Jefferson to act. The second is what motivated him to take such a personal and detailed part in the prosecution. At the beginning of the year, he wrote to a correspondent who was not a politician, "Burr's enterprise is the most extraordinary since the days of Don Quixote. It is so extravagant that those who know his understanding [of it] would not believe it if the proofs admitted doubt. He has meant to place himself on the throne of Montezuma." Such grandiose dreams were not real threats; the nature of a quixotic quest is that it can never be fulfilled.

Jefferson was less concerned about Burr's progress than what Burr's travels left in their wake. On September 4, for example, Jefferson wrote Hay: "the criminal is preserved to become the rallying point of all the disaffected and the worthless of the United States, and to be the pivot on which all the intrigues and the conspiracies which foreign governments may wish to disturb us with." Burr had to be pursued and prosecuted ruthlessly, or the disaffected who found his message intriguing might find a way to achieve the sundering of the nation.

Bear in mind that Jefferson and the nation were still surrounded by enemies. The war scare with Spain had abated, but England and France were at war, and Royal Navy ships patrolling American waters regularly and sometimes violently intercepted American merchant vessels, boarded them, and inspected their cargo. Contraband — war materials allegedly headed for Napoleonic France — were confiscated and suspected deserters carried off by force. Napoleon too seized

American shipping. Diplomacy abroad, particularly in England and France, brought no relief. The two nations, locked in mortal combat, regarded the American diplomats as nullities. Closer to home, Jefferson knew that even nominal Republicans in the West wanted him to declare war on the various Indian peoples who occupied lands within and abutting the United States, suspecting, quite correctly, that the British egged on the natives. Burr's travels and exaggerated plans, though mere shadows of treason, projected on this screen grew large and menacing. As Jefferson wrote during the trial, "Burr's conspiracy has been one of the most flagitious of which history will ever furnish an example."

Consider as well that the West held a special place in Jefferson's thinking about the republic. He believed that the settlement of the West by independent farmers would ensure that the republican form of government in the rest of the country survived. He had proposed a system of survey and land use for the Northwest Territory in 1784 that maximized the access that farmers would have to land that they could own, and at the same time provided space for public use. Jefferson had jumped at the chance to add the Louisiana Territory to the national domain and had authorized and took special interest in the Lewis and Clark expedition to survey the new acquisition. Although at one time in the 1790s he had speculated that the West might seek some form of independence, as president, Jefferson did not favor such a prospect.

But Jefferson was not only motivated by disinterested public concern. The tone of his personal involvement went beyond national security needs. Jefferson did not like Burr and never saw his merits. As soon as he was elected president, Jefferson had begun undermining Burr, not only in Washington but also in New York. He gave to Burr's enemies in the state confidential letters from Burr listing the men Burr wished appointed to federal posts. As a result, men allied to Burr, with one exception, gained nothing from Burr's elevation to the vice presidency. Jefferson may have suspected Burr of too long and too cunning a dalliance with the Federalists in the winter of 1800–1801, but he never once confronted Burr about it. Instead, he left Burr without patronage or honor in his own party.

Hay's first witness for the grand jury was Bollman. Bollman's interview with Jefferson was now revealed to the court, and as Hay feared, Bollman did not accept the proffered pardon. This put off Hay's plans to introduce evidence in chronological order. Hay wanted chronological presentation so that he could show how Burr put together the conspiracy. This in turn would establish the intent to overthrow the government. Then Hay could place Burr virtually at Blennerhassett on the night of December 9, even though Burr was two hundred miles away.

There was a complex legal question involved in Bollman's refusal to accept the pardon, for in effect the pardon was a kind of transactional immunity. Today, a witness given this immunity cannot refuse it. If he declines to testify, he is in contempt of court and can be jailed until he testifies. Martin argued that Bollman could reject the offer of the pardon and then refuse to testify lest he incriminate himself. No man "can be forced to incriminate himself." Hay agreed, but he insisted that Bollman be pardoned, whether he accepted it or not. Bollman's own counsel had books piled up on the desk with citations to cases to prove that whether pardoned or not, Bollman could not be made to testify against himself.

Hay needed Bollman's testimony nevertheless, and he sent Bollman off to the grand jury to answer their questions. On June 16, Wilkinson went to the grand jury. Hay alone oversaw these sessions. Defense counsel was not present when the grand jurors interrogated the witnesses, nor were the judges. No record of those conversations survives, as none was taken. This was standard practice at the time and was observed throughout this stage of the Burr case. The grand jury, as it were, was on its own, asking what questions they might, though they could ask the assistance of the court at any time.

Hay had also presented the grand jury with the treason charge. Wilkinson must have been persuasive, for the grand jurors voted the indictment on both the treason and the Neutrality Act charges on June 24. On June 26, the grand jury reported true bills against Dayton, Senator John Smith of Ohio, Comfort Tyler, Israel Smith, and David Floyd, the latter men having been present at Blennerhassett Island when the boats were loaded. But none could be found guilty until Burr was, and that was far from certain. Harman Blennerhassett was arrested on July 14 and brought to Richmond. All the threads of the garment Jefferson had designed were coming together.

During the latter stages of the grand jury hearings, Joseph Alston and Theodosia arrived, with young Aaron, in Richmond. They roomed with Luther Martin and Burr. The family did not have much time together. A week later, Burr was ordered confined on the third floor of the new federal penitentiary in Richmond until the trial, set for the first Monday in August, the third of that month.

CHAPTER 7

The Trial of the Century
U.S. v. Burr

From the start of Burr's treason trial, it proved very hard to find an impartial trial jury. Jury selection began on August 4. After a week's time, only four jurors had been seated. Potential trial juror after juror wriggled off the hook of what promised to be a very long trial by asserting that they had read the newspapers and concluded Burr must be guilty. One said that Burr "deserved to be hung." He was dismissed by Marshall. Some offered to serve under the twisted logic that, although they had expressed an opinion about his guilt in the past, they were "unwilling to subject themselves to the imputation of having prejudged the cause." No gentleman would be so dishonorable.

Hay was at his wits' end. "I most seriously apprehend that we shall have no jury at all." He wanted to allow a juror to sit who simply asserted he would be open-minded, although he had notoriously prejudged the case. Hay: "I believe that any man can, who is blessed with a sound judgment and integrity," serve. Wirt asked another juror whether, despite the "hostile impressions he had taken up from newspaper reports," these impressions so fixed in his mind that they could be called "opinions"? But even Hay and Wirt did not try to seat the juror who, running for office on the Republican ticket, told the voters that Burr was guilty.

On August 10, Blennerhassett was brought to court and charged with treason, but his trial would wait until the principal in the alleged plot had been convicted. He and Burr had little contact, though he was still Burr's ally.

Marshall intervened in the jury selection quagmire on August 11, 1807. "The great value of the trial by jury certainly consists in its fairness and impartiality. Those who most prize the institution, prize it because it furnishes a tribunal which may be expected to be uninfluenced by an undue bias of the mind." Surely a jury of Richmond vicinity voters — all white, propertied men — had read about, discussed, and formed opinions about the Burr affair. How could a panel of impartial triers of fact have been assembled in the vicinity from which to select a jury if *impartial* meant having no opinions?

So long as the jury was "composed of men who will fairly hear the testimony which may be offered to them, and bring in their verdict according to that testimony, and according to the law arising on it," the requirements for impartiality would be met. It did not matter whether they had read the newspaper accounts and expressed, in heat, an opinion. By contrast, a juror who had "deliberately formed and delivered an opinion that the person whom they are to try is guilty or innocent of the charge alleged against him" before the juror had heard the testimony should be excused from serving.

Even with such a broad definition of impartiality, Marshall had to make some delicate distinctions. If, for example, a prospective juror had said that Burr might have had treasonable designs but he did not know whether Burr had carried those designs into effect, that would not be grounds to remove that juror for prejudice. "But if the juror has made up and declared the opinion that to the time when the fact laid in the indictment is said to have been committed the prisoner was prosecuting the treasonable design with which he is charged, the court considers the opinion as furnishing just cause of challenge."

The examination of Edward Carrington was typical. He had "formed an unfavorable opinion" of Burr, "but those opinions were not definitive." Burr asked, "have you any prejudice of a more settled kind and ancient date against me?" Carrington replied, "none at all." Burr cried out that Carrington was fine with him. At last Burr broke the logjam. Speaking as his own counsel once again, he agreed to seat the remaining eight members of the jury randomly. The court consented, and trial began in earnest on August 17.

Charles Lee arrived and sat with the defense team. The chairs behind the table were now all occupied with what may be argued was the finest legal talent assembled in any trial in the history of the young nation. Indeed, Burr, Lee, Martin, and Randolph were the living history of law in the new nation. District attorney Hay must have sensed that he, MacRae, and Wirt were overmatched. Local counsel had joined both sides, but the scales tilted toward the defense.

Hay had the indictment read. It found that "Aaron Burr, at the

Island of Blennerhassett, on the tenth day of December 1806 . . . did compass, imagine, and intend" to levy war against the United States, and with at least thirty persons well armed, assembled, and gathered together, "Aaron Burr with the said persons . . . traitorously assembled . . . did ordain, prepare and levy war" against the United States. The next day, the indictment continued in a second count of treason, Burr and his armed band proceeded down the Ohio River to "take possession of New Orleans."

Hay began for the prosecution in high dudgeon, personally offended that the defense counsel made "Many observations . . . extremely derogatory to the character of the government . . . and injurious to the feelings of the counsel concerned in the prosecution." He conceded what everyone knew: that the indictment alleged that Burr was present at Blennerhassett when the armed men climbed into the boats, but that Burr was hundreds of miles away, in Kentucky. He was not present the next day, when the expedition was supposed to set off (though in fact it never did because of the intervention of the Ohio militia). No matter, for "his absence at the time when the people assembled is totally immaterial."

No matter, because being part of the conspiracy, procuring the arms, commissioning the building and delivery of the boats, and recruiting the men was enough. "It is obvious that the interval between the first movement towards a conspiracy, and actual hostilities or a battle fought, may be immense." He conceded that a plot, a plan, and an assembly were not enough under the Constitution and *Bollman*, but "common sense and principles founded on considerations of national safety" did not require a treason "to be completed" for it to be real. "An assemblage of men convened for the purpose of effecting by force a treasonable design . . . is treasonable."

This reading of *Bollman* II's dictum made the gathering of men with a treasonable design into the "ripening" act of treason. A conspiracy matured to the edge of action, though no violence against the United States had occurred, constituted an overt act. Hay was not concerned that he stood on the edge of a slippery slope, that everyone who had anything to do with the act, before or after, in any way, might also be guilty of treason under his rationale. Did the men have to be armed if their plan included arming themselves at a later time? No.

Did they have to number more than a few if their plan included the addition of numbers later? No.

Hay's authority was English cases, in which intent to commit treason allowed the prosecution to construct scenarios not in evidence. "I trust, that I have shown, that the treason is completed the very instant that they assemble together with a treasonable design." Hay's argument was perfectly circular, as well as slippery, for the evidence of the treasonable design of Burr's men was their assembling.

American precedent ran against Hay. Marshall had cited and confirmed that precedent in *Bollman*. Some purposeful violence against the United States must occur to turn a gathering into overt levying of war. Mere plot or design, accompanied by an assemblage, even an armed assemblage, was not an overt act of levying war. Hay squirmed under this burden, continually returning to the more friendly English precedent. For example, he had to concede, for Marshall was listening intently, "that the doctrine which shall let in treason, not defined by the [federal] Constitution, by mere arbitrary constructions, influence or analogy, as in England formerly, ought not to be countenanced." But Hay though he had a safe harbor in the last lines of *Bollman* II: "if war be actually levied, all those who perform any party . . . however remote from the scene of action, and who are actually leagued in the general conspiracy, are to be considered as traitors." Every time Hay returned to Marshall's words, the chief justice must have squirmed.

Hay told the jury (though his real audience was the bench) that he was not trying to adopt the doctrine of constructive treason. He merely expanded the concept of levying war to its proper and needful extent. From the effort he expended to make this point, it can be inferred that he was not hopeful. "Perhaps it will be said that the decision of the Supreme Court is not correctly understood or stated by me. I may be incorrect in my exposition of it." But what else could he say if the prosecution were to proceed?

Hay's next step down the slippery slope was even more precarious. If Burr "intended to take New Orleans at all, he is completely guilty of the treason." Hay had done what he promised not to do: make intent into action, and conspiracy into an overt act. Burr's travels became evidence of intent. The Washita settlement "was merely a cover to the real design," the same assumption Jefferson included in his message to Congress. Burr's announced intention of invading the Spanish territory further hid his purposes. The different messages he left with people in the East and in the West were proof of his duplicity. Only Wilkinson's timely intervention prevented the treason from coming to fruition.

To prove all this, Hay had to get Burr's conversations with Eaton, Truxton, and others into evidence. He had to convince the jurymen that what they had read in the newspapers was true. But Burr objected. Before the motive testimony could come in, there must be proof of an overt act. Hay must start with Blennerhassett on December 9, not sometime in the previous year. Burr's counsel joined him: there was no war, not one single act of violence. The prosecution could not prejudice the jurors' minds with inflammatory character assassination until it had proved the key element of the offense.

Wirt replied. He professed to be astounded that the prosecution was interrupted in the presentation of its opening arguments. "If the whole evidence may be adduced, the result will be the same, in whatever manner it may be arranged." Wirt's posture of offended dignity—in fact, posturing in general—was common in the Virginia courts where lawyers used the methods of evangelical preachers to sway juries. Patrick Henry was the most famous practitioner of the art of swaying juries when the law was not on his side. It was not by accident, then, that Wirt would become Henry's first biographer. Or perhaps Wirt did not fully understand that the one man he had to persuade sat not in the jury box but on the bench.

Lee understood that point, however, for he had lost *Marbury* in just such manner. The law was with him this time, and that was enough. No blustering oratory was needed, only a few minutes for the prosecution to show "an open deed of war," and the defense would subside. Martin made a similar point by analogy. In a murder trial, "a great deal of the time of the court might be taken up to prove malice on the part of the person indicted, which in truth no act could be proved . . . this would be a fruitless waste of time . . . if there be no evidence that the man is dead." Hay wanted to call Eaton to show that Burr had from early in 1806 formed a traitorous design. Burr's team objected again. Evidence of the overt act was necessary at the start of the trial.

The prosecution was barred from bringing in the evidence of motive until an overt act could be established.

On August 18, 1807, Marshall chimed in: "Although this is precisely the same question relative to the order of evidence which was decided by this court on the motion to commit [Burr to jail], yet it is now presented under somewhat different circumstances, and may, therefore, not be considered as determined by the former decision." Marshall bent over backward to be fair to the prosecution, for "there is now an indictment specifying the charge which is to be proved on the part of the prosecution, there is an issue made up which presents a point to which all the testimony must apply, and consequently it is in the power of the court to determine with some accuracy, on the relevancy of the testimony which may be offered."

Eaton's testimony might be probative, but only "So far as his testimony relates to the fact charged in the indictment, so far as it relates to levying war on Blennerhassett's island, so far as it relates to a design to seize on New Orleans, or to separate by force the Western from the Atlantic states, it is deemed relevant and is now admissible." The most outrageous of Burr's fulminations to Eaton against Jefferson and his party were not to reach the jurymen's ears.

Eaton repeated a portion of what he had communicated to Jefferson. He did not mention Burr's sneering about the weakness of the Jefferson administration. Truxton was next. He knew about the filibustering expedition, should war arise, but he never heard Burr mention the severing of the union. Burr hoped that war with Spain would come, and that he and Truxton could take part. Otherwise, he merely wished to exploit his Washita land purchase. Peter Taylor, Blennerhassett's gardener, recalled the gathering of men on the island but could not say whether they were heavily armed. His testimony inculpated Blennershassett but did little to prove Burr's role. Morgan testified that Burr was trying to repeat the Spanish conspiracy of the 1780s.

Jacob Albright was on the island, and he testified that he saw many armed men as well as the militia commander, Edward Tupper, arrive to arrest them all. But Tupper was among the 140 witnesses summoned to Richmond, and Burr wanted to know why Albright had to testify to what Tupper was far better placed to know. In fact, Burr had in hand Tupper's affidavit. He had not arrested anyone but had chatted amiably with Blennerhassett, then left. Albright had impeached himself on the stand.

More witnesses were called who that December night saw, or did not see, guns and ammunition, men armed or merely busy, warlike preparations, or nothing of the sort. Burr and his counsel approached the bench, as did Hay and his cohorts. Nothing had been adduced to show Burr committing an overt act. The defense moved that the court admit no further evidence unless it proved Burr committed the overt act. The prosecution responded. The defense rejoined. The air crackled with the finest display of lawyerly erudition and oratorical skill that the young republic could produce.

Wickham summarized the prosecution case from the defense perspective. No war was levied on the island or the river against anyone. The prosecution, however, had repeatedly asserted that Burr was guilty, replacing evidence with assertion. Burr was not there, and that was that. The Constitution was crystal clear — he had to levy war. There was no precedent whatsoever for convicting a man who did not take part in the overt act of making war. Even the English cases, which Wickham now rehearsed at length, provided no comfort to the prosecution on this point. But Wickham went a step further. His dismissed as irrelevant all the English precedent. "Now as there is no general common law of the United States, the act of Congress must be construed without any reference to any common law, and treason is to be considered as a newly created offense, against a newly created government."

Marshall thought that the Constitution could be read with the common lawbooks open alongside, a stance somewhat at odds with his comments in *Bollman* I. The Constitution imported key concepts from common law. All the counsel in the hall had quoted from English precedents. Wickham then proposed another way of reading the Constitution based on plain meaning: "the language [the framers] have used for this purpose is plain, simple, and perspicuous. There is not occasion to resort to the rules of construction to fix its meaning. It explains itself."

Wickham preferred a history of the framing of the Constitution to more distant English history. Sitting quietly, perhaps occasionally nodding in confirmation of Wickham's argument, Edmund Randolph's presence lent gravity and credibility to Wickham's historical foray. "With the great volume of human nature before them, [they] knew that perjury could easily be enlisted on the side of oppression; that any man might become the victim of private accusation; that declarations might be proved which were never made."

That is why the Constitution required two witnesses to an overt act. Consider the alternative — to be sure a hypothetical construction: "Without that plain and simple requirement, a man who is selected to be a victim is dragged from one end of the continent to the other, before a judge who is the creature of the government, appointed at the pleasure of the government, liable to be thrown out of office, if he offend the government" and put at peril of his life. Wickham here borrowed Martin's argument against any suspension of habeas corpus. What if the judge were corrupt? The jury affrighted? The prosecution prejudiced? Only the Constitution itself could save a defendant.

Argument on Burr's motion to bar presentation of evidence on motive until the prosecution could show an overt act continued over the course of a week from August 22 to August 29. In the course of that argument, Wirt and Martin pronounced two of the most famous orations in the history of American rhetoric. Together, the speeches absorbed almost three days of the court's time.

Wirt began with a profession of his disinterest. He did not act from sullied motives, for "I would not plant a thorn, to rankle for life in my heart, by opening my lips in support of a prosecution which I felt and believed to be unjust." Neither would he intentionally hurt the feelings of the defendant or his counsel. They were "too sensitive," and needed gentle handling.

To "cut off" all evidence that led up to the act of treason would leave that act without motive. The evidence was "as naked as a sleeping venus." Wirt, whose flowery tones here matched his published essays, knew "that by adopting these arts" of oratory he might offend, but he did not wish it so. So often did Wirt smear the defense counsel, followed by a false apology, that one might compare Wirt's effort to that of another great legal orator, the ancient Roman Cicero. In fact, Cicero's attacks on Mark Antony seem to have been the model for Wirt's on Burr.

Next, Wirt "brought Wickham to England" and treated him to a discourse on the law of felony, proving that all conspirators in a crime were equally culpable. Burr was there, on Blennerhassett Island, in the eyes of the law. Just as Marshall had written in *Bollman* II, one need not be present to be guilty if the crime was ripening.

Wirt insisted that common-law principles and common-law cases were relevant to Burr's case. "The majority" of the federal judges had said so in a wide variety of cases. Chief Justice Ellsworth, Justice Bushrod Washington, Judge Richard Peters, and (unmentioned at the time but certainly understood by all) Chief Justice Marshall all believed as Wirt did. The language of the Constitution was "borrowed" from English legal speech. The word *felony* used in congressional acts would have no meaning were it not defined in the common law. So treason, in the Constitution, derived from an English statute, and the words *levying war* similarly derived from common law.

Even if actual presence was required, should not this question go to the jury? Should they not decide whether Burr was there in spirit? "Is this not a question of fact proper to be settled only by a jury? Will this court say it will take place of the jury?" Wirt's was a gauntlet thrown down at Marshall's feet. If he ruled that no further evidence might be presented unless it bore directly on Burr's participation in the overt act, was he taking the case from the jury?

Wirt had tried this tactic before, and failed. In 1800, Wirt, along with Hay and Nicholson, defended Republican publicist James Callender on a charge of violating the Seditious Libel Act. Callender was a nasty fellow and had run afoul of the act when he wrote that "The reign of Mr. Adams has been one continued tempest of malignant passions. As president, he has never opened his lips, or lifted his pen without threatening and scolding; the grand object of his administration has been to exasperate the rage of contending parties, to calumniate and destroy every man who differs from his opinions." At the circuit court trial in Richmond, Justice Samuel Chase presided. His conduct was horrid. He interrupted the defense counsel repeatedly, denied them the chance to gather the evidence they needed and assemble the witnesses they wanted, and so embarrassed them that they could not finish their address to the jury at the end of the trial.

At issue was Wirt and Hay's claim that Virginia procedural precedent, which should have governed the conduct of the trial, allowed the lawyers to inform the jurors they could interpret the law. They told Chase that "The laws and customs of the state of Virginia were in favour of the motion." Chase, from the bench of the circuit court, denied the motion. Hay "was mistaken in supposing that the jury had a right" to decide matters of law. "It may be conformable . . . to your local state laws, but it is a wild notion as applied to the federal court. It is not the law. . . . I will not permit the counsel for [Callender] to offer arguments to the jury, to urge them to do what the constitution and law of this country will not permit; and which, if I should allow, I should, in my judgment, violate my duty, disregard the Constitution and law, and surrender up the judicial power of the United States, that is, the power intrusted by the constitution to the federal courts, to a petit jury, in direct breach of my oath of office." The Callender case was one of the reasons why Chase was impeached, so partisan was his handling of the Republican defendant and his counsels, but Chase's ruling on counsel instructing the jury in the law, and idea of the jury interpreting law as well as finding fact, stood.

Finally, Wirt insisted that Burr was never merely an accessory to the offense. "Will any man say that Blennerhassett was the principal, and Burr but an accessory. . . . Will any man believe that Burr, who is soldier bold, ardent, restless and aspiring . . . should sink down into an accessory?" Burr was the ultimate seducer of men, who "draws into his plan, by every allurement which he can contrive, men of all ranks and descriptions. To youthful ardor he presents danger and glory; to ambition, rank and titles and honors; to avarice the mines of Mexico." Wirt was so carried away with his own rhetoric that he failed to notice the implication of it: Eaton was motivated by what? Wilkinson by what? If Burr approached them, did he not think them eager for rank and riches? If he were such an astute judge of human failings, might the jury not discard the testimony of those very same prosecution witnesses?

Wirt raced on to the most famous part of his speech. "Who is Blennerhassett? A man of letters, who fled from the storms of his own country to find quiet in ours. . . . He carried with him taste, and science and wealth," and on his island he "rears . . . a palace and decorates it with every romantic embellishment of fancy." Flowers, music, and "all the secrets and mysteries of nature. Peace, tranquillity and innocence shed their mingled delights around him." He recreated an Eden itself, completed by "a wife, who is said to be lovely even beyond her sex." Had Wirt forgotten that the grand jury had indicted Blennerhassett along with Burr? That Wirt was supposed to be prosecuting both of them?

Not really, for Blennerhassett was Burr's first victim. A "stranger" came into the Blennershassetts' garden. Satanic Burr "comes to change this paradise into a hell." He pours poison into the ears of the innocent Blennerhassett, "the poison of his own ambition." Blennerhassett no longer has time to smell the flowers or listen to the music. "His imagination has been dazzled by visions of diadems, of stars and garters and titles of nobility. He had been taught to burn with restless emulation" of Burr.

Pause one moment before turning to Luther Martin's two-day reply to Wirt. Why did both Hay and Wirt take such pains to deny that they were importing the English concept of constructive treason? They certainly skirted it, hinting that conspiracy was tantamount to action. But they could not import the English common-law doctrine of conspiracy because all good Republicans had opposed the Sedition Act for that very reason. At the heart of the Sedition Act was the common-law notion that "if any persons shall unlawfully combine or conspire together, with intent to oppose any measure or measures of the government of the United States," they were guilty of sedition. The Republicans, with Jefferson in the lead, hotly and repeatedly denounced the common-law definition of sedition as a "bloody code." To reintroduce the language of that code, even to catch the satanic Burr, would have required a somersault beyond the most agile advocate's abilities.

While Burr's counsel dismissed Wirt's words as "a speech manufactured out of tropes and figures," on Friday, August 28, and Saturday, August 29, Luther Martin closed out the argument for the motion in a bravura performance rising to the same flowery eloquence as Wirt. Until this moment Martin rarely participated in the back and forth of counsel, saving himself for the final act. Now he claimed to speak not as Burr's advocate, but as the exponent of "great principles." These reached out beyond the trial at hand to the very core of the legal system.

The "great question" was the sanctity of the law and the fairness of the courts. Corrupt that system out of eagerness to convict Burr, and the courts would lay every citizen's life and property at the feet of the government. Instead of that supine and partisan default, the court must exclude "irrelevant . . . illegal evidence."

Martin insisted that government prosecutors should not represent a party, a faction, or a national leader's personal bias. They should be interested only in finding the truth. The prosecution of Burr had become a persecution, dragged out over time, by all the organs of the Republican Party. Finding no evidence of an overt act, the prosecution delayed month after month. Witnesses arrived at last, but their testimony proved nothing. "During all this time, colonel Burr must remain in confinement . . . oppressed."

What was left? "Will o' the wisp treason . . . here and there and everywhere, yet it is nowhere." There was no violence, no "actual war," whatever words may have passed, whatever groups of men might have assembled. To be "legally present" at a crime required that the crime actually be committed. Treason was no different from other crimes in this respect. Conspiracy, even if proven, was not treason under the constitutional definition of that crime. It was not treason to have a treasonable intention.

Wirt here interjected that he had never said this; treason required "intention and action." Martin rejoined: "the gentleman cannot make the case better" for the defense. There had to be an act, and that act must include violence against the United States, its officers, or the government.

Martin too had his books of precedents, and one can see him opening them to the pages to quote from this case and that — the same cases that Hay and Wirt cited, reread to a different purpose. He even cited the pages from which he took his excerpts, as though he and opposing counsel were taking a final examination in English criminal law.

Martin had followed Hay and Wirt's citation of English cases closely. Martin might simply have said that the English cases did not matter. Wickham had. The letter of the Constitution and the intentions of the framers diverged from the English practice specifically to omit constructive treason and conspiracy to commit treason. Why, then, the hours of tedious recapitulation, the long spirals through English cases?

Perhaps the point of the exercise was not to convince the bench to allow or dismiss the defense motion, but to sway the jury. In effect, Hay, Wirt, and Martin were bringing in evidence without having to call witnesses. What was more, a long recitation of the same citations as Hay's and Wirt's, read to opposite effect, would nullify the impact of English precedents, as Hay and Wirt had read those precedents, on the jury. The jurymen would just balance one set of interpretations against the other and ignore them all.

There is a third reason why Martin had to respond to the prosecution's English case law. Marshall's closing words in *Bollman* II had cracked open a door that the prosecution crashed through. So Martin had to follow Hay and Wirt through every page of the English law books to demonstrate that a treasonous act had to occur before any of the parties to a conspiracy were liable.

Could the charge of treason be general — that is, laid without specifics such as Burr's actual attendance at the gathering, the arms the body possessed, whether they displayed those arms to the Ohio militia? Martin said no, no, no. Treason must be specific in its indictment and its proofs. The indictment was specific about time and place, but general about Burr's part.

The prosecution had argued that Burr was an accessory, and in all treasons, every accessory was a principal. Was Burr an accessory, pulling strings though two hundred miles away? Was he legally there and physically afar? A general charge might, if allowed, bring in everything that Burr had ever done, shaped and formed by the prosecution to resemble a treason. Overt acts long before December 10 and far afield might become, constructively, tied into the specifics of the indictment. All this could happen if Burr's motion to suppress Wilkinson's evidence was denied.

Martin had a final point directed to the bench. Wirt had said that the question of the admissibility of Wilkinson's testimony should be left to the jury to decide. Martin rejected that proposal. "What is law and common sense? That the court shall decide the law; and the jury the facts upon the evidence." The prosecution would have "the jury . . . encroach 1000 miles on the rights of the judges, rather than the court should encroach a hair's breath on the province of the jury." Martin did not cite Chase's ruling in *U.S. v. Callender*; no doubt Hay and Wirt were grateful not to have to relive the time they spent in front of Chase.

But Martin was not being charitable to the opposition. He quoted Wirt's incautious words that judges "are men, and mingle in the politics of their country. . . . Their very patriotism will subject them to the influence of party spirit. Hence he infers, that this party spirit will render the judges partial; that they will favor only men of their own party." Wirt and Martin both knew that Wirt was referring to Chase, but Martin was reminding Marshall, by the indirect means of repeating Wirt, that Wirt had impugned the impartiality of the bench. Wirt had the good sense not to interrupt this time.

Randolph had a few words to add — about two hours' worth. Martin had left him only "the gleanings" of the law to harvest. What concerned him most was the question of principal and accessory. He insisted that in defending Burr the defense had never said or implied that Blennerhassett was guilty. He was innocent. "I have done . . . I find myself hurt, that I could not give a greater scope to my feelings." No doubt the jury was gleeful that Randolph had no intention of going on as long as Martin. But Randolph could not forbear one last remark: "Popular effusion and the violence and clamor of party" must not sway judges. "We look up to the judiciary to guard us," a sentiment that Federalists, having lost Congress and the presidency, could all share.

On August 31, Marshall ruled on the motion. Although technically the ruling was not binding on later courts, because the circuit court was a trial court, not a court of appeal, Marshall's ruling had all the trappings of such an opinion. Indeed, it was the longest he ever wrote. He began with his customary courtesy. "The question now to be decided has been argued in a manner worthy of its importance, and . . . a degree of eloquence seldom displayed on any occasion has embellished a solidity of argument and a depth of research by which the court has been greatly aided in forming the opinion it is about to deliver." Marshall was a master of the polished manner of the gentlemen and the proprieties of lawyers to one another. It is easy to see how he achieved unanimity on the High Court so often.

The opinion was notable, however, because it was the fastest overruling of a High Court precedent in its history — a mere six months. Moreover, that overruling did not come from the High Court itself, but from an inferior federal court, something that simply should not have happened in the American legal system. On top of all that, it constituted a rare occasion in which a Supreme Court justice publicly and definitively implied that he had gotten the law wrong in one of his earlier decisions.

Marshall had allowed the possibility of constructive treason in a dictum at the end of *Bollman* II. Indeed, on June 29, he had confided to Justice Cushing and the other members of the High Court that "the opinion of the supreme court [in *Bollman* II] certainly adopts the doctrine of constructive treasons. How far does that case carry this doctrine? Ought the expressions in that opinion to be revised?" Marshall, as was his habit, was consulting the other justices, but Marshall answered his own question now. He reversed himself.

"The testimony adduced on the part of the United States, to prove the overt act in the indictment" admitted "that the prisoner was not present when the act, whatever may be its character, was committed." Marshall asked himself, "What is the natural import of the words 'levying war?' And who may be said to levy it?" Levying meant raising, creating, making, or carrying on war. "Those only who actually constituted a portion of the military force appearing in arms could be considered as levying war." But this required that "an army should be actually raised for the avowed purpose of carrying on open war against the United States and subverting their government."

What did the common law say of the term? After all, for Marshall, the key terms in the Constitution had common-law derivations. "It is scarcely conceivable that the term [levying] was not employed by the framers of our Constitution in the sense which had been affixed to it by those from whom we borrowed it. . . . Principles laid down by such [English jurists] as Coke, Hale, Foster, and Blackstone, are not lightly to be rejected. These books are in the hands of every student. Legal opinions are formed upon them, and those opinions are afterwards carried to the bar, the bench, and the legislature." Did a glimmer of hope flicker in Hay's breast when Marshall read these words? It was soon extinguished. Alas, "It is to be regretted that [the English authorities] do not shed as much light on this part of the subject as is to be wished."

The notion that all were principals in a conspiracy to commit treason may have been part of the common law, but "the terms of the Constitution [defining treason] comprise no question respecting principal and accessory, so far as either may be truly and in fact said to levy war." You either did it or you didn't.

"It does not follow that he alone can have levied war who has borne arms. All those who perform the various and essential military parts of prosecuting the war which must be assigned to different persons, may with correctness and accuracy be said to levy war." But, and a very big but, "It will be observed that this opinion does not extend to the case of a person who performs no act in the prosecution of the war, who counsels and advises it, or who being engaged in the conspiracy fails to perform his part . . . the Constitution having declared that treason shall consist only in levying war."

At last Marshall arrived at his own concluding words in *Bollman* II. "It is said [by Burr's counsel] that this opinion in declaring that those who do not bear arms may yet be guilty of treason, is contrary to law, and is not obligatory, because it is extra-judicial, and was delivered on a point not argued. This [circuit] court is therefore required to depart from the principle there laid down." Marshall agreed with the defense argument, but he had to find a way to save face. Simply saying "I got it wrong; I should not have added the dictim" would not do, because in February he spoke for the High Court, and in August he spoke only as a member of the circuit court. A circuit court judge, though in person a Supreme Court justice, could not dismiss, ignore, or overrule a Supreme Court holding, even if he wrote that opinion himself.

But Marshall was entitled, he supposed, to interpret the meaning of his own words. The result was a passage as twisted and filled with double negatives as a Virginia snake fence. "The Court [that is, Marshall] had [in *Bollman* II] employed some reasoning to show that without the actual embodying of men, war could not be levied. It might have been inferred from this, that those only who were so embodied could be guilty of treason. Not only to exclude this inference, but also to affirm the contrary, the court proceeded to observe, 'It is not the intention of the court to say that no individual can be guilty of this crime who has not appeared in arms against his country. On the contrary, if war be actually levied, that is, if a body of men be actually assembled for the purpose of effecting by force a treasonable object, all those who perform any part, however minute, or however remote from the scene of action, and who are actually leagued in the general conspiracy, are to be considered as traitors.'"

If the core of this admission — the concept that remote persons were just as guilty as men who had a hand in the act — was applicable to Burr, Hay could begin to celebrate. The entire High Court had signed on to *Bollman* II. It was precedent on point and binding on the court in *U.S. v. Burr*. Had Marshall been counsel for Burr, "I would certainly use any means which the law placed in my power to carry the question again before the Supreme Court, for reconsideration, in a case in which it would directly occur and be fully argued." Ouch.

Still, only four justices had actually been present at *Bollman*. "I have since had reason to suspect that one of them, whose opinion is entitled to great respect, and whose indisposition prevented his entering into the discussions, on some of those points which were not essential to the decision of the very case under consideration, did not concur in this particular point with his brethren." Thus only three justices had actually signed the opinion, out of the seven in commission. "Should the three who were absent concur with that judge who was present, and who perhaps dissents from what was then the opinion of the court, a majority of the judges may overrule this decision."

But until that event came to pass, Marshall still had to deal with his own words. "Those only who perform a part, and who are leagued in the conspiracy are declared to be traitors. To complete the definition both circumstances must concur." Evidence on whether Burr performed a part in the overt act was necessary, for "the person who comes within this description, in the opinion of the court, levies war." Did Burr?

"In opening the case it was contended by the attorney for the United States, and has since been maintained on the part of the prosecution, that neither arms nor the application of force or violence are indispensably necessary to constitute the fact of levying war." In all the examples the prosecution gave, from England and from America in the 1790s (but not, for obvious reasons, from the Revolutionary War), the assembly of armed men clearly had the purpose of levying war. Proof came from and at the gathering itself. There was no doubt about motive. "If a rebel army, avowing its hostility to the sovereign power, should front that of the government, should march and countermarch before it" even without firing a gun, it would be levying war. Even if the armed body did not have weapons in hand, the crime of treason would be proved.

There was in those cases an overt act of violence, and the purpose of the overt act was to pull down the government. But this did not mean that "any assemblage whatever for a treasonable purpose, whether in force, or not in force, whether in a condition to use violence, or not in that condition, is a levying of war . . . war could not be levied without the employment and exhibition of force." Saying something was not enough. Planning something was not enough.

The "intention to go to war may be proved by words, but the actual going to war is a fact which is to be proved by open deed." Marshall read all of the English authorities to confirm his reading of the constitutional requirements. Thus even were the circuit court to entertain (according to the dictum in *Bollman*) a constructive treason, an overt act of violence must be proved. "It must be a warlike assemblage, carrying the appearance of force, and in a situation to practice hostility." One can only sit back and admire the way in which Marshall labored to escape from the trap his own dictum had laid for Burr. Having thrown the actual deployment of violence out the front door in *Bollman* II, Marshall retrieved it through the back door in *Burr*.

Marshall could now revisit the holdings of earlier circuit courts and find them in consonance with his own views. "In his charge to the grand jury, when John Fries was indicted, in consequence of a forcible opposition to the direct tax, Judge Iredell [a Supreme Court justice sitting with a circuit court] is understood to have said, 'I think I am warranted in saying, that if in the case of the insurgents who may come under your consideration, the intention was to prevent by force of arms the execution of any act of the Congress of the United States altogether, any forcible opposition calculated to carry that intention into effect, was a levying of war against the United States, and of course an act of treason.'" From this, Marshall concluded, "To levy war then, according to this opinion of Judge Iredell, required the actual exertion of force." Actually, that conclusion did not follow logically. Marshall was reasoning from the converse: if no violence, then no treason.

More logic chopping followed. "Judge Paterson [another High Court justice writing in his capacity as a circuit court judge], in his opinions delivered in two different cases, seems not to differ from Judge Iredell. He does not, indeed, precisely state the employment of force as necessary to constitute a levying of war, but . . . combining actual force with a treasonable design, 'the crime is high treason.'" Again, finding treason from a combination of act and design does not logically mean that the absence of an overt act defeats the prosecution.

"Judge Chase has been particularly clear and explicit" on this point. Chase was the justice who, through indisposition, did not press his dissent from Marshall's opinion in *Bollman*. As delicately as he could, Marshall gave Chase a chance to speak now. "In an opinion which [Chase, at a circuit court session] appears to have prepared on great consideration, he says, 'The court are of opinion, that if a body of people conspire and meditate an insurrection to resist or oppose the execution of a statute of the United States by force, that they are only guilty of a high misdemeanor: but if they proceed to carry such intention into execution by force, that they are guilty of the treason of levying war.'"

Marshall's conclusion entirely vitiated his dictum in *Bollman* II: "The court are of opinion, that a combination or conspiracy to levy war against the United States, is not treason unless combined with an attempt to carry such combination or conspiracy into execution, some actual force or violence must be used in pursuance of such design to levy war." Unlike English jurists, "Our judges seem to have required the actual exercise of force, the actual employment of some degree of violence."

Marshall returned to his own words in *Bollman* II once again. "But it is said all these authorities have been overruled by the decision of the Supreme Court in the case of the United States against Swartwout and Bollman. If the Supreme Court have indeed extended the doctrine of treason, further than it has heretofore been carried by the judges of England, or of this country, their decision would be submitted to. At least this court could go no further than to endeavour again to bring the point directly before them." But that was not necessary. "Had the intention [of the High Court] been . . . to make so material a change in this respect, the Court ought to have expressly declared, that any assemblage of men whatever, who had formed a treasonable design, whether in force or not, whether in a condition to attempt the design or not, whether attended with warlike appearances or not, constitutes the fact of levying war. Yet no declaration to this amount is made [in *Bollman* II]."

What had led to the confusion? The High Court—that is, Marshall—had failed to state that the assembly had to be using force, an excusable oversight because that issue was "not in the mind of the Court when the opinion was drawn, which passages are mingled with others, which at least show that there was no intention to depart from the course of the precedents in cases of treason by levying war." Oops. But it was an oversight that should not have led the prosecution in *Burr* astray. "Every opinion, to be correctly understood, ought to be considered with a view to the case in which it was delivered. In the case of the United States against Bollman and Swartwout, there was no evidence that even two men had ever met for the purpose of executing the plan, in which those persons were charged with having participated." Instead, "it is fairly to be inferred from the context [of the opinion], and nothing like dispensing with force appears in this paragraph."

It was a simple misunderstanding — so simple that Marshall spent another half hour unraveling it. He traversed the whole of the Court opinion freeing Bollman and Swartwout, showing how a reader insufficiently attentive to the context and nuance of the opinion might get the wrong impression. In other words, it was not his fault if Hay and Wirt misread *Bollman* II. Traveling to such an assembly, or from it, was not the same as participating in the assembly, for even if an army were marching from place to place in arms with the intent of rebellion, "a solitary individual traveling to any point, with any intent, could not, without a total disregard of language, be termed a marching detachment."

Finally, in the matter of circuit court judge Marshall presuming to correct Supreme Court Chief Justice Marshall: "The opinion of a single judge certainly weighs as nothing if opposed to that of the Supreme Court; but if he was one of the judges who assisted in framing that opinion, if while the impression under which it was framed was yet fresh upon his mind, he delivered an opinion on the same testimony, not contradictory to that which had been given by all the judges together, but showing the sense in which he understood terms that might be differently expounded, it may fairly be said to be in some measure explanatory of the opinion itself." If one is going to eat one's words, one should season them as tastefully as Marshall did that last day in August 1807.

Marshall could have finished here, but there was one more point to be made. "Before leaving the opinion of the Supreme Court entirely on the question of the nature of the assemblage which will constitute an act of levying war, this court cannot forbear to ask, why is an assemblage absolutely required?. . . . Why is it that a single armed individual, entering a boat and sailing down the Ohio, for the avowed purpose of attacking New-Orleans, could not be said to levy war?" Why, in short, could Burr not be levying war all by himself?

He could, but that was not what the indictment alleged. The overt act for which Burr was deemed treasonable was the assemblage of men at Blennerhassett Island, and "when there is an assemblage of men, convened for the purpose of effecting by force a treasonable object, which force is meant to be employed before the assemblage disperses, this is treason." Marshall had hoisted the prosecution by its own petard. "This indictment having charged the prisoner with levying war on Blennerhassett's island and containing no other overt act, cannot be supported by proof that war was levied at that place by other persons, in the absence of the prisoner, even admitting those persons to be connected with him in one common treasonable conspiracy. . . . In point of fact, the prisoner was not on Blennerhassett's island, nor in the county of Wood, nor in the district of Virginia."

Marshall was not quite done with his commentary on the insufficiency of the indictment. "The place in which a crime was committed is essential to an indictment, were it only to shew the jurisdiction of the court. It is also essential for the purpose of enabling the prisoner to make his defence." Although the prosecution might insist on the legal fiction that Burr was virtually present at Blennerhassett Island because everyone was acting on his orders, for him to be part of the overt act, he had to be physically, not fictionally, present. "It is conceived by the court to be possible that a person may be concerned in a treasonable conspiracy, and yet be legally, as well as actually, absent, while some one act of the treason is perpetrated. If a rebellion should be so extensive as to spread through every state in the union, it will scarcely be contended that every individual concerned in it is legally present at every overt act committed in the course of that rebellion." But the defendant had to take an actual part in one of the overt, violent acts of rebellion to be legally culpable. "In point of law then, the man who incites, aids, or procures a treasonable act, is not, merely in consequence of that incitement, aid or procurement, legally present when that act is committed."

A jury so instructed in the law might decide that Burr was at hand, or close enough, or on his way to be a part of the gathering at the island. So the case could go to the jury. "But if he was not with the party at any time before they reached the island; if he did not join them there, or intend to join them there," then the indictment ought to say so. There were or might be other grounds to attach Burr to an overt act of levying war. In fact, the indictment contained a second count. So long as witnesses put him and a band of armed men together at any time with the established purpose of levying war against the United States, that would be sufficient for an indictment. But the prosecution's case rested on that sandy slip of land in the Ohio River. "In conformity with principle and with authority, then, the prisoner at the bar was neither legally nor actually present at Blennerhassett's island; and the court is strongly inclined to the opinion, that without proving an actual or legal presence by two witnesses, the overt act laid in this indictment cannot be proved."

Marshall offered the following hypothetical notion to drive home his point: "Suppose the law . . . is as contended by the counsel for the United States. Suppose an indictment, charging an individual with personally assembling among others, and thus levying war, may be satisfied with the proof that he caused the assemblage. What effect will this law have upon this case? The guilt of the accused, if there be any guilt, does not consist in the assemblage, for he was not a member of it. The simple fact of assemblage no more affects one absent man than another. His guilt then consists in procuring the assemblage, and upon this fact depends his criminality." But that was not what the indictment alleged.

Juries in trials are not asked to speculate. They are asked to find which set of facts is true. To do this, as in all treason trials, they must have two witnesses. What could such witnesses testify to — that the apparition of Burr hovered over the island on the night in question? The jury would have to speculate rather than report the facts as they knew them. No evidence, no testimony, would suffice to establish the prosecution's case.

Marshall was starting to enjoy himself, having at last extricated himself from the toils of *Bollman* II. He was even willing to venture a little whimsy. An "accused cannot be truly said to be 'informed of the nature and cause of the accusation,' unless the indictment shall give him that notice which may reasonably suggest to him the point on which the accusation turns, so that he may know the course to be pursued in his defence." How could a defendant prove anything about his presence when he was absent?

Which claim brought Marshall back to the opinion in *Bollman* II for the last time. "That opinion is, that an individual may be guilty of treason 'who has not appeared in arms against his country . . . if war be actually levied," but "this opinion does not touch the case of a person who advises or procures an assemblage, and does nothing further," for such a man has not "appeared in arms" at all. "It is further the opinion of the court, that there is no testimony whatever which tends to prove that the accused was actually or constructively present when that assemblage did take place. Indeed the contrary is most apparent."

To hammer down the last nail in the prosecution coffin, Burr could not be found guilty of being an accessory to a crime if the principals, the men at Blennerhassett, were not already convicted. "The legal guilt of the accessary depends on the guilt of the principal; and the guilt of the principal can only be established in a prosecution against himself." If the assemblage at Blennerhassett Island was not a crime, then "those who perpetrated the fact be not traitors, [and] he who advised the act cannot be a traitor."

Marshall had not lost sight of the purpose of the defense motion. Wilkinson's testimony might sway the jury to believe anything of Burr, but it could not put him at the scene of the crime — even if there were a crime. "No person will contend that in a civil or criminal case, either party is at liberty to introduce what testimony he pleases, legal or illegal, and to consume the whole term in details of facts unconnected with the particular case. . . . The counsel for the prosecution offer to give in evidence subsequent transactions, at a different place, and in a different state, in order to prove what?" — nothing relevant to place Burr at Blennerhassett in December. "The testimony, then, is not relevant."

Marshall closed with his customary courtesy. "In a case the most interesting, in the zeal with which they advocate particular opinions, and under the conviction in some measure produced by that zeal," the two sides may have pressed "their arguments too far . . . be[en] impatient at any deliberation in the court . . . [and] suspect[ed] or fear[ed] the operation of motives to which alone they can ascribe that deliberation." Such suspicion of the court "is perhaps a frailty incident to human nature." But Marshall's ruling was based only on what was "prescribed by duty and by law."

The testimony of Wilkinson and the others as to Burr's scheme was inadmissible. "No testimony relative to the conduct or declarations of the prisoner elsewhere and subsequent to the transaction on Blennerhassett's island, can be admitted." Testimony "that the meeting on Blennerhassett's island was procured by the prisoner" was admissible. "The jury have now heard the opinion of the court on the law of the case. They will apply that law to the facts, and will find a verdict of guilty or not guilty as their own consciences may direct."

Marshall's August 31 opinion in particular and the entire course of the Bollman-Swartwout-Burr prosecution in general anticipated many of the modern rules of evidence at trial. The general rule for admissibility is that relevant evidence has the direct tendency to establish a fact material to the prosecution or defense. The offense charged was the levying of war, and the count in the indictment was the assembly of armed men at Blennerhassett Island. Evidence whose impact is primarily prejudicial, whose probative value — its value to establish the facts in the indictment — is outweighed by its nonprobative, prejudicial effect on the triers of fact, will not be admitted. Wilkinson's testimony and the letter he claimed he received from Burr may or may not have had some distant relevance to the charge in the indictment, but the prejudice against Burr they would have aroused far outweighed the proof they contributed that he had ordered and supervised the arming of men at the island for the purpose of overthrowing the federal government.

For many years after Marshall reversed the constructive treason portion of *Ex Parte Bollman* in his ruling on the admissibility of Wilkinson's evidence in *Burr*, commentators have struggled to describe the shift. Many, perhaps the majority, find it hard to excuse. They suggest that it evidenced Marshall's strong feelings about Jefferson's presidency, or more likely his strong antipathy to Jefferson's conduct. Marshall never had much use for Jefferson. He was too radical, too revolutionary. "I have felt almost insuperable objections" to Jefferson, Marshall wrote Hamilton in 1801. If such prejudice underwrote Marshall's rulings in *U.S. v. Burr*, then they did him no honor.

In this light, some historians have read the end result of Marshall's exhaustive opinion as having the sole purpose of embarrassing Jefferson. Although the opinion never mentioned the conduct of the executive branch in the prosecution, Marshall had already made his views on that matter public. Jefferson had far exceeded any kind of disinterested or impartial conduct, and his interference in judicial matters (not for the first time) would have rankled Marshall.

One might, in the alternative, take Marshall's convoluted argument at face value: there was no contradiction between the two opinions. They both rest on the constitutional definition of the offense. Wirt, arguing against the motion, insisted that it should be read in light of common-law precedent, appealing to Marshall's long-standing and often-expressed view that the Constitution might be read in light of the common law. But the Constitution sharply diverged from the common law in the matter of treason, rejecting the idea of the constructive treason.

One could also note, as Marshall did, that the indictment itself was faulty. Such technical dodges about deficient indictments were often used by the High Court to avoid interpreting the Constitution — for example, in the concurring opinions in the Voting Rights Cases of 1875 and 1876. These cases denied that the Fourteenth Amendment and Fifteenth Amendment provided a basis for federal courts prosecuting individuals who prevented freedmen from voting. Had Burr actually contracted for men or arms for the venture, Hay could have added additional counts to the indictment. But all Burr did was arrange for the construction of boats and call for men willing to crew them.

The best explanation, however, must concede that Marshall had gotten the law wrong in *Bollman* II. He admitted being perplexed about the case, had asked for further argument, and at conferences with his brethren had come away only more confused. Without further evidence, one must also suspect that the final passages of the second *Bollman* opinion were a concession to other justices, particularly Johnson, in order to get a majority. As Johnson hinted in his dissent in *Bollman* I, there was no clear agreement on what constituted treason. It was typical of Marshall's style as chief justice to add a conciliatory passage at the end of *Bollman* II. He did not like dissents. What Marshall should have foreseen was that the compromise on the High Court would come back to haunt him when he presided over the Burr trial in the circuit court.

In the interim between February 21 and August 31, Marshall had to rule on a series of motions and charge the grand jury. In all of these he kept the door open to the prosecution. But in the process, as he examined evidence and rethought the law, he realized that his concession in February was not the right interpretation of the Constitution. Not having to concede anything to Justice Johnson in Richmond, as Marshall had in *Bollman* II, the chief justice simply went back and got the law right.

Why, then, spend so much time explaining his second pose? A circuit court judge, even when he was the Supreme Court justice who wrote the opinion, cannot simply ignore a precedent on point from a higher court. So Marshall the judge had to explain what Marshall the chief justice had meant in such a way as to reverse the earlier opinion while claiming to follow it.

On September 1, 1807, Hay announced that he had no more evidence to present, and the defense rested as well. The jury retired and twenty-five minutes later, surely a record of sorts even in a time when juries did not have the comfort of "fire, meat, and drink," much less air-conditioning and catering, its foreman announced: "We of the jury say that Aaron Burr is not proved to be guilty under this indictment by any evidence submitted to us." When a motion is argued in modern trial court, the jury is often asked to leave the courtroom. There is no evidence that the jury left the Delegates Hall, however, and much of the argument of counsel was clearly directed to the jury, even though the lawyers were supposedly speaking to the court.

Carrington, the jury foreman, was palpably unhappy that the jury could not hear further evidence from Wilkinson and others among the 140 witnesses that Hay had summoned. Burr objected to the form of the verdict, however, demanding that it be recorded as a "not guilty." Hay insisted that it be recorded as Carrington had read it. Marshall ruled that the verdict would stand, and then told the clerk to note that the verdict was "not guilty." Vintage Marshall.

CHAPTER 8

Concluding Acts

Predictably, Jefferson was furious at the outcome of the trial. He wrote to Hay that Marshall had exceeded his powers as a judge by effectually taking the case away from the jury. His purpose, Jefferson surmised, was to "prevent evidence from going to the world" of Burr's perfidy—though accounts real and fanciful, including the president's, had filled the newspapers for months. Jefferson told Wilkinson that the nation would judge the judges, though in the meantime the Richmond court had issued "a proclamation of impunity to every treasonous combination."

As himself a lawyer who had practiced in Virginia courts, Jefferson knew that state judges had generally conceded to juries the power to decide questions of law as well as fact—or to be more precise, how the facts of a particular case fit the law. At the same time, judges could and did hear and allow motions to suppress certain kinds of evidence, or to require that a particular fact be proved before another particular fact was asserted.

St. George Tucker summarized the practices: "When the evidence is gone through on both sides, the judge in the presence of the parties, the counsel, and all others, sums up the whole to the jury; omitting all superfluous circumstances, observing wherein the main question and principal issue lies, stating what evidence has been given to support it, with such remarks as he thinks necessary for their direction, and giving them his opinion in matters of law arising upon that evidence." Insofar as the judiciary acts of 1789 instructed federal judges to use the procedural law of the state in which they sat (the reason why Marshall kept asking counsel about Virginia practice), all of these questions were relevant to Marshall's August 31 ruling, but they do not prove that he had gone too far in barring certain kinds of testimony.

Only the intercession of attorney general Caesar Rodney, who had removed himself from the trial at the outset, prevented Jefferson from making even stronger comments about Marshall. Rodney told Jefferson, "Our counsel at Richmond had acted like men and have acquitted themselves with honor. But it is vain to struggle against wind and tide." Jefferson put a good face on and told Congress that "the enterprises against the public peace which were believed to be in preparation by Aaron Burr and his associates, of the measures taken to defeat them, & to bring the offenders to justice. Their enterprises have been happily defeated." But Jefferson's private correspondence showed a different face. On September 26, he wrote to a friend, "We had supposed we possessed fixed laws to guard us against treason and oppression. But it now is apparent that we have no law but the will of the judge."

Jefferson also asked Rodney to supervise "the selection & digestion of the documents respecting Burr's treason, which must be laid before Congress in two copies (or perhaps printed, which would take 10 days)." In fact, the transcription by Virginia law reporters William Hening and William Munford was not ready until the next year. Jefferson also ordered Giles to prepare and present to the Senate a bill to make conspiracy to commit treason a federal offense, and he proposed that Bollman and Swartwout be indicted for it. Giles complied, and so did the Republican majority in the Senate, but the bill died in the House. Such a step would have violated the Ex Post Facto Clause of the Constitution, prohibiting prosecution for an act committed before it was made illegal.

The day after Burr was acquitted of treason, Jefferson also ordered Hay to bring charges against Burr for violating the Neutrality Act. Jefferson wrote Hay, "It is now, therefore, more than ever indispensable that not a single witness be paid or permitted to depart until his testimony has been committed to writing." In the pretrial jousting on that offense, the other shoe of the subpoena duces tecum dropped. Burr, suffering from depression and a stomach ailment, demanded to see the Wilkinson letter to Jefferson that Jefferson had sent to Hay. Jefferson once again agreed to supply the letter, "omitting only certain passages . . . entirely confidential." Jefferson told Hay that the president must be "unwilling . . . to set a precedent which might sanction a proceeding so preposterous" as to put the presidency at the disposal of a federal district court.

In effect, Jefferson was simply reiterating the reason that Washington had given Congress for not supplying it with the Jay Treaty correspondence. But claiming executive privilege against a federal court subpoena in a criminal matter was not exactly the same as claiming that privilege against Congress in a diplomatic matter. The Constitution's Article II, section 2, gave to the president "Power, by and with the Advice and Consent of the Senate, to make Treaties." Other than the pardoning power, the president had no privilege against the constitutional actions of the federal courts. That point was settled in the first trial.

Nevertheless, in court, Hay objected that showing the Wilkinson letter would violate executive privilege. Marshall ruled that the letter was material. Hay offered to provide that portion of the letter sufficient to show that it would not help Burr's case. Marshall informed Hay that the court would make that determination, not the prosecution. The grand jury had already found a true bill on this indictment, and trial began on September 9.

After six days and ample testimony from some fifty witnesses whose recollections varied, Hay bowed to the inevitable. On September 14, Marshall had ruled out evidence by third parties "not forming a part of the transactions," and the next day, he asked pointedly whether the prosecution might not be "wasting the time and money of the United States, and of all those persons who are forced to attend here, whilst they are producing such a mass of testimony which does not bear upon the cause." Hay moved for a dismissal. Marshall would have granted it, but Burr insisted that the jury reach a verdict on the evidence already admitted. It took a short time to acquit him—five minutes less than the jury took to acquit Burr of treason.

Jefferson's wearied persistence had not spent itself. Following Jefferson's instructions, on September 16, Hay brought Burr, Blennerhassett, and one of their comrades into court to show cause why they should not be charged with violating the Neutrality Act when they came together on the Cumberland River in late December. This would have been (would have to have been) a separate offense from the gathering at Blennerhassett Island. Hay might have filed a series of indictments in various federal courts targeting the flotilla of boats all the way down the Mississippi. Committal hearings (to hold Burr) did not end until October 20, with Burr and his counsel arguing that the plan to invest the Spanish side of the Mississippi was contingent on a war with Spain. Wilkinson, Burr truthfully insisted, knew all about the plan. Wilkinson, allowed to testify in the Neutrality Act prosecution in September, had to step lively under cross-examination not to expose his own double dealing. He would spend the next three years trying to dig out from the dirt that Burr dumped on him that fall.

Although an Ohio grand jury did find a true bill on the indictment for violating the Neutrality Act, the federal government did not prosecute on it. Not only had it become prohibitively expensive (with the federal government paying for all those witnesses), the prime witness against Burr, Wilkinson, had been discredited. Observers concluded, as Daveiss had a year previously, that Wilkinson was a conniver. Moreover, the final stages of the Neutrality Act violation trial revealed something of Wilkinson's dealings with the Spanish. Burr could now put Wilkinson on trial, the offense being his dishonesty. With Wilkinson's self-dealing open to public disapprobation, the Jefferson administration itself became vulnerable. Jefferson had relied on Wilkinson, and now that reliance was an embarrassment.

Had Jefferson gone too far in his pursuit of Burr, or was the president simply trying to prevent the most dangerous man in America from getting off scot-free? On the one hand, Jefferson's personal view of Burr was never entirely trusting. As Jefferson wrote in his 1818 "Anas," a compendium of personal recollections, "I have given to the whole a calm revisal, when the passions of the times are passed away, and the reasons of the transactions act alone upon the judgment . . . [and Burr's] conduct very soon inspired me with distrust. I habitually cautioned Mr. Madison against trusting him too much. I saw afterwards, that under General Washington's and Mr. Adams's administrations, whenever a great military appointment or a diplomatic one was to be made, he came post [hastily] to Philadelphia to show himself, and in fact that he was always at market, if they had wanted him." Did Burr's perpetual solicitation of offices reveal him as a man capable of inciting a war with Spain to fill his own coffers? Perhaps — so long as war with Spain was a possibility. Jefferson surely hoped that the Richmond jury would find Burr guilty of something.

On the other hand, Jefferson was aware that Burr might win in Richmond. On May 26, 1807, Jefferson wrote Hay, "if there be no [grand jury] bill, and consequently no examination [of witnesses] before [the] court [at trial], then I must beseech you to have every man privately examined by way of affidavit, and to furnish me with the whole testimony." From this and other evidence it becomes plain that in the course of the trial, Jefferson's fear had shifted from the Western unrest Burr stirred to Burr himself. If he could not be convicted, he must be discredited in the public mind.

Another possibility in the May 26 instructions to Hay was that Jefferson intended laying the entire record before Congress. After the trial ended, Jefferson ordered such a transcription be prepared and given to Congress. Burr was safe from impeachment and trial in Congress, for he was no longer a federal official, and there was little likelihood that he would ever stand for office again. But Marshall was still exposed. Perhaps Jefferson planned to have Marshall impeached and removed in 1805 but dropped the plan when the Senate refused to remove Justice Chase. Marshall's rulings at the Richmond trials revived Jefferson's interest in impeaching the chief justice. The written testimony would then have become part of the evidence against Marshall.

In 1809 Jefferson passed the presidency, and the leadership of the Republican Party, to his trusted lieutenant, Secretary of State James Madison. In his two terms in office, Madison would have to deal with much of Jefferson's unfinished business—what to do with the Louisiana Territory, how to protect American interests in the Napoleonic wars, how to handle a chaotic banking system, and how to negotiate the discontent of the Federalists.

Jefferson himself, still a figure of controversy, retired to Monticello. From his hilltop mansion, he managed his plantation, helped make the University of Virginia into an exemplar of publicly funded higher education, and fretted that the sacrifice and the principles that animated the Revolutionary generation would be forgotten. Lest that occur, he ordered his tombstone to read, "Here was buried Thomas Jefferson; Author of the Declaration of American Independence; Of the Statute of Virginia for Religious Freedom; And Father of the University of Virginia." He need not have worried. Americans still honor his name and his achievements.

At the close of the trials, Jeffersonian newspapers accused Marshall of partisanship and worse. The *Baltimore Whig* opened its publication history with a scathing attack on Marshall, calling him a "wretch . . . deep in crime" and partisan corruption. His effigy was burned in Baltimore, so upsetting his already nervous wife, Polly, that she took to her bed. When Congress met again, Jefferson presented it with the hastily printed stenographic record of the trials, commenting that he hoped they knew what to do with it. The only thing that Congress could do with the transcript was impeach Marshall, and that did not happen. Dumas Malone, Jefferson's premier biographer and a man highly sympathetic to Jefferson's views, doubts that Jefferson had a direct role in the campaign of public vilification of Marshall, but Malone admits that "he did not call off" the bloodhounds.

Marshall's composure throughout the nearly nine-month ordeal of *Bollman* and *Burr* never cracked. He had ruled incorrectly on a number of motions, but he rectified his own errors, usually within a day or two. He prepared these rulings with great care, wrote with impressive speed and thoughtfulness on a number of novel and complex questions, and directed the proceedings with impartiality and good humor. But he regarded the entire affair with sorrow. He had no love lost for Burr, who was a "man to be feared," as Marshall wrote Hamilton. Nor did Marshall look forward to locking horns with Jefferson. Some of the legal issues, particularly those involving relations among the three branches of the federal government, had caused him much anxiety already. He had previously and would again defend the judiciary against the more powerful executive and legislative branches, but unlike Hamilton and Jefferson, Marshall did not relish such combats.

Each day of the trial, Marshall, exhausted, returned to his townhome in the city. There his fellow citizens saw him shopping at the farmer's market, taking his morning constitutional, and even down on his hands and knees helping his servants clean house. He went to great lengths to prevent Polly from suffering from noise and other distractions, for her health grew ever more delicate. Always willing to stop and share gossip in the street, still a genial host at home, the unprepossessing chief justice was happy to put the Burr trial behind him. In the following twenty-eight years of his service on the High Court (he died in office), Marshall compiled a record of judicial leadership and principled adjudication rivaled only perhaps by Chief Justice Earl Warren.

Still, Marshall was no slacker when it came to defending himself, or to defaming others. Although it cannot be said that his rulings in *Burr* were intended to strike at Jefferson, after the trials Marshall got his revenge indirectly. Daveiss was Marshall's brother-in-law, and shortly after the trials had concluded, he published *A View of the President's Conduct, Concerning the Conspiracy of 1806.* Daveiss slammed Jefferson for ignoring the Burr conspiracy from its inception (that is, from the moment in January 1806 when Daveiss first denounced Burr to the president), and throughout the pamphlet, he slurred Jefferson's character and abilities. The fact that Jefferson had not reappointed Daveiss to his post might have contributed something to his venom.

Wilkinson was another target of Daveiss, who claimed that the general was a tool of Spain. The first of a breed of "men of destiny" (the sobriquet was first applied to the young Napoleon Buonoparte) in the new nation who looked to military adventure for gain and fame, Wilkinson's sense of personal injury grew over time. After facing a "court of enquiry" in 1808, and again in 1810 nearly losing his command because of his suspected dealings with Spain, he prepared and published a series of *Memoirs*. In them he pled he was "entirely innocent" of any intrigue with Burr. The only reason he had any dealings with Burr was because Burr had "represented himself as being on the best footing with the [Jefferson] administration." No one who knew anything about Republican politics in Washington at the time that Wilkinson rekindled his acquaintance with Burr would have believed such a tale.

Wilkinson next blamed the administration for ignoring his "warning in September" 1806 — the warning that neglected to mention Burr's name. Burr was the snake in the garden, deceiving and concealing. (Wilkinson had taken to heart Wirt's eloquence.) "I could not penetrate the veil, which the main objects of letter [of April 16, 1806] concealed, and, of course, was at a loss how to act." Only through deciphering the July letter, and his clever interrogation of Swartwout, and later Bollman, did Wilkinson learn Burr's true purpose. "My conduct immediately on the receipt of these letters, will best expound the part I determined to take, and the world will bear me witness, that I did not for a moment waver in the line of my duty."

When the War of 1812 erupted, Madison sent Wilkinson to invade Canada. The expedition failed disastrously. Wilkinson faced court-martial in 1815, but again emerged unscathed, though his defense cost him whatever loot his double dealing had gained. He removed himself to Texas, and there tried his hand at sugar planting and political intrigue. He died in 1825, still protesting his honorable conduct in the Burr conspiracy.

Hamilton's ghost roved about its usual haunts in lower Manhattan, occasionally appearing as a martyr to an age gone by. He had feared the democracy, but its time had come with Andrew Jackson's smashing victory in 1828. Hamilton despised dangerous men who pandered to the mob, and some very much fitting that description would come to lead America into a civil war. His belief in industry, banking, and central government planning survived his death, though it would be many years before the federal government adopted his ideas of administrative expertise in managing currency and finance.

Luther Martin's role in the Burr defense had gone beyond simple advocacy for a fee. He had put up bail for Burr and had housed Burr when the defendant was not in close custody. When he returned to his home in Baltimore, Martin wrote a report of the trials for the *Federal Gazette*. Hardly a man to hide his own light under a bushel, he boasted that "we have proved that in America there are lawyers who cannot be intimidated by fear of presidential vengeance." Vengeance of a sort soon arrived in the persons of a mob. They broke the windows of his town house and might have done more had his friends not protected him.

Martin continued to argue cases, including *McCulloch v. Maryland* (1819), before the High Court. A massive stroke shortly thereafter did not kill him, but cost him his wits. For a time, with no brief to argue and no client to represent, he would appear in the Supreme Court and take his place with the other attorneys. He said not a word. Marshall understood and let Martin remain. Just as Martin had provided quarters, care, and sustenance for Burr in Richmond, so Burr made a place in his New York City household for Martin. Martin died in 1826.

By the fall of 1807, Burr's creditors had caught up with him. His travels through the West had delayed their demands but not quieted their ardor. He faced civil suits for nearly $40,000. Blennerhassett wondered aloud where all the money had gone, for Burr had collected at Lexington alone more than the creditors wanted. At first, Blennerhassett was buoyed by Burr's good spirits, confiding to his diary "September 13, 1807. I visited Burr this morning. He is as gay as usual, and as busy in speculations on reorganizing his projects for action as if he had never suffered the least interruption. He observed . . . that in six months our schemes could be all remounted." But as the days, then weeks, then months passed without repayment of his loans to Burr, he became "openly disillusioned with a man who appeared to be 'careless' with money, and with the truth." Burr promised to pay Blennerhassett what he owed but never did — promises coming much easier than payments to Burr.

For the rest of the decade, Blennerhassett, hardly the simple farmer that Wirt extolled, sought Burr out high and low, and when Burr could not be found, wrote angry letters to Joseph Alston demanding payment. Blennerhassett would remove himself and his wife to the Mississippi territory to grow cotton, and when that failed, they returned to New York, then Canada, then Britain. He died there in 1831, once again in obscurity.

Alston had guaranteed Burr's debts and would pay off most of them, but Theodosia's fragile health and her apparently inherited inability to settle down — she was constantly on the move — occupied his attention. His son, Burr's grandson, much beloved, finally succumbed to his many infirmities at age eleven. The blow devastated Alston, Theodosia, and Burr. Alston wrote to his father-in-law that "With my wife on one side and my boy on the other, I felt myself superior to depression. The present was enjoyed, the future was anticipated with enthusiasm. One dreadful blow has destroyed us; reduced us to the veriest, the most sublimated wretchedness. That boy, on whom all rested; our companion, our friend — he who was to have transmitted down the mingled blood of Theodosia and myself — he who was to have redeemed all your glory, and shed new lustre upon our families — that boy, at once our happiness and our pride, is taken from us." Alston still rested his hopes for the future in Theodosia. "I will not conceal from you that life is a burden, which, heavy as it is, we shall both support, if not with dignity, at least with decency and firmness. Theodosia has endured all that a human being could endure; but her admirable mind will triumph. She supports herself in a manner worthy of your daughter."

Theodosia wrote her father, "there is no more joy for me" as she planned to rejoin him in New York. A half year later, at the start of 1813, she was lost at sea in a shipwreck that is still mysterious. Perhaps a squall took the ship, for the Hatteras was then and still remains a graveyard of ships. Perhaps a British squadron patrolling the shore during the War of 1812 sank it. Theodosia had chosen for the voyage, according to Alston, "the privateer *Patriot*, a pilot-boat-built schooner, commanded by Captain Overstocks, with an old New-York pilot as sailing-master. The vessel had dismissed her crew, and was returning home with her guns under deck." Alston, bereft of Theodosia's companionship, soon lost his own compass. He died in 1817, aged thirty-seven. The tragedy of the Burr trial had fallen on his family.

Burr himself returned to Philadelphia after the trials, assigning his legal business to Nicholas Biddle, son of his old friend Charles Biddle. Nicholas Biddle would become in 1823 the director of the Second Bank of the United States and a leading anti-Jacksonian. Burr still talked boldly of exploiting his Washita lands, but no one was listening. Still, Biddle kept Burr out of debtors' prison with Alston's help, freeing Burr to travel to England. There he was welcomed by the intellectual circle around the English reformer Jeremy Bentham, but almost penniless and without powerful patrons, he had to leave. Travel through Europe, finally to France during the last of the Napoleonic wars — was no easy matter, particularly for a man as notorious and penurious as Burr, but he managed it. His adventures, kept in a coded notebook, reveal that his satyrlike appetites, at last unchecked by political prospects, took over.

He returned to New York City in 1812, still poor, to law practice, another marriage, and as quiet a retirement as a man as adventurous as Burr could manage. When Texas rebelled against Mexico, an older and wiser Burr remarked that he had been right all the time — just ahead of it. He suffered a series of strokes in the early 1830s, reducing a still dapper and graceful body to a pitiful shell. Removed from his New York City home to a seaside hotel on a hill above the village of Port Richmond, Staten Island, Burr spent his last few days looking east, not west. He died on September 14, 1836, aged eighty, and was buried in the cemetery of his beloved College of New Jersey, by then renamed for its home, Princeton.

In death, Burr took on a new life as the man without a country. His precipitous flight in 1808 became the model, according to legal writer Robert Ferguson, of the most reprinted and best-known short story of the late nineteenth century. Edward Everett Hale's 1863 "The Man

Without a Country" fashioned a tragic fate for a man, young Philip Nolan, convicted of abetting Burr. In law, the story made no sense, for a conspirator or accessory cannot be convicted when the principal in the alleged crime is acquitted, but no matter. Nolan, who cried out "damn the United States," was sentenced to a unique and fanciful exile — forced to forever sail the seas without setting foot on American soil. The story, written by a Union publicist, taught patriotism, a commodity that Burr, a character in the story, lacked. The Burr conspiracy became the Confederacy, and Burr the avatar of national disunion and disgrace.

The charges against Dayton, Smith, and the other alleged coconspirators were dropped, although Smith faced expulsion from the Senate in 1808. Massachusetts Senator John Quincy Adams led the campaign. A trial in 1808 failed by a single vote to remove Smith, but he resigned at its end. Facing bankruptcy, Smith did what many, including Wilkinson and Burr, did: he went west. He died in Louisiana in 1824. Jonathan Dayton returned to New Jersey, served in the state legislature, and died in Elizabethtown in 1824. Brown left the Senate and returned to law practice in Frankfort, where he died in 1834.

Samuel Swartwout traveled with Burr in Europe, fought for his country in the War of 1812, dabbled in Texas lands and later in railroad stock, and gained from newly elected President Andrew Jackson in 1830 the coveted post of collector of the port of New York. He served until 1838. Whether through inadvertence or the need for investment capital, he took some of the collections with him when he departed the office. He died in 1856.

Bollman settled down in New Orleans, a city given to epidemic sicknesses, to practice medicine, failed, removed to New York City, and failed again. His notions for finance and civil engineering were ahead of his time. Perhaps under the right circumstances his fame might have rivaled German immigrants like the banker Jacob Schiff or John Augustus Roebling, who designed the Brooklyn Bridge.

In 1808 Jefferson had no choice but to turn his attention away from Burr. Britain was impressing American sailors on the high seas, and on one occasion in 1807 fired at and boarded a U.S. naval vessel, taking from it alleged deserters from the Royal Navy. The incident occurred in sight of the shoreline, and the demand for war rose like a storm tide. Jefferson sought other means to bring the British to their senses, and he eventually convinced Congress to pass an Embargo Act. Enforcement of the act included the threat of treason indictments, and one of these cases came to the circuit court in 1808.

In *U.S. v. Hoxie*, a Vermont smuggler was caught trying to ship goods to Canada in violation of the embargo. When the officials set a guard over the evidence on the suspect's raft, Hoxie and a party of his friends tried to wrest it from them. He was indicted for treason. Supreme Court Justice Brockholst Livingston, sitting with the circuit court, rendered the decision. "The only occasion on which the supreme court of the United States has delivered any opinion on the doctrine of treason was, on the return of a habeas corpus, in the Case of *Bollman* who had been committed on a charge of that nature. 'To constitute this crime,' says the court, 'war must be actually levied against the United States. However flagitious may be the crime of conspiring to subvert by force the government of our country, such conspiracy is not treason.'"

But here, "stripped of its artificial dress, and technical appearance, [it] is nothing more than the forcible rescuing of a raft from the custody of a military guard placed over it by a collector. It is impossible, to suppress the astonishment which is excited at the attempt which has been made to convince a court and jury of this high criminal jurisdiction, that, between this and levying of war, there is no difference." The defendants' "conduct shows it to have been of a private nature, and that no further violence was contemplated, than to smuggle a raft which had been seized by the collector, and was then lying at a small distance from a guard, into Canada."

Livingston was mindful of Jefferson's charge against Marshall — that the judge had wrongly taken the case from the jury. "You have been reminded, in the course of this trial, that in criminal cases, a jury has a right to take upon itself the decision of both law and fact. There is no design in the court to dispute this position, or in any degree to encroach on your prerogatives. The trial by jury, whatever doubts may exist as to its excellence in civil actions, has uniformly received, and is most eminently entitled to the highest praise, as a mode of determining between the public and a party accused . . . But while you have this right, the court has also its duties to perform. As judges, we are not sent here merely to preside at trials, to preserve order, and to regulate the forms of proceeding; we have a much higher and more important trust committed to us: it is our right and our duty to expound the law to a jury."

The overbroad and hasty charge of treason, with its obvious implications to quiet those who loudly assembled to oppose the policy of an administration, and those who carried out some lesser offense that an administration wished to highlight, had withdrawn itself into the dragon's cave. It would reappear in times of national danger, when other administrations beckoned it.

United States v. Burr was cited 383 times in federal court since 1807. Most of the citations concerned the use of evidence, a key part of Marshall's rulings. In *U.S. v. Valenzuela-Bernal* (1982), Justices William Brennan and Thurgood Marshall, in dissent, cited John Marshall's ruling in *Burr* to support the argument that a criminal defendant has a constitutional right, under the compulsory process clause of the Sixth Amendment, to interview eyewitnesses to his alleged crime before they are whisked out of the country by a prosecutor.

Burr also proved that no one was above the law, not even (or especially) the president of the United States. In it, Marshall ruled "that the president of the United States may be subpoenaed, and examined as a witness, and required to produce any paper in his possession, is not controverted." In *Nixon v. U.S.* (1974) and *Jones v. Clinton* (1997), this principle would be tested and found essential to our system of government.

The Burr trial also set precedent for self-incrimination and search and seizure rules. In *Mason v. United States* (1917), the High Court noted that "During the trial of Aaron Burr . . . Chief Justice Marshall announced the applicable doctrine as follows: 'The principle which entitles the United States to the testimony of every citizen, and the principle by which every witness is privileged not to accuse himself, can neither of them be entirely disregarded . . . it belongs to the court to consider and to decide whether any direct answer to it can implicate the witness. If this be decided in the negative, then he may answer it without violating the privilege which is secured to him by law. If a direct answer to it may criminate himself, then he must be the sole judge what his answer would be.' "

Burr should have been sufficient, coupled with *Bollman* I, to establish the rule that the writ of habeas corpus could not be summarily denied by the executive branch. But *Bollman*, like *Merryman* and *Mil-*

ligan, is too easily ignored when chief executives believe that they are above the law, and compliant attorneys general, like Caesar Rodney, or Edward Bates, Lincoln's first attorney general, or John Ashcroft and Alberto Gonzales, President George W. Bush's attorneys general, provide excuses to ignore the constitutional limitation on the suspension power, or ways to dodge it. Thus the most important precedent that *Burr* set was that federal courts must be, and could be, above politics.

Although the majority of historians who retell the Burr trial story quite appropriately set it in a political context, the political lesson must be intertwined with a legal one. Political animus, particularly when hurled from the heights of the presidency, can crack the soundest foundations of law. No one is safe from presidential persecution. Often the political process itself may provide a remedy in time — the party in power may overstep its popular mandate — but when the legislative and the executive branches are in accord in some desperately proclaimed campaign to root out evil, every individual's rights are imperiled.

Constitutional limitations on prosecution and constitutional guarantees of procedural rights fail before such combined onslaughts on the rule of law. Administrations conceal their violations, and congressional majorities put their seal upon the violations. The only bulwark against such illegality is the independent judiciary. As Hamilton wrote in the *Federalist* defending the new judiciary, it was their job to keep the executive and the legislative branches "within the limits assigned to their authority." If the judiciary is itself suborned, corrupted, bows to the other branches against its better judgment, or gives in to the same indifference to due process and fair play as the other branches, then our constitutional democracy will fall.

The canary in the mine is the unpopular suspect. What happens to that suspect warns of what any opponent of government may next face. Whether it is color, religion, place of national origin, or political viewpoint that draws the ire of the executive and the legislative branches down on the defendant, he will be denied counsel, as Burr was, or kept in close confinement without the chance to confront those who accuse him, as Burr was. Where, then, is his safety? Against this engine of persecution, what can save a defendant? Burr had friends, means, and his own skills to defend himself. What weapons of truth or law can far less well-off prisoners deploy? Who will risk career or reputation to defend those whom the government has already condemned?

In *Cramer v. U.S.* (1945), a case that came to the High Court at the end of World War II, Anthony Cramer appealed to the U.S. Supreme Court to reverse his conviction on a charge of giving aid and comfort to our enemies in time of war. In 1942, he had provided housing and other comforts to an old friend, who happened also to be a Nazi saboteur. Cramer, a German immigrant who divided his loyalties between his adopted country and his fatherland, did not know about the sabotage plans and had no desire to levy war against the United States. But who would speak for him when so many Americans had died to end the Nazi reign of terror?

Representing the government, solicitor general Charles Fahy argued, "We believe in short that no more need be laid for an overt act of treason than for an overt act of conspiracy . . . Hence we hold the overt acts relied on were sufficient to be submitted to the jury, even though they perhaps may have appeared as innocent on their face." Let the jury decide whether the law included conspiracy and unwitting aid and comfort was an overt act—if the jurors were willing to stand up against the entire weight of the federal government in a time of great national struggle.

Justice Robert Jackson, formerly attorney general of the United States, read the opinion of the Court. Relying on research that legal scholar James Willard Hurst and others had done in preparation for Cramer's defense, research that included the Burr trial, Jackson began with a history of American treason law. "When our forefathers took up the task of forming an independent political organization for New World society, no one of them appears to have doubted that to bring into being a new government would originate a new allegiance for its citizens and inhabitants. Nor were they reluctant to punish as treason any genuine breach of allegiance, as every government time out of mind had done. The betrayal of [George] Washington by [Benedict] Arnold was fresh in mind. They were far more awake to powerful enemies with designs on this continent than some of the intervening generations have been."

The framers of the Constitution intended the charge of treason "as an effective instrument of the new nation's security against treachery that would aid external enemies." But the framers were also aware of the misuse that a partisan executive might make of treason and imposed "every limitation" possible. Overt acts must be just that—so visible that two witnesses to each act could clearly testify to the nature of the act as well as the participants in it. Jackson's reading of these limitations came directly out of Marshall's earlier opinion.

To prevent "perversion [of treason prosecutions] by established authority to repress peaceful political opposition; and conviction of the innocent as a result of perjury, passion, or inadequate evidence," the Court had to define the offense as narrowly as possible and limit what juries might hear. "A citizen intellectually or emotionally may favor the enemy and harbor sympathies or convictions disloyal to this country's policy or interest, but so long as he commits no act of aid and comfort to the enemy, there is no treason. On the other hand, a citizen may take actions which do aid and comfort the enemy—making a speech critical of the government or opposing its measures, profiteering, striking in defense plants or essential work, and the hundred other things which impair our cohesion and diminish our strength—but if there is no adherence to the enemy in this, if there is no intent to betray, there is no treason." Marshall would have been proud to have written these lines.

In a democratic republic, there will always be cabals of dissidents. People angry with government will say angry things about killing politicians or overthrowing the government they do not mean, or that they mean at the time but will never act on. Had Burr been convicted, a precedent would have been set to arrest, try, and convict for treason anyone who said anything that the regime in office thought gave aid and comfort to an enemy or constructively levied war.

Over and over in our history, the courts have proven the reliable last resort in the struggle to prevent such perversions of law by hasty politics. So, in *Watts v. United States* (1969), an anti–Vietnam War protester's statement "at [a] small public gathering that if inducted into Army (which he vowed would never occur) and made to carry a rifle 'the first man I want to get in my sights is L.B.J.,' was held to be crude political hyperbole which in light of its context and conditional nature did not constitute a knowing and willful threat against the President."

A trusted colleague asked me, not long before these words were written, whether Aaron Burr mattered. Had his participation in the politics of the day changed anything? Would not the larger story of the nation have been the same without him? Perhaps — were it not for the events of 1807. For Burr's trials proved that a judiciary defending the rule of law could stand up to the president and a Congress bent on revenge, and that judges had the power to deny to the other branches ill-founded prosecutions of unpopular and even dangerous men. This is the most important precedent of the Burr treason trials, the most important story we can tell about law in the early republic, and one we have to remember.

Afterword
What Was Burr Really After?

Burr was a man of real ability, genuine charity, and kindness; he was capable of friendship and loyalty to those who needed help. He was an insecure man, looking for respect, love, and a home, sometimes in all the wrong places. He was a vain man, polished in manner but with no sense of money. Burr was ambitious, but it was ambition without a star, fixed ideology, or goal. In the service of a great ideal like the American Revolution, he could be a hero. In his own service, he could be secretive, obsessive, and given to poor judgment.

Perhaps worse, certainly for a would-be "usurper," at key moments, Burr hesitated. When he might have appeared in person in Washington in the winter of 1801 and swayed key state delegations to vote for him instead of Jefferson, he stopped in Trenton. When he was presiding officer in the Senate, he might have jumped in to save the Judiciary Act of 1801 and pleased the Federalists enough to become their man, he simply presided over the Senate debates on repeal. When he might have endeared himself to the Republicans in the Chase impeachment by tilting the playing field in their favor, he refused to aid them in any way. In the end, his public conduct was always above reproach, but hardly helpful for a man reputed to be unscrupulous.

Was Burr then guilty of treason, the most public of all crimes? If not, then what was his aim? According to Nancy Isenberg, the object was "a filibuster." Nathan Schacter adds that it was "not an ordinary filibuster" but one driven by "the dazzling possibilities of a career of arms and glory, of personal aggrandizement at the expense of Spain." Roger Kennedy sees the ultimate goal of the filibuster as not to divide the nation, but to add territory to the United States — perhaps Florida, Texas, and even Mexico.

But there is another possibility, perhaps no more, as Nancy Isenberg warns, than "barstool chatter." I had, until I undertook this study, taught Burr's travails as a republican tragedy, the rise and fall of a man whose pride and grandiose self-confidence blinded him to the meaning and consequences of his actions. I may have been wrong, however, just as Burr's detractors and later historians may have been wrong all along. There is the possibility that Burr was not guilty of any of the offenses with which he was charged, but instead of fraudulent misrepresentation—a sweeping entrepreneurial shell game, a confidence scam.

One question that has bothered historians of the Burr episode is why a man of such consummate political skills, even a man down on his luck, would lend himself to such harebrained schemes as Burr proposed. True, Burr never really made clear what his objective was. In this light, let us review his conduct from the middle of 1805 though the winter of 1807.

He traveled incessantly, and at every stop, he asked for funding. He named different projects to different potential donors. To the British minister, he discussed a war with Spain, if only the British would provide funding. With the Spanish minister, he revealed a plan to separate the West from the East, if only the Spanish would grease his palm. With Blennerhassett, Smith, and other Westerners, he promised the land and gold of Texas, New Mexico, and beyond. With his New Orleans backers, he hinted that New Orleans would become the capital of a great empire, and there would be glory and wealth enough for everyone. They need only bankroll his plans. To Jefferson, Burr suggested that a remunerative office, whose fees and patronage Burr could ply, would buy him off. When Daveiss once again indicted Burr, he dropped the mask a little and wrote, on November 27, 1806, to William Henry Harrison: "I have no wish or design to attempt a separation of the Union," but "it is true that I am engaged in an extensive speculation and that with me are associated some of your intimate and dearest friends."

When rumors of Burr's various plots and plans circulated and newspapers published hints of dire treason, a man who had political aims, whether or not they involved criminal activities, would have ceased and desisted. A conspiracy, if such it was, is supposed to be a secret. Revealing the existence of a conspiracy should quiet it. If Burr intended to filibuster in Spanish territory, the notoriety his plans had gained would have put the Spanish on alert. The Spanish were certainly aware of the entire scheme.

But Burr seemed unperturbed by the rumors. The more rumors spread, the more scope his plans seemed to gain—which made it easier to approach more potential donors. All they had to do was fund his small army, buy arms, pay for boats, and on and on the list grew. As Thomas Abernathy concluded, "Burr at this time experienced no great difficulty in raising funds." As Blennerhassett asked, after the trial to be sure, what was Burr doing with all that money? A good question, for Burr was never there. Like McCavity, the master criminal cat of the T. S. Eliot poem, Burr was far away, soliciting more funds. Luther Martin was right—Burr's was no more than "will o' the wisp" treason, for he wanted nothing to do with armies and armed camps, nothing to do with filibustering raids down rivers or violent incursions in the Spanish provinces. He simply wanted the money to fund these.

But where did the money go? No one was paid for "revolutionizing" Louisiana or anyplace else that Burr touched. Did the money go to Burr's creditors? They were dunning him when he went west and dunning him when he returned. They dunned him after he was acquitted and after he came home from Europe. And now the outrageous surmise: Had he only been allowed to fail!

Perhaps—pure speculation on my part—Burr anticipated the plot of the Mel Brooks movie *The Producers*. If a play is a Broadway success, all the backers whose money has paid for the production have to be repaid. Sell 1,000 percent of the profits, and you go to jail if you cannot pay all the backers tenfold. But if the play is a flop, then no backer expects to be paid—there is nothing, no receipts, no gate, with which to pay the backer what is owed. All the money the producers have raised vanishes. So in a failed coup, there is nothing to repay the conspirators and sponsors and investors. They have to swallow their loss. In the movie, Max Bialystock and his accountant, Leo Bloom, go to jail because their surefire flop, *Springtime for Hitler*, becomes a hit. It may be that, like Bialystock, Burr never meant to succeed. Had he been given a little more time and space, he could have done what "the producers" had hoped to accomplish.

If Burr was driven to a confidence game by his penury and his fear of debtor's prison, he went about the con in outrageous fashion. The conspiracy to create an empire, or sever the union, or invade the Spanish Empire, was never more than a shadow play, but the shadows were cast upon an IMAX screen. With his entourage, Burr traversed the Western country by boat and horseback, manipulated the greed of former U.S. senators, the adventurism of men like Blennerhassett and Adair, and the swagger of Wilkinson to advance Burr's own far more ordinary aims.

Seen in context, scams like Burr's were a national pastime. Burr was in debt, but so was everyone else in the new republic. No form of wealth (save one) was secure. There was no legal tender — paper money depreciated in value as soon as it was printed. Ownership of land was worthless without labor, rents, and crops. Banknotes and stocks could be printed and sold without any capital reserve, and were. Indeed, forgery and counterfeiting were major business enterprises. Banks and companies went into and out of business so regularly that no one's deposits in such institutions and enterprises were safe.

One's own abilities as a craftsman or a professional, for example a lawyer or doctor, could earn one a living, so long as one's customers and clients paid what they owed, and the income exceeded the expense of running the business. In the end, all business, retail, wholesale, import, export, from the biggest warehouser to the solitary peddler with his wares on his back, depended on a network of credit. A man's name and reputation gained him credit, but even the greatest of men, financiers like Robert Morris, Supreme Court justices like James Wilson, and leading lawyers like Luther Martin could (and did) end up penniless. Worse, if creditors wanted, debtors faced prison until they paid what they owed. Aaron Burr was a victim of this economic system as well as a villain in it. Only the very rich slave holders of the South — men like Alston — could be secure in their holdings. Slaves kept their value, and as the country moved west, that value appreciated. Burr would have done better as a slave trader than a land speculator.

Nor was Burr the first man of repute to come up with a grand scheme for self-advertisement, wealth, and independence in the American story. The beginning of English colonization in North America rested on just such visionary greed. Walter Raleigh promised Queen Elizabeth everything — gold, silver, security against the aggressive Spanish Empire — if she would bankroll his "Virginia Colony" on Roanoke Island. John Smith, who like Raleigh brimmed with self-confidence, wrote and rewrote the history of the Jamestown colony, each time figuring larger in the account. What he did not revise he invented, selling himself along with copies of his *History of Virginia*. Land speculators, town builders, trading company founders, colonizers, and empire builders all exaggerated the riches that investors and settlers had waiting if they bought lottery tickets, stock issues, and bonds to underwrite a thousand ventures as wild-eyed as those that Burr waved in front of Alston, Blennerhassett, Dayton, Brown, Smith, and the rest of the assembly of confederates and dupes.

If Burr's real crime was attempted fraud, not treason or conspiracy to commit treason, then the almost complete disappearance of the Burr plot from the public eye soon after Marshall announced his opinion makes perfect sense. Had the plot been real, then surely during the War of 1812 the principals had another opportunity to press for Western independence. For the last year of the war, New Englanders had openly spoken of secession. Federal troops and military were otherwise occupied. The Indian threat, spurred by the British, had again worsened. There was no better time for plotters to hatch their plot. But nothing happened because the alleged chief architect of the plot never plotted to do anything — except gather money from foreign governments and solicit contributions from investors. Perhaps. As Washington Irving said of Burr, shortly before the essayist died, "Burr was full of petty mystery. He made a mystery of everything."

1756	Aaron Burr is born in Newark, New Jersey, to a ministerial family.
1759	Burr is orphaned and finds himself part of his uncle's extended family.
1769	At age thirteen, Burr matriculates at the College of New Jersey, where his father had been president.
1772	Burr graduates from college, travels to Connecticut, and prepares first for a ministerial career, then for the bar.
1775–1776	At the siege of Boston, Burr seeks a commission in the Continental army. As a private citizen, he joins Benedict Arnold's assault on Quebec and distinguishes himself in battle.
1776–1779	Burr gains a command, rising to the rank of colonel.
1782	Burr marries Theodosia Prevost, a widow, buys Richmond Hill, and is admitted to the New York bar.
1784	Burr is elected to the New York State Assembly, where he will serve on and off throughout the rest of the century. He begins to build the first modern political machine.
1791	Burr is selected as U.S. senator from New York. His political ideology is never clear, as ideologies do not interest him, but he runs as a Jeffersonian Republican.
1796	Burr campaigns as Jefferson's vice presidential candidate on the Republican ticket.
1800–1801	Burr and Jefferson again run, now getting an equal number of electoral votes. Burr stays silent as Jefferson wins the contest in the Congress. Jefferson, upset with Burr's lack of loyalty, denies Burr New York patronage, though Burr carried New York for the ticket.
1804	Burr loses a race for the governorship of New York. An on-and-off rivalry with Alexander Hamilton escalates into a duel, and Hamilton is fatally wounded. Burr flees from New Jersey to Philadelphia and then Washington.

1805

February 4–March 1	As vice president, Burr presides over the Senate impeachment trial of Judge Samuel Chase and the swearing in of Jefferson.
March 2	Burr departs the Senate after a deeply moving farewell speech. It will be his last official act.
January–April	Burr confers with James Wilkinson and others, eyeing Western opportunities.
April–October	Burr's first tour through the West, down the Ohio and the Mississippi. Returns to Philadelphia on horseback. Meets the Blennerhassetts, General Andrew Jackson, and Edward Livingston, as well as leading Ohio, Kentucky, Tennessee, and Louisiana politicians.
October 1805–January 1806	Burr returns to Philadelphia and Washington. Two meetings with President Jefferson.

1806

Winter and Spring	Burr's plans for Ouashita (Washita) land deal, possible filibuster in Spanish Empire begin to form. He asks William Eaton and others if they are interested. He also seeks financial aid from Britain and France.
July 22–29	The drafting of the cipher letter, two copies to Wilkinson, sent for hand delivery with Samuel Swartwout and Erick (or Erich) Bollman.
August–September	Second Western tour. In Washington County, Pennsylvania, Burr confers with Morgans; visits Blennerhassett Island in September and contracts for boats. Stops in Nashville, where he contracts for additional vessels. He also purchases 400,000 acres of land on the Washita River.
October–November	Wilkinson receives Burr's ciphered letters, changes his mind about the expedition, arranges a truce with the Spanish forces on the Sabine River, and sends letter to Jefferson denouncing Burr. Joseph Daveiss, federal attorney for Kentucky, asks for a grand jury in Frankfort to investigate Burr. Burr appears, represented by Henry Clay, to answer questions. John Graham sent by President Jefferson to follow Burr and gather evidence.

November 27	Jefferson proclamation about attack planned on Spanish Empire.
December 1–5	A second Frankfort, Kentucky, grand jury hears evidence against Burr and finds no bill. Graham convinces Ohio governor to send militia to Blennershassett Island.
December 7	Four boats and about thirty men from Pennsylvania arrive at Blennerhassett Island.
December 9	Boats at Blennerhassett Island seized by the Ohio militia. Blennerhassett and others leave.
December 14	Wilkinson arrests Bollman, Swartwout, and James Alexander in New Orleans.
December 20	The secretary of the navy sends a letter ordering navy officials in New Orleans to "intercept and if necessary destroy" boats under the command of Burr.
December 22	Burr leaves Nashville, heading down the Cumberland River.

1807

January 5	Wilkinson proclaims martial law in New Orleans.
January 14	Word of Burr's arrival at Bayou Pierre reaches Natchez. A force of 275 men is dispatched to capture Burr and his comrades.
January 25–February 4	Burr surrenders to territorial governor Cowles Mead for trial. A grand jury impaneled in the Mississippi Territory refuses to indict Burr for "any crime or misdemeanor against the United States."
February 5–19	Burr flees from Wilkinson's agents, is arrested by Gaines and Perkins near the Tombigbee River in Alabama. He is taken to Fort Stoddart, where he is imprisoned for two weeks.
March	Burr, under a guard of nine men, is taken to Richmond by horseback. He arrives on March 26.
March 30	Burr appears before Chief Justice John Marshall.
April 1	Bail hearing for Burr. Marshall allows the prosecution to prepare an indictment for a grand jury on Burr violation of Neutrality Act, but not on treason.
May 22	Grand jury proceedings open in Richmond, Virginia.
June 12	Jefferson papers sought by Burr.

June 13	John Marshall ruling on the Jefferson papers. Wilkinson arrives. Marshall allows the grand jury to consider bill against Burr for treason.
June 14–26	Grand jury deliberates and finds true bill against Burr, Blennerhassett, and others for treason and misdemeanor.
August 3	The trial of Aaron Burr opens in Richmond, Virginia.
August 17	Jury selection is completed and prosecution opens its case.
August 22–29	Arguments on Burr's motion to exclude evidence not related to an overt act of levying war.
August 31	Marshall allows the Burr motion to exclude evidence unrelated to the gathering on Blennerhassett Island.
September 1–October 20	Burr acquitted. Retried on the violation of the Neutrality Act, but the prosecution asks for a dismissal of the case. Burr seeks and gains a jury not guilty verdict.
1808–1812	Burr travels in Britain and Europe.
1812–1813	Burr returns to New York City to practice law. His grandson, followed by his daughter, die.
1836	Burr dies.

BIBLIOGRAPHIC ESSAY

Note from the series editors: The following bibliographic essay contains the primary and secondary sources that the author consulted for this volume. We have asked all authors in the series to omit formal citations in order to make our volumes more readable, inexpensive, and appealing for students and general readers. In adopting this format, Landmark Law Cases and American Society follows the precedent of a number of highly regarded and widely consulted series.

I have modernized the most awkward spellings in the primary sources, as well as followed modern capitalization and punctuation rules.

The definition of political trials comes from Michal Belknap's introduction to his edited collection of essays, *American Political Trials*, rev. ed. (Westport, Conn.: Praeger, 1994).

Burr wrote fulsome letters to his daughter and others, but during and about the trials, he was almost sphinxlike. When near death, he allowed Matthew L. Davis access to his papers. The result is the *Memoirs of Aaron Burr* (New York: Harper, 1837), 2v. The few letters he composed to Wilkinson and others during 1806 and 1807 are tantalizingly vague. Primary sources on Burr include Mary-Jo Kline et al., eds., *The Political Correspondence and Public Papers of Aaron Burr* (Princeton, N.J.: Princeton University Press, 1983), 2v., and *The Papers of Aaron Burr*, 27 rolls of microfilm, edited by Mary-Jo Kline under the auspices of the New-York Historical Society.

The direct precedent, alongside *Ex Parte Bollman*, is the trial of John Fries. A stenographic account is available in Thomas Carpenter, *The Two Trials of John Fries on an Indictment for Treason* . . . (Philadelphia: Woodward, 1800). The case itself was reported at 9 F. Cas. 826. Though far less useful as precedent because Justice Paterson did not discuss the law, *U.S. v. Vigol* (1795) can be found at 28 F. Cas. 376 and 2 U.S. 346. *U.S. v. Hamilton* (1795), equally terse and unhelpful, appears at 3 U.S. 17. Speeches of counsel and rulings of the court from the 1795 and 1799 cases can be found in Francis Wharton, ed., *State Trials of the United States during the Administrations of Washington and Adams* (Philadelphia: Carey and Hart, 1849). A very fine essay on the Whiskey Rebellion and Fries's Rebellion treason trials is Stephen Presser, "A Tale of Two Judges: Richard Peters, Samuel Chase, and the Broken Promise of Federalist Jurisprudence," *Northwestern Law Review* 73 (1978): 26–52.

The formal report of Burr's case is *United States v. Burr*, 25 F. Cas. 187 (No. 14,694) (C.C.Va. 1807). *Ex Parte Bollman* and *Ex Parte Swartwout* can be found at 8 U.S. 75 (1807).

I have taken additional material on the cases and opinions from Herbert

Johnson, followed by Charles F. Hobson, eds., *The Papers of John Marshall* (Chapel Hill: University of North Carolina Press, 1974–), of which 12 volumes were available at this writing. Volume 7 covered the year 1807. For Hobson's views on Marshall as a chief justice, including his reading of the Marshall-Cushing letter of June 29, 1807, see Charles Hobson, "The Chief Justice and the Institutional Judiciary: Defining the Office," *University of Pennsylvania Law Review* 154 (2006): 1421–61. The stenographic compilation of testimony and arguments at the treason and misdemeanor trials and hearings I used is David Robertson, *Reports of the Trials of Col. Aaron Burr . . .* (Philadelphia: Hopkins and Earle, 1808), 2v. A selection of documents, drawn from these sources, along with a chronology of the trial, appears in Douglas Linder's Web site on famous American trials (http://www.law.umkc.edu/faculty/projects/ftrials/burr/Burr.htm).

In his own defense, James Wilkinson composed a series of reports; these are available in *Memoirs of My Own Times* (Philadelphia: Small, 1816), 3v. George Campbell's circular letter to his constituents on the Burr plot, dated February 25, 1807, along with other congressmen's reports, appears in volume 1 of Noble E. Cunningham Jr., ed., *Circular Letters of Congressmen to Their Constituents, 1789–1829* (Chapel Hill: University of North Carolina Press, 1978), 1:494, 495, 496 (for Campbell).

Older works, like James Parton's *The Life and Times of Aaron Burr* (Boston: Houghton, 1856), 2v., a collection of anecdotes gathered from surviving Burr intimates mixed with narratives of the times, is generally favorable to Burr and to Jefferson, but not to Hamilton. Samuel L. Knapp, *The Life of Aaron Burr* (New York: Wiley, 1837), is a derivative work. More recent and reliable works defending Burr are Milton Lomask, *Aaron Burr: The Years of Conspiracy and Exile, 1805–1836* (New York, 1982), and Joseph Wheelan, *Jefferson's Vendetta: The Pursuit of Aaron Burr and the Judiciary* (New York, 2005). Whelan contends that the whole affair was part of the president's assault on his political enemies.

Robert Ferguson, *The Trial in American Life* (Chicago: University of Chicago Press, 2007), devotes a chapter to the Burr trial. He concludes that "the politics of the time were the controlling elements" (80). This is more than a little unfair to Marshall. He reports that "Burr had called Hamilton out with single-minded ruthlessness" (80). This is more than a little unfair to Burr (ignoring Hamilton's relentless campaign of vilification, and Burr's attempts to end the ritual of the duel short of actual combat). "Burr was also a known sexual predator" (80) is more than a little unfair to the times; it uses terminology that is anachronistic, and it ignores Burr's remarkable respect for women. Burr was not "imperiously aristocratic in bearing" (80), and no one who knew him found him so. He was not "filled with entitlements" (81), and in fact grew up living in fairly uncertain, if not dire, circumstances.

Ferguson's contribution to the literature on the trial thus lies not in his reading of the history, but his reports on the notoriety of the case at the time, and the reputation that it gave Burr long after the verdict was reported.

Ferguson's introductory essay is worth reading, however, for its insights into trials generally (for example, everyone on the witness stand tells lies; the lawyers are not interested in the truth either; the rules of evidence preclude the introduction of much of the story): "This all-or-nothing approach leads to a devastating conclusion. Most stories told in a courtroom are true only in an instrumental sense" (13). Or not at all. Certainly, the jury at Burr's trial wanted to hear more from Wilkinson, but Marshall closed that door. Ferguson also reminds us that trials can be immensely boring to the uninitiated. Arcane points of law like those marking much of the arguments of counsel in the Burr trial have little resonance for the average juror—or reader. I have tried to add drama to what must have been sleep-inducing hours of technical pleading, perhaps falling into Ferguson's trap of manipulating the truth in order to enliven the story. On the other hand, Ferguson argues here and elsewhere that the law is a form of literary event and the trial a performance. Perhaps he would overlook the liberties I have taken.

Most historians—like most of Burr's contemporaries—find Burr's actions interesting, if hard to explain, and believe that at least one strand of them included a conspiracy to sever the Western portions of the country from the Eastern states. See, for example, Francis F. Beirne, *Shout Treason: The Trial of Aaron Burr* (New York: Hastings, 1959), whose verdict is guilty, guilty, guilty, but offers amusing vignettes of Richmond life at the time; Thomas Perkins Abernathy, *The Burr Conspiracy* (New York: Oxford, 1954), quotation in the text from 72, a work of significant scholarship that finds Burr guilty as charged, but reveals the full extent of Wilkinson's betrayal of his country's interests to the Spanish (as well as his role in Burr's affairs); the chatty and sometimes flippant Donald Barr Chidsey, *The Great Conspiracy: Aaron Burr and His Strange Doings in the West* (New York, 1964), offering more than a few sharp words about the character and motives of everyone in the episode; and Buckner F. Melton Jr., *Aaron Burr: Conspiracy to Treason* (New York, 2002). Melton's close reading of the conspiracy side of the indictment finds Burr culpable. Perhaps more important, like Abernathy, Melton fits the conspiracy into a pattern of Western speculative ventures. Melton, like Parton, knows his way around all the protagonists' stories, but unlike Parton, he does not take them at face value. The result is Melton's belief that "The ultimate version—if anyone ever writes it—will be massive, full of fact and conjecture . . . yet it will still fall short of the truth, for the truth died with Burr" (235).

Biographies of the principals are numerous. A solid biography of Burr is Nathan Schachner, *Aaron Burr: A Biography* (New York: Barnes, 1961), quotations in the text from 517, 288, 282. More recent are Lomask, *Aaron Burr* (New York: Farrar, 1979–82), 2v., Herbert S. Parmet and Marie B. Hecht, *Aaron Burr: Portrait of an Ambitious Man* (New York: Macmillan, 1967), quotation from page 17, and the beautifully written Nancy Isenberg, *Fallen Founder: The Life of Aaron Burr* (New York: Viking, 2007), quotations from which come from pages 2, 7, 307, and personal correspondence from the author. Isenberg and Lomask are friendly to their subject. Every politician should have a biographical defender as fierce as Isenberg. Gordon S. Wood, *Revolutionary Characters* (New York: Penguin, 2006), 225, 231, takes a far more dour view of Burr, as does Edward J. Larson, *A Magnificent Catastrophe: The Tumultuous Election of 1800, America's First Political Campaign* (New York: Free Press, 2007), 87, 88.

Gore Vidal's *Burr: A Novel* (New York: Random House, 1973), is 428 pages of marvelous speculation told by an invented character, young Charlie Schuyler, about a man — Burr — whom the novelist saw as spiritual kin. In an afterword, Vidal writes, "Why a historical novel and not a history? To me, the attraction of the historical novel is that one can be as meticulous (or as careless!) as the historian and yet reserve the right not only to rearrange events, but most important, to attribute motive — something the conscientious historian or biographer ought never do" (429).

As the foregoing pages indicate, I have violated Vidal's rule, attributing motive to all the major characters, but I take his message seriously. Motive is the most inward and the most human of all characteristics. History without motive is mindless narration — one damn thing after another, as Robin Winks (and countless others) have put it. In any case, Vidal wants his cake after he has eaten it: "the story told is history, and not invention" (430). Except for most of the dialogue, the subplots, and the anachronisms of law and politics, Vidal has gotten it right, or not, as the case may be.

On Jefferson, whose biographies are four times as numerous as Burr's, I have relied on Nobel E. Cunningham Jr., *In Pursuit of Reason: The Life of Thomas Jefferson* (Baton Rouge: Louisiana State University Press, 1987), Dumas Malone, *Jefferson and His Time* (Boston: Little, Brown, 1948–81), 6v., especially volume 5, with quotations in the text from xvi, 256, and 355. Merrill Peterson, *Thomas Jefferson and the New Nation: A Biography* (New York: Oxford, 1970), and, for me the most interesting, Joseph J. Ellis, *American Sphinx: the Character of Thomas Jefferson* (New York: Knopf, 1997).

Two old collections of very select Jefferson letters and writings are Andrew Lipscomb and Albert E. Bergh, *The Writings of Thomas Jefferson* (Washington, D.C., 1903), 20v., and Paul L. Ford, *The Works of Thomas Jefferson* (New York: Putnam, 1905), 12v. The modern, authoritative edition was begun by Julian P. Boyd in 1950 and continues to this day, just now reaching into his presidency: *The Papers of Thomas Jefferson* (Princeton:

Princeton University Press, 1950–), 33 volumes to date. There are in addition three volumes in the series on his retirement, a volume reprinting his Commonplace Book, and in the works a much-awaited edition of his legal writings. Jefferson's messages to Congress appear in James D. Richardson, *A Compilation of the Messages and Papers of the Presidents, 1789–1897* (Washington, D.C.: U.S. Government, 1896–99), 1:404–5, 412.

On Hamilton, the old classic is Broadus Mitchell, *Alexander Hamilton* (New York: Macmillan, 1957–62), 2v. The modern classic is Ron Chernow, *Alexander Hamilton* (New York: Penguin, 2004). Harold C. Syrett was the editor of the *Papers of Alexander Hamilton* (New York: Columbia University Press, 1961–79), 25v. To Syrett is attributed the legendary quotation, among editors of the founders' papers at least, "thank God for Aaron Burr." Julius W. Goebel Jr. and J. H. Smith edited *The Law Practice of Alexander Hamilton* (New York: Columbia University Press, 1964–79), 5v.

On Marshall, the first great biography was Albert J. Beveridge's *The Life of John Marshall* (Boston: Houghton, 1944), 4v. Everyone who tells the story of the trials has dipped into this well. More recent are Leonard Baker, *John Marshall: A Life in Law* (New York: Macmillan, 1974), Charles F. Hobson, *The Great Chief Justice: John Marshall and the Rule of Law* (Lawrence: University Press of Kansas, 1996), R. Kent Newmyer, *John Marshall and the Heroic Age of the Supreme Court* (Baton Rouge: Louisiana State University Press, 2001), and Jean E. Smith, *John Marshall: Definer of a Nation* (New York: Holt, 1996). All of the foregoing are fine works, but Hobson's expertise and insight are unparalleled, in part because he is the editor of the Marshall papers.

Roger G. Kennedy, *Burr, Hamilton, and Jefferson: A Study in Character* (New York: Oxford University Press, 1999), with quotations in the text from 11, 10, 281, and 146, is beautifully written but quirky, jumping from person to person and time period to time period. Its "sympathy for losers, and the underappreciated" (389) hints where Kennedy's heart lay—with Burr. Director of the Smithsonian's Museum of American History and then of the U.S. Park Service, Kennedy both feels and knows history. Like Parton, who interviewed men and women who had known Burr, Kennedy sees a great man with a tragic flaw—perhaps the wrong man for an age of transparent virtues. I think that Kennedy did not see into Jefferson's character as he did into Burr's, and in the end, he had no wish to see what lay beneath the surface of the radical land- and slave-owning gentleman. Kennedy's Hamilton is simply the opposite of Burr, impetuous and candid. I only wish that Kennedy had included Marshall more fully, that we could know what Kennedy thought of the chief. Oh, and yes, I wish that I could write half as incisively and sympathetically as Kennedy about the men and the times.

Jonathan Daniels, *Ordeal of Ambition: Jefferson, Hamilton, Burr* (Garden City, N.Y.: Doubleday, 1970), 4, 347, finds Burr the best of the three men.

On Robert Goodloe Harper, see Joseph W. Cox, *Champion of Southern Federalism* (Port Washington, N.Y.: Kennikat, 1972). On Luther Martin, see Paul S. Clarkson and R. Samuel Jett, *Luther Martin of Maryland* (Baltimore: Johns Hopkins University Press, 1970). On Randolph, see Moncure D. Conway, *Omitted Chapters of History Disclosed in the Life and Papers of Edmund Randolph* (New York: Putnam, 1888). The epitome of Jonathan Dayton comes from David Hackett Fischer, *The Revolution of American Conservatism: The Federalist Party in the Era of Jeffersonian Democracy* (New York: Harper and Row, 1965), 327, a source for observations of Robert Goodloe Harper and Luther Martin as well.

Did the Constitution incorporate English common-law criminal precedent? See Gary D. Rowe, "The Sound of Silence: *United States v. Hudson & Goodwin*, the Jeffersonian Ascendancy, and the Abolition of Federal Common Law Crimes," *Yale Law Journal* 101 (1992): 919–48; and Kathryn Preyer, "Jurisdiction to Punish: Federal Authority, Federalism and the Common Law of Crimes in the Early Republic," *Law and History Review* 4 (1986): 223–60.

On the Whiskey Rebellion, see Thomas P. Slaughter, *The Whiskey Rebellion: Frontier Epilogue to the American Revolution* (New York: Oxford University Press, 1986). For John Fries's Rebellion, see Paul Douglas Newman, *Fries's Rebellion: The Enduring Struggle for the American Revolution* (Philadelphia: University of Pennsylvania Press, 2004).

The classic scholarly work on the American law of treason, evidence, presidential prosecutions (and defenses), and jury trial is James Willard Hurst's "Treason in the United States," *Harvard Law Review* 53 (1944): 226–72, (1945): 395–444, 806–57, prepared for the defense in *Cramer v. U.S.* Students can also consult Albert W. Alschuler and Andrew G. Deiss, "A Brief History of the Criminal Jury in the United States," *University of Chicago Law Review* 61 (1994): 867–928; Suzanne Kelly Babb, "Fear and Loathing in America," *Hastings Law Journal* 54 (2003): 1721–44; Eric M. Freedman, "Milestones in Habeas Corpus, Part I," *Alabama Law Review* 51 (2000): 531–600; Stewart Jay, "Origins of the Federal Common Law," parts 1 and 2, *University of Pennsylvania Law Review* 133 (1985): 1003–116, 133 (1985): 1231–332; Randolph Jonakait, "The Origins of the Confrontation Clause," *Rutgers Law Journal* 27 (1995): 77–168; and John C. Yoo, "The First Claim: The Burr Trial, *United States v. Nixon*, and Presidential Power," *Minnesota Law Review* 83 (1999): 1435–79.

English treason and evidence law were mainstays for the counsel and the court in the Burr trials. They are also the subject of Thomas Bayly Howell's *A Complete Collection of State Trials and Proceedings for High Treason and Other Crimes and Misdemeanors from the Earliest Period to the Year 1783* (London: Longman, 1816), 21v. There one can find the More, Perrot, and Raleigh Cases (at 1:392 [1538], 1:1315 [1592], and 2:1 [1603], respectively).

Scholarly pieces that connect the English to the American story include T. P. Gallanis, "The Rise of Modern Evidence Law," *Iowa Law Review* 84 (1999): 499–559; L. M. Hill, "The Two-Witness Rule in English Treason Trials," *American Journal of Legal History* 12 (1968): 95–111; Stanton D. Krauss, "An Inquiry into the Right of Criminal Juries to Determine the Law in Colonial America," *Journal of Criminal Law and Criminology* 89 (1998):111–214; John H. Langbein, "Shaping the Eighteenth-Century Criminal Trial," *University of Chicago Law Review* 50 (1983): 1–136; Stephen Landsman, "The Rise of the Contentious Spirit: Adversary Procedure in Eighteenth-Century England," *Cornell Law Review* 75 (1990): 497–605; Craig S. Lerner, "Impeachment, Attainder, and a True Constitutional Crisis: Lessons from the Strafford Trial," *University of Chicago Law Review* 69 (2002): 2057–101; Conrad Russell, "The Theory of Treason in the Trial of Strafford," *English Historical Review* 80 (1965): 30–50; and, generally, Barbara J. Shapiro, *Beyond "Reasonable Doubt" and "Probable Cause": Historical Perspectives on the Anglo-American Law of Evidence* (Berkeley: University of California Press, 1991).

On the court reporters, see Craig Joyce, "The Rise of the Supreme Court Reporter," *Michigan Law Review* 83 (1985): 1291–391.

James Wilson's views of treason appeared in his law lectures, reprinted in volume 2 of *The Works of James Wilson*, ed. Robert Green McCloskey (Cambridge: Harvard University Press, 1967). Randolph's contributions to the drafting of the Treason Clause can be found in Max Farrand, ed., *The Records of the Federal Convention of 1787* (New Haven, Conn.: Yale University Press, 1911), 2:345, 347.

On Marshall's apparent volte-face from *Ex Parte Bollman* II to *Burr*, there is a cottage industry of scholarly opinion. Robert K. Faulkner, "John Marshall and the Burr Trial," *Journal of American History* 53 (1966): 247–58, Hurst, "Treason in the United States," Bradley Chapin, *The American Law of Treason* (Seattle: University of Washington Press, 1964), and Leonard Levy, *Jefferson and Civil Rights: The Darker Side* (New York: Cambridge University Press, 1963), all find the second opinion compelling. Marshall biographers, starting with Beveridge and most recently including Hobson, Newmyer, and Smith, find nothing untoward in Marshall's motives. By contrast, Edward S. Corwin, *John Marshall and the Constitution* (New Haven, Conn.: Yale University Press, 1919), Charles Haines, *The Role of the Supreme Court in American Government and Politics, 1789–1835* (Berkeley: University of California Press, 1944), 1:279–88 (Marshall's shift exhibited "the exigencies of political strife"), Abernathy, *Burr Conspiracy*, and Melton, *Burr*, are more critical of Marshall's motives.

On the law practices of Virginia generally, see Edward Dumbauld, *Thomas Jefferson and the Law* (Norman: University of Oklahoma Press, 1978), and F. Thornton Miller, *Juries and Judges Versus the Law: Virginia's Provincial*

Legal Perspective, 1783–1828 (Charlottesville: University Press of Virginia, 1994). The two bibles of Virginia precedent were William Walker Hening, *The New Virginia Justice, Comprising the Office and Authority of a Justice of the Peace, in the Commonwealth of Virginia. Together with a variety of useful precedents adapted to the laws now in force. To which is added, an appendix containing all the most approved forms of conveyancing, commonly used in this country. Also, the duties of a justice of the peace, arising under the laws of the United States* (Richmond: Davis, 1799), and St. George Tucker, *Commentaries on Blackstone with Notes of Reference to the Constitution and Laws of the Federal Government of the United States and of the Commonwealth of Virginia* (Philadelphia: Birch and Small, 1803), 5v., especially volume 4. On the jurisprudence of treason law reform, see Alexander H. Shapiro, "Political Theory and the Growth of Defensive Safeguards in Criminal Procedure: The Origins of the Treason Trials Act of 1696," *Law and History Review* 11 (1993): 215–55.

Washington Irving's recollection of Burr appears in *The Life and Letters of Washington Irving*, ed. Pierre Irving (New York: Putnam, 1864), 4:301. For the argument that the opening of the Alabama, Mississippi, and Louisiana lands was a slave holders' project, see Adam Rothman, *Slave Country: American Expansion and the Origins of the Deep South* (Cambridge: Harvard University Press, 2005). On disorder in those lands, see Patrick Griffin, *American Leviathan: Empire, Nation, and Revolutionary Frontier* (New York: Hill and Wang, 2007), and Abernathy, *Burr Conspiracy*.

With a few exceptions, I have tried to avoid making what seem to me obvious comparisons between the Burr case and the handling of the prisoners at Guantánamo Bay after the Afghan and Iraq wars. For an explicit comparison, see Carlton F. W. Larson, "The Forgotten Constitutional Law of Treason and the Enemy Combatant Problem," *University of Pennsylvania Law Review* 154 (2006): 863–926.

INDEX